The Millennium

Past, Present, or Future?

The Millennium

Past, Present, or Future?

A Biblical Defense for the
40 Year Transition Period

Joseph M. Vincent II

JaDon Management Inc.
1405 4th Ave. • N.W. #109 • Ardmore, OK. 73401

Published 2012, by JaDon Management Inc.

Foreword © 2012 by Don K. Preston, D. Div.

Copyright © 2012 by Joseph M. Vincent II

Cover Design by Joseph M. Vincent II (Author)

Printed in the United States of America

ISBN-13:   978-1-937501-08-2

Dedication

This book is dedicated to my father, who God placed into my life to shape, mold, and make me the person that I am today. Dad, you are my hero, and despite our differences I am eternally grateful for how you were used to impact my life. I am the man I am today mostly because of you. While at times that can be my downfall, I am thankful to have had a dad who instilled the values in me to make me the man I am today; a man who loves God, who loves his family, and who desires above all else to lean on God's understanding and to make a difference in the world according to His will and desire. I look forward to spending the rest of eternity getting to love and hang out with you here on earth, and in heaven, and to one day being able to say, "I told you so!"

Acknowledgments

Extra special thanks goes to my wife, Lauren, who held down the fort while I spent countless hours writing this book. Without you my love, I would be nothing, and this book would not have happened. I love you, and I thank you for everything. Love always, Your Pig.

Special thanks also goes out to the many people who have helped mentor and shape me, in addition to all those who have spent hard and long hours reviewing this book and counseling me whenever I have needed guidance, help, or a little encouragement. For all those who were involved in this process, you know who you are and your contributions to this book have been just as important as me writing it. Thank you so much!

CONTENTS

FOREWORD

Joseph Vincent has produced what is, in my mind, an excellent treatment of one of the most difficult of theological issues; The Millennium.

Contrary to what many believers seem to think, wildly divergent speculation about the definition, duration and even the beginning of the millennium has run rampant for, well, millennia! Vincent revealingly documents this often confusing situation throughout church history and aptly concludes: "So divergent and different was one writer from another on the subject of end-times and eschatology that it is any wonder that the Church ever developed any consistent views at all. Some might argue that even 2,000 years later, they still haven't."

Indeed, the theological world of the 21st century is as divided and confused on the issue of the millennium as ever. We have premillennialism in its various forms, amillennialism, postmillennialism, and the true preterist view of the millennium, developed herein by Vincent. I think Mr. Vincent has made a solid contribution to this entire study.

What Vincent brings to the table is not a polemic examination of the various millennial views, although he does interact with them enough to demonstrate the weakness of the varying views, rather, he primarily offers the reader a positive exegetical presentation based on what the text of scripture says. One of the things that is revealing and helpful is the study showing that "1,000 years" is not referent to either a literal 1,000 years, or, significantly, even necessarily a long period of time. This is very, very important, yet, overlooked by the majority of exegetes and theologians.

Another aspect of the millennium investigated by Vincent is the interrelationship between the Garden of Eden, the death of Adam, the resurrection and the millennium. This is a wonderful, foundational study and more than worth the price of the book all by itself. In fact, this study is critical to any understanding of the millennium. And while all three futurist views of eschatology and the millennium give lip service to these subtopics in the available commentaries today, they all begin with false presuppositions that Vincent powerfully exposes. Good stuff here!

I am honored and pleased to recommend Joseph Vincent's book to lay readers, theologians, and scholars alike. While there are always more questions to be asked and other issues to investigate, Joseph Vincent has provided the reader with some solid exegesis, excellent logic, and plenty of food for thought.

Don K. Preston D. Div.
President Preterist Research Institute
Ardmore, Ok. 73401
www.eschatology.org
www.bibleprophecy.com
www.store.bibleprophecy.com

Easy to read, easy to understand, hard to ignore. A serious challenge to Christian history on the subject of the millennial reign of Christ. In this book, Joseph Vincent demonstrates the deficiencies in both pre-millennial and post-millennial views and provides a convincing argument for what he calls the trans-millennial view (not necessarily after Max King) - the idea that places the end of the millennium in or around the time of A.D. 66-70.

Bryan E. Lewis
B.Th. in Theology
Master of Theological Studies Candidate
Vanderbilt University, Nashville, Tennessee
www.orthodoxwars.com

ADDENDUM

"Then from the Speaker of the Empire, in a scolding tone, said that his [Luther's] answer was not to the point, and that there should be no calling into question of matters on which condemnations and decisions had before been passed by Councils. He was being asked for a plain reply, without subtlety or sophisticated speech, to this question: Was he prepared to recant, or no? Luther then replied: Your Imperial Majesty and Your Lordships demand a simple answer. Here it is, plain and unvarnished. Unless I am convicted [convinced] of error by the testimony of Scripture or, since I put no trust in the unsupported authority of Pope or councils, since it is plain that they have often erred and often contradicted themselves, by manifest reasoning, I stand convicted [convinced] by the Scriptures to which I have appealed, and my conscience is taken captive by God's word, I cannot and will not recant anything, for to act against our conscience is neither safe for us, nor open to us." – **Luther, AD1521**

The Westminster Confession of Faith – AD1646

Chapter 1, Paragraph IV. The authority of the Holy Scripture, for which it ought to be believed, and obeyed, depends not upon the testimony of any man, or Church; but wholly upon God (who is truth itself) the author thereof: and therefore it is to be received, because it is the Word of God.

Chapter 1, Paragraph IX. The infallible rule of interpretation of Scripture is the Scripture itself: and therefore, when there is a question about the true and full sense of any Scripture (which is not manifold, but one), it must be searched and known by other places (scriptures) that speak more clearly.

Chapter 1, Paragraph X. The supreme judge by which all controversies of religion are to be determined, and all decrees of councils, opinions of ancient writers, doctrines of men, and private spirits, are to be examined, and in whose sentence we are to rest, can be no other but the Holy Spirit speaking in the Scripture.

Chapter 31, Paragraph IV. All synods or councils, since the apostles' times, whether general or particular, may err; and many have erred. Therefore they are not to be made the rule of faith, or practice; but to be used as a help in both.

PREFACE

Anyone who has lived in a typical Bible belt town has surely been exposed to the modern prophecy pundits on television, in Christian book stores, and they have likely heard sermons from their church pastors who talk about the end times, or the coming of the Lord at any moment. Even secular programs on television are inundated with prophecy speculation about the end of the world. The History Channel, A&E, and others are filled with countless programs about Revelation, the Apocalypse, Nostradamus, the Mayan Calendar and 2012, and people who supposedly receive prophetic signs about things near in our future. But tucked away in all of that speculation is arguably the most significant doctrine of end times theology that can shape, reform, or change your interpretation of eschatology (the study of last things) altogether.

Often the most ignored topic of end times prophecy commentary is the topic of the millennium, or the thousand years. In most commentaries and books on this subject, the thousand year period is often mentioned as an afterthought, and it is simply alluded to as the period of time when Jesus reigns on the earth once again. In Dispensational Premillennial circles, the millennium is simply the period after the seven year great tribulation and the rapture, and in this scheme little attention is typically given on the subject of the millennium. Often times the assumption is made that it has not yet begun, and that it is still in our future, with little to no explanation.

In reformed circles, that is, Christians who are typically Amillennial or Postmillennial, the millennium is addressed somewhat more thoroughly, but commentary that is typically offered on the subject from this group are arguments for the number "thousand" as a vague, symbolic period of time that is supposedly to last a very long time. There is no specific period of time or duration in question concerning the millennium in the reformed schemes and it is thought to be the age during which the Church reigns with Jesus on His heavenly throne until the end of time; whether that is thousands, millions, or billions of years or longer, no one really knows.

The lack of critical inquiry by the church, even throughout its history, is quite telling as to the problem with trying to properly understand the doctrine of the millennium. Is it really something we still await in our future? Is it a period of time we currently live in? Or was it a period of time in the distant past? And whatever the answers are to these questions, does it make a difference with regard to how we live as Christians, and how we view the world around us? Does it change our hopes, our joys, our future, and our mindset as believers in Jesus?

This book is an attempt to address many of the loose ends concerning the doctrine of the millennium. I attempt to return to the original audience of the first century and to gain insight into the meaning and literature of the texts in question. A grammatical, historical analysis is required for any serious student of Biblical interpretation, and so it is that I have tried to seriously inquire about what the Scriptures really have to say about the doctrine of the millennium, and also, how the first-century audience would have understood, taught, and interpreted this doctrine when they had listened to or read about the teaching of the millennial period by John, Peter, or even Jesus himself.

My journey first began as a young boy, converted to believing in Jesus at the age of five. My father, truly the hero of my life, was saved in his mid 20's just before the time I could ever remember. At the age of five I can remember my dad praying with me and teaching me about God's Word, and it would have been sacrilegious to miss a Sunday service. I grew up early on in charismatic churches that my father had attended, and to my recollection he was a hard core, Bible thumping, on fire Jesus freak. He regularly spoke about end times, heaven and hell, and other issues that a young child formulates in dramatic pictures in his head. At that age, understanding Scripture, or the world for that matter, was only through the eyes of what I had been taught or told. Hermeneutics and the science of Biblical interpretation were as foreign to me as African dance routines.

My dad's primary motives were to simply light the world on fire for Jesus and to allow God to use him as a tool for planting seeds and making new converts. But underlying those motives were his beliefs that the world could end at any moment, and that he only had so much time to make believers out of the lost people in the world. My dad used to say that he believed the rapture would take place before he was thirty; he's now in his 50's, and he's a far cry from his early years of charismania. I must say, sometimes I look back on those years, and I miss the passion my father had for Christ, but I often wonder if that passion had more to do with his expectation of getting taken out of the world and into heaven, rather than a simple zeal for the love of God. I don't doubt his love for the Lord, and to this day my father still talks about the greatness of God in his life if you ask him, but unless you really knew him, you might not know it about him anymore.

Needless to say, everything I knew about the Bible was indoctrinated from anything my father had ever learned from his large book library, or from whatever I had heard from him or the pastor each Sunday, or from the long drives I had with my dad when he came to pick me up every other weekend where we would frequently listen to the Bible Answer Man broadcast together, or to other Christian programs or music. Those were some VERY fun car rides and discussions, and I always looked forward to having those dialogues with my dad. Some of my favorite moments were jamming to songs with him, like Petra's "This Means War" album in the car, and learning through music about the heavenly battle between God and Satan until Jesus returns. But as the years came and went, and life began to happen as it always does, my father's zeal steadily died down. Eventually we moved on to more conservative churches, and finally my father stopped going to church altogether in 2004, and to this very day he still hasn't returned.

In my early 20's I had joined the Marine Corps, and after a short stint of rebellion in my post teenage life, I married and finally moved back to my home town after my military tour was over. In my teens and early 20's I had grown tired of end times failed predictions, and constantly having to keep an eye out for the latest headlines to figure out what was supposed to happen next on the eschatological calendar. Y2K ramped up, and then came and went as I turned 21, and it all happened as though New Year's Day of 2000AD were just any other day of week, on any average New Year. I had studied the Bible nearly all of my life, read more books on theology by this time than most seminary graduates, and yet, I still couldn't figure out how to piece the end-times puzzle together. Every time I thought I had one thing figured out, it always seemed to contradict another part of Scripture. I watched my father go through the teeter tottering between the premillennial pretribulational view, the midtribulational view, the prewrath view, and then a more panmillennial approach to end-times (I just don't know, and it will all "pan out" one way or the other).

So I did what any good Christian would do who wanted to really understand what the Bible was talking about. I attended Seminary. My thinking was that a person would have to be a scholar to truly understand what the Bible was saying. I mean, in all those years of attending churches and listening to the radio, and watching TV programs by supposed "scholars" of the Bible, they always seemed to teach on issues like eschatology as if they were certain and sure of their particular view. I wasn't, but I wanted to be.

And then it happened. In 2005, during my second semester of graduate seminary school, I was driving in my car one afternoon and happened to be listening to a Hank Hanegraaff Bible Answer Man program where he was interviewing Steve Gregg. The discussion was on end-times, but this particular show was different than anything I had ever heard before. Instead of attempting to provide new insights into the latest world headlines compared with Bible prophecy, Mr. Gregg was answering Hank's questions, in addition to questions from the listening audience, from a "preterist" perspective. I had never heard of this view before despite all my years of reading and studying. End-times, or eschatology, was one of the more prominent subjects I had studied growing up, and yet, why had I never heard of this view before, or if I had, why couldn't I recall knowing anything about it?

Another hour later, sitting in my car in the driveway of my home, I couldn't get out. I was glued to everything I was hearing, and astounded at what seemed so simple! Mr. Gregg was talking about certain passages and how they fit into first-century fulfillment. He mentioned AD70, and the Jewish war with the Romans, and he began talking about "audience relevance" and "time statements." All of a sudden, things that had been utterly confusing to me for all my life were instantly becoming easy to understand and as clear as glass. How was this possible? How could I have missed this? How could everyone else be missing this? Either this guy was nuts, and the Bible Answer Man had lost it, or there was a major problem with what the majority of popular churches in America were teaching.

And so began my journey into preterist understandings of eschatology. For two years I wrestled with different aspects of eschatology trying to unwrap my brain from things I had learned growing up. My family thought I was going crazy, and even our home church rejected the idea that I was considering that Jesus had returned in some way in AD70. No one could understand why I was so determined and focused on studying end-times and eschatology. At a point, no one wanted to be around me because every discussion turned into preterism and the end-times.

But why was this endeavor such a big deal for me? What no one could understand was that the experience of being able to now understand Scripture in ways I had never before been able to understand it was like being born again, all over again! Reading the Bible had become fresh and new once again in my life like never before, and no longer was I constantly stumped on things that before were complete mysteries to me. I no longer expect people to understand that time in my life, and so I've learned to not bring up the issue to people who just don't care, or who don't see it as a very big deal, but to me, it was a big deal, and it impacted my life in very big ways, and it truly changed me from the inside out.

Near the end of my two year journey I had become an ardent partial preterist with a postmillennial understanding of end-times, and Scripture. I still couldn't fathom thinking that Jesus wasn't going to come again in our future, and so I clung to this as an anchor of orthodoxy (traditionally held views in Church history) in order to tell myself that I wasn't crazy, and that I hadn't completely lost my mind. There were after all "some" Christians in the church today who had a similar view as me, and so it was still acceptable as long as this stuff was taught in church history, and accepted by other "mainstream" Christians today. No one wants to feel like an outsider, and having met with people who had left extremist cult groups or faith organizations like Mormonism, or Jehovah's Witnesses, I knew the kind of rejection that accompanied those who have left their former faith behind. I certainly didn't want to have anything to do with that, and I just knew that I was too smart to fall for some cult, unorthodox doctrine.

My main objections to becoming a full preterist (believing that ALL prophecy had been fulfilled in the first century) was that I still couldn't figure out how to interpret the Resurrection of 1 Corinthians 15 in light of preterist understandings, in addition to Acts 1:11 which said that Jesus was to come in the same manner that he left (physically I assumed was the correct interpretation here), and also the millennium and judgment. Surely the millennium could not be limited to the first century. That's just insane! Anyone who believes that a millennium (that's a thousand years right?) could be limited to a few years in the first century is crazy! That's heresy! That was my immediate reaction. The millennium had to be a very long time, I just knew it. How long, I wasn't exactly sure, but by this time I was convinced that we (the Church) were living in the millennial period, reigning with Christ while He sits on His throne.

The Dispensational, Premillennial view was laughable at this point, sadly, and it almost seemed cultish to me by now. I nearly placed the popular views of the church into the same category as other Christian cults like Jehovah's Witnesses, Mormons, and others. It wasn't quite the same, I mean after all, these Dispy Premillers (as they're called) read the same Bible as I did, but how they managed to mangle and twist the Word of God into such a confusing scheme of Zionist fervor was astounding to me, and how so many Christians bought into that theological thinking hook line and sinker was a shocking reality about the culture of American Christianity today. My dad bought into it early on in his Christian life, and I was raised and spoon fed on this stuff. It's no wonder people are apathetic about end-times when nothing they believe is supposed to happen actually ever does! I had family members who regularly attended these types of churches, and I now felt like they were trapped in the same cult like atmosphere as other cults. But what was I to do or say without offending them or sounding arrogant? I mean, we are taught as Christians to fight against false doctrines, and to grow and mature in God's Word as Bereans, but how do you approach someone you love and tell them that you believe they are following cult doctrines taught in their churches?

In one breath the average Christian will tell you that end times stuff just doesn't matter all that much, and in the next breath, all they can talk about is how much they can't wait for the coming of the Lord at any moment, for the rapture of the church, and for the millennial reign of Jesus to begin. Many of these people invest enormous amounts of time and money into sending Jews back to their homeland of Israel so that God's prophetic clock can wind down sooner, and so that Jesus can return quicker! I mean, well meaning and devout Christians actually pay for this stuff! And you're supposed to tell me that end-times views don't matter? Absurd!

Most Christians today, when asked about their end-times view, can typically ramble on about the basic synopsis of events…you know, the rapture, the Great Tribulation, the anti-Christ coming on to the scene, the battle of Armageddon, the millennial reign of Christ, maybe even a rebuilt temple, and finally, the second coming of Jesus and the transformation of the cosmos. But when you ask the majority of these people to actually point out the Scriptures that teach about this stuff, typically you get a deer in the head lights stare, or some cop out statement about how none of it really matters…it will all pan out one way or the other, right?

So there I was, locked in as a partial preterist and conforming to the reformed views of Kenneth Gentry, Gary DeMar, R.C. Sproul, James Jordon, and renowned writers and theologians of my new partial preterist view, and adamantly against the traditions I had been taught as a Charismatic, and then as a Southern Baptist Christian. But something still wasn't quite right. The thing that bothered me the most was that the Apostles' and the first disciples of Jesus expected all the things they predicted and spoke about to happen at any moment and within their lifetime. They said that those things would happen very soon, very quickly, and that they eagerly waited for all those events to fully transpire. But how is that possible? Weren't these men inspired by God? Weren't they filled with the Holy Spirit and given divine ability to proclaim the Gospel and to reveal what had been hidden, or to unlock what had been sealed for centuries and ages before in the Old Testament?

How could they have been wrong and inspired at the same time? A few pastors and teachers tried to explain to me that what they were preaching and writing about in the New Testament, well, they just didn't understand what it was they were saying. God just wanted all of us to be ready "as if" he would come at any moment, but "soon" could really be a very long time in the future since time to God is meaningless. Of course, when I had asked if something in the Bible that said an event was very far in the future, if that could really be very close at hand, once again, I got the deer in the head lights look, or maybe something like, "Well, when it comes to end-times passages, time is in God's eyes; everywhere else, it means what it says." And preterists were the ones guilty of spiritualizing the Bible, and picking and choosing how and when to interpret the Bible when it fits your needs? Come on! Talk about being inconsistent. You know that feeling down in your gut when something just isn't right and you know it? That's called Spiritual discernment, and I was getting a gut check.

What I was being told was impossible and downright ridiculous, and I wasn't buying it. I knew that Jesus had told his disciples in Luke 21 not to listen to or follow anyone who said that the time of the end was near when it really wasn't, and yet, 25-30 years later, there they were in the New Testament, proclaiming that the time was near over and over again. Were they false prophets? Were they guilty of doing exactly what Jesus told them not to do? The inspiration of

Scripture and of the Apostles was at stake here, and I wasn't going to settle for a "panmillennial" explanation (I'm just not sure, but it's gotta be true).

But where did I start? How would I overcome this dilemma? Well, I had to start with the unresolved issues that I couldn't quite figure out. First it was Acts 1:11. That didn't take very long. A few months later and some intensive research and I was able to see that the cloud language and context of what Luke was writing about had nothing to do with Jesus returning in his physical body to planet earth. Not to belabor that topic, but I was surprised that I had never given that passage any other consideration. It's amazing what you'll believe when someone tells you what they think a passage means, and it "seems" to make sense. But like a faithful Berean, I had to know for myself, and doing the homework paid serious dividends.

Then I was on to figuring out the Resurrection and passages like 1 Corinthians 15. Surely there was no way around the fact that this hadn't happened yet…right? I mean, in the New Testament Hymaneaus and Philetus said the resurrection had already happened, and Paul called them heretics! Surely I wasn't going to jump on that bandwagon, was I? But wait, all Paul had to do was tell his audience that those guys were crazy…I mean, look around right? The grave yards are still full! But did he do that? No! Not once! But if resurrection was about physical bodies being raised, and if it was about the world physically being transformed at the end of time, why didn't Paul just make that as clear as day for us and the rest of the world? Why was he using such cryptic language from the Old Testament to explain his doctrine of the resurrection? Why was he only concerned with correcting the "time" of the resurrection, and not their understanding of the nature of the resurrection, if they had it wrong? If all those guys got wrong was the time of the resurrection, and not the nature of it, what does that mean about what kind of resurrection Paul and the other Apostles and first-century disciples had in mind when they spoke and wrote about it?

Once again, a few months and some intensive research later and I was utterly convinced that this passage had nothing to do with physical bodies coming up out of the ground and from their graves to receive new glorified bodies! Oh the indoctrination I had received! Ouch! I can't explain the entirety of my conclusions here, or the process I took to get there, but it should be enough to simply say that I knew that the resurrection had taken place already, and that the entire context of Paul's teaching was nothing but the hope of Israel, and that his whole teaching in 1 Corinthians 15 had primarily come from Isaiah 25 and the book of Hosea, and from the Old Testament. The language of the "body" (Greek – Soma) in chapter 15 was the same "body" in chapter 12-14. How did I miss this before? The "dead" had nothing to do with physical bodies, but was referring to the Jewish Theocracy which, even though the Jewish leaders in it were physically alive, they were in fact dead to God! All the faithful "dead ones" from the Old Testament were waiting for the future "gathering of Israel" where even though Israel had been divorced by God hundreds of years earlier, Israel would be brought back, remarried, and raised to life again along with the rest of the gentile nations!

Either way, however the doctrine of the Resurrection was supposed to be worked out, it was not a future event for us today. That much was certain. Certain aspects of the nature of the Resurrection were still up for grabs, and it was a process to come to the conclusions I have now grown to believe, but I knew that there was no way on God's green earth that the Resurrection was a future event. It was a future event for the first-century Apostles who wrote about the Resurrection (or at least it was a process that was "being" fulfilled during their ministry), but it wasn't future for me, and it was not for us today.

Now that didn't mean that I still didn't expect some sort of resurrection when I died. Surely I would put off this body someday, and God would give me "something" else at that time. But the doctrines of "Resurrection" in the Bible had nothing at all to do with this, and I had finally settled that issue once and for all. My personal feelings about the afterlife and a new body at death were simply just that, personal ideas and feelings. All I knew was that the Bible said that I would live for eternity with God and that although I might physically die, I would live forever. How that is worked out, and what kind of body or existence that might entail or look like, I have no idea, nor do I really care to speculate (although it is fun to think about). But the resurrection wasn't a matter of physical bodies, or the afterlife. It was about Israel and the New Covenant marriage between God and His people once again.

You see, when you begin to understand that God was divorcing his harlot (prostitute) bride, Judah, in the Jewish system, a cheating wife had to be stoned, burned, and killed. Once she was dead, the old marriage contract was void and destroyed. At that time the husband could then remarry his new bride. The cool thing about God was that when he divorced and killed his ex-wife (unfaithful Israel), he then raised her to life, he redeemed her and forgave her sins from the past, and he then remarried her as a new bride (true Israel, the Church)! How cool was that? Doesn't every bride wish her husband had the power to raise the dead? This was what Paul's teaching of the resurrection was all about. Whew…what an eye opening experience this was.

Then there was the final hurdle. What about the millennium? Since the resurrection takes place after the millennium, how was I going to figure that out now? If I was in the millennium now (as a post-millennial, partial preterist), I had a problem. Since I now believe the resurrection was in the past, my view of the millennium had to be flawed! Before delving into this subject, first I had to deal with the question of orthodoxy. Was anything that I now believed orthodox in the history of the Church? Did it even need to be?

At first there was great opposition to my views by certain friends, family members, and even people within the mainstream church that I had conversations with. Even partial preterist idols I had come to adore like Gentry were berating Christians who were adopting full preterist interpretations due to what they considered to be "unorthodox" and "heretical" positions. But a few studies in historical literature led me to several early church writings from men who adopted forms of my preterist understanding, in one way or another. Sure, none of them ever fully adopted every position I had accepted as a complete or whole system, but all the parts and pieces were there in the different writings of the early church fathers, and also in many of the later church historians.

For example, Athanasius applied the resurrection texts to life in Christ, and believed in ultimate fulfillment of those passages to be in the first century. Other men gave extensive commentary to the AD70 events and applied the majority of the prophetic passages in the Bible to the first century as well. When the historical preterist statements were combined, I found no problem with accepting and adopting a full preterist hermeneutic or interpretation of Scripture. For one thing, I had never found a single consistent interpretation in the history of the Church regarding end-times from a futurist understanding.

The fact that nearly all Church historians expected "something" to occur in the future was not compelling at all, since few of them ever agreed on what was or was not fulfilled or unfulfilled, or even when or how end-times was to be worked out. Even if they had given commentary about their views, rarely did any of them ever agree on the passages they applied to future events. So the question of orthodoxy was no longer a problem. After all, the Westminster Confession of Faith was clear that the only standard of Biblical theology that a person should cling to is Scripture itself.

Sola Scriptura (Scripture Alone) is the only creed or confession that should truly be adopted; and that creed means that NO CREED should be adopted unless it comes from Scripture itself. So if I was finding major problems in modern teachings of "end-times," or even historical problems in the popular views of the church at any given period in church history, that really wasn't a major problem as long as I relied on, and clung to the words of Scripture, and used some form of consistent hermeneutical approach (the method of interpreting the Bible).

Finally, the doctrine of the millennium had to be worked out. Why was this issue so hard to understand? Well, the first thing I discovered was that the only specific or direct mention of the millennium was in Revelation 20. That was quite telling. In fact, the word "millennium" wasn't even used. It was a vague Greek word used to define "thousand years," but it didn't specify how many thousand years. Without a number in front of it, the Greek word is vague. But what did it mean? How could the Apostles and first-century disciples have expected a soon and near end, resurrection, and judgment if they understood the millennium in ways that the majority of Christians today understand it? They couldn't have! But if that is true, then how did they understand it, and how has the Church missed this for so long? As you read this book, please keep this fact clearly in the back of your mind. Whatever the true doctrine of the millennium actually is, the Apostles and disciples of the first century believed that the Lord was going to come very soon in their lifetime to fulfill all that he said concerning the resurrection and judgment, and to establish His Kingdom forever. If those events aren't completed until after the millennium, then how could the Apostles or disciples have viewed this period of time as lasting beyond their own generation?

And so this book is my first attempt at a final analysis of the past few years of research on the doctrine of the millennium. It may be imperfect, incomplete, or even flat out wrong in some areas, but until I can be shown that my analysis and research is incorrect, I believe that this book is the most concise and well developed, consistent, and true interpretation ever produced to date on the timing, nature, and language of the subject of the millennium. Whether you agree or disagree, I hope and believe that you will be amazed at some of the simple, logical truths that I have discovered in my own journey while coming to a better understanding of exactly what the millennium is, what it isn't, and how that impacts our lives today.

Whether you agree with futurist, preterist, or other views of end-times prophecy, I think that you will find something of value in this book which you might have otherwise never known or learned about. Don't be afraid to challenge your traditionally held views, and take the same journey that I did as a faithful Berean, and study this issue out for yourself. You might not jump ship and join my theological boat of understanding, but at least you'll have a better understanding and respect for why I've chosen to paddle down the river in this direction!

─────── *Introduction* ───────

THE QUESTION OF HERMENEUTICS

In order to perform a study of this magnitude concerning such a critical topic, we need to discuss a matter of great importance, and that is the question of hermeneutics. Biblical hermeneutics is the study of the principles of interpretation concerning the books of the Bible, and how a person approaches the study of Scripture. It is the "science" of Biblical interpretation. It is part of the broader field of hermeneutics which involves the study of principles for the text and includes all forms of communication: verbal and nonverbal, including the historical, grammatical, cultural, linguistic, contextual, and other factors that bring an individual to a particular conclusion about the text in question.

Each mainstream view of the millennium within the church comes with a particular bias that is formed because of the hermeneutical approach used to arrive at whatever conclusion one might come to. Dispensationalists claim to hold to a primarily "literal" or "straightforward" interpretation of Scripture, ignoring many of the claims by postmillennialists or amillennialists that there is a need and precedent to view certain passages within a more symbolic, metaphoric, apocalyptic, idiomatic, or some other way that is and was never intended to be understood in a simply straightforward manner. "That a great deal of the Bible is given in figurative or symbolic language, which by no stretch of the imagination can be taken literally, should be apparent to everyone."[1]

"The question of hermeneutics raised by the millennium issue, however, moves beyond the book of Revelation. In its most comprehensive scope, of course, it encompasses the proper approach to the Bible as a whole. But more

─────────────────

[1] Boettner, Loraine, *The Meaning of the Millennium.* (Downers Grove, IL: InterVarsity Press, 1977). 136.

specifically, the millennium debate raises hermeneutical questions concerning Old Testament prophecy, literalism and the relation of the Old Testament to the New."[2] Whatever the case may be, Christians from various backgrounds use different methods or hermeneutical rules of interpretation to come to whatever conclusion they arrive at. What's more important than trying to arrive at a viable conclusion about the millennium is trying to establish or prove which method of interpretation is correct to get you to the most accurate conclusion possible! In other words, rather than focusing on when, how, or what the millennium is, we should first be focused on how we read the Bible as a whole, and what principles of interpretation we use to understand it. For example, when a person says, "I read the Bible literally," what does that really mean? The appropriate meaning of this statement is to say that you interpret every aspect of the Bible within the appropriate "literature" or "literary genre" in which it was intended to be understood by its original writer and audience, whether it is spiritual, symbolic, metaphoric, hyperbolic, idiomatic, historical pros, chiastic, or strictly straight forward.

However, what is often meant by someone making this statement is that whatever they read in English should be understood in a strictly straightforward sense. If Jesus said in Matthew 24 that he will return on a cloud, then a literal understanding would have a 6 foot Jew returning in the sky on a cumulous cloud over Mount Zion for all the physical people of the earth to see all at once some day in our future! However, a "literal" understanding of this passage could simply have Jesus referring to similar "coming" language as it was used in the Old Testament, such as in Isaiah 19, when God came riding on a swift cloud in judgment upon Egypt. Both could be seen as "literal," but what is meant by each person is something altogether different. And that is why understanding your hermeneutical approach is so important. What terms are you using, and what do they mean?

---

[2] Grenz, Stanley J., *The Millennial Maze: Sorting out Evangelical Options.* (Downers Grove, IL: InterVarsity Press, 1992). 181.

It must be further stated that while we might come to vastly different conclusions than our Christian brothers and sisters who disagree with us, "equally evangelical scholars who accept the Bible as the inspired Word of God should be able to disagree without the accusation of [being unorthodox, or unbiblical, or unchristian]...I am prepared to accept whatever I can establish as biblical teaching...Let this be clear: the Bible and the Bible alone is our one authority."[3] Ladd demonstrates clearly the differences that exist in our understanding from one another. "Here is the basic watershed between a dispensational and a nondispensational theology. Dispensationalism forms its eschatology by a literal interpretation of the Old Testament and then fits the New Testament into it. Nondispensational eschatology forms its theology from the explicit teaching of the New Testament." Thus, in his argument, anyone who does not teach dispensationalism should attempt to understand the Old Testament in light of the New Testament, whereas a dispensationalist will use Old Testament predictions to help understand New Testament prophecies.

In the example given above, they both cannot be correct. Which is it? Do we understand the Old with the New Testament, or do we understand the New with the Old Testament? "That believing Christians through the ages, using the same Bible and acknowledging it to be authorative, have arrived at quite different conclusions appears to be due primarily to different methods of interpretation...Evidently the individual reader must use his own judgment, backed by as much experience and common sense as he can muster. And that, of course, will vary endlessly from individual to individual."[4]

There are many more differences than this, but they range in a wide variety of methods and scientific principles. It is not our goal here to prove one over the other; rather, we wish to express the methods we will be using to arrive at our own conclusions. Exhaustive books have been written already

---

[3] Ladd, George Eldon, *The Meaning of the Millennium*. (Downers Grove, IL: InterVarsity Press, 1977). 20.
[4] Ibid, 134, from Loraine Boettner.

concerning the appropriate methods of interpretation one ought to use to read Scripture. We hope that you have done your homework, and that as you read this book, even if you use a different method than us, that your inquiry into this matter will at least help you understand why we have arrived at the conclusions we have come to hold.

Our main focus is not that you necessarily agree with this systematic study, but that you recognize and understand why your particular view of eschatology matters, and how it can change the way you live, and how you view the world around you, and the future. Erickson explains the importance of eschatology this way, "[T]he eschatological so interpenetrates the rest of Christianity's themes that one cannot extricate, eliminate, or ignore it without ruining the whole." And he is absolutely correct. In fact, it is my belief that the reason Christianity has arrived to date with thousands of denominations and cult variations, is primarily because eschatology has never been worked out in the church throughout the centuries.

While most people lay this topic on the sidelines as if it doesn't influence their overall essential beliefs, the truth is, your eschatological view impacts some of those essentials in ways that directly changes them, or it changes the way you apply them in a practical sense. Basic elements of the Christian faith such as fasting, communion (the Lord's Supper), baptism, salvation, spiritual gifts, and many more theological subjects are directly impacted by your eschatological view, either in the meaning they take on, or in the way you interpret the application of those doctrines.

One way or the other your eschatological view is of great importance because it is the one doctrine that changes all other doctrines to a large extent. If you get this wrong, you'll get a great deal of Scripture wrong. Ultimately, this may not change your salvation, but it will change the way you practice your faith, how you view the church, how you view "going to church," how you view Christian education and higher learning, and how you interact with other Christians and non-Christians in your day to day life.

"The question of the nature and time of the millennium envisioned by the seer of the Apocalypse has been debated, rehashed and rehearsed ad nauseam within evangelicalism. Having grown tired of the disagreements and speculations about matters that only the future will resolve, many believers are disdainful of eschatology in its entirety. How often have Christians repeated the glib, even ignorant, response: 'I'm a panmillennialist. I believe it will all pan out in the end.' Such simplistic dismissal of the discussion merely fails to understand the importance of the world-view issues at stake."[5]

"[H]ow could the inscripturated disclosure of the future not be important and practical for God's people? Does not 2 Timothy 3:16-17 teach us that 'all Scripture is God-breathed' (hence important) and profitable in preparing us for 'every good work' (hence practical)? Eschatology's considerable task is to explore the whole revelation of the inerrant Word of God in order to discern the divinely ordained, prophetically revealed flow of world history from creation to consummation with a view to issuing 'a call to action and obedience in the present.'"[6] How we view the past and the future necessarily affects how we conduct ourselves in the present. If our eschatological view is incorrect, and if we treat the task of attempting to properly grasp its meaning as though it doesn't matter, then how can we possibly fulfill and practice the commands and teachings of the Lord with any real assurance that we are "doing the right thing" if we don't care?

Sure we can love (and we are always to love), but do we love by praying in tongues, or warning our brothers and sisters in Christ through prophecy, or do we love by not doing those things? Do we love by practicing all of the spiritual gifts, or are they already fulfilled, and simply a matter of manipulative self-proclamation, without any real substance? Should we tithe, and if so, how should we do it? Should we fast, and if so, what meaning does that have today? Should we baptize, and if so, what meaning does it hold, and how should we do so? Should we take communion together, and if so, what is the full meaning of this sacrament? Should we fulfill the Great

---

[5] Grenz, Stanley J., *The Millennial Maze: Sorting out Evangelical Options.* (Downers Grove, IL.: InterVarsity Press, 1992). 209.
[6] Gentry, Kenneth L. Jr., Three Views on the Millennium and Beyond, (Grand Rapids, MI.: Zondervan, 1999). 13.

Commission and witness to our neighbors and friends, or was this already fulfilled? And if it was, what do we do now? If not, how do we properly go about performing this task? These are only a few of the many questions that arise when we think of the significance of how eschatology impacts our Christian life, both spiritually and practically.

The Analogy of Scripture

Before we begin a critical analysis of the millennium, we must first recognize and utilize one of the most important hermeneutical[7] rules of Biblical interpretation. That rule is the "Analogy of Scripture."[8] The function of this rule is to cause the student of the Bible to carefully interpret Scripture with Scripture; not interpreting hard to understand portions of the Bible apart from the more clear ones. That is to utilize the easier to understand passages to help with understanding the not so easy ones.

When Scripture is not so clear in one area we are not to form doctrine solely on the basis of these hard to understand passages; rather, we are to instead apply clearly understood passages within the text to help with understanding the other unclear passages. This is also how proper exegesis is performed (the art of dissecting the Word of God, properly understanding its meaning, and applying what it says in the correct manner).

With the book of Revelation we must at all times learn to interpret Scripture with Scripture and not attempt to interpret Scripture with newspaper headlines (also known as "newspaper exegesis"), or the latest modern theories that do not employ sound Biblical principles. It is not the book of speculation, imagination, or alteration. The book of Revelation was written to be revealed with full disclosure and to take the cover off or to "lift the veil" for its contemporary audience and readers.

---

[7] See "Glossary" at the end of this book for a definition of the term "hermeneutics."

[8] See "Glossary" at the end of this book for a definition of the term "analogy of scripture."

The word "Revelation" itself literally means "the revealing" or the lifting of the veil. It is to be seen clearly in light of its genre (it is an apocalyptic[9] work) and its' symbols and imagery were to be clearly understood by the audience to whom it was written. The book was not written for a distant audience 2,000 or more years into the future that has no way to understand it until the events begin to unfold. If it were, then the Book of Revelation could not possibly say that anyone who reads and keeps its teachings would be blessed (cf. Revelation 1:3). How could anyone be blessed by it if they can't keep or apply its teachings if it only applies to a distant generation of readers? If that were true, then only the final generation who could possibly understand it could ever be blessed by the book!

On the other hand, a more accurate and scholarly approach to understanding the context of the Book of Revelation is to realize that the book can be properly learned when the reader gathers the appropriate information relating to its historical background, its occasional context, and when the reader uses a proper hermeneutical approach which the writer (John) originally intended his audience to use and apply (or "keep"). By properly interpreting the contents of John's apocalyptic book, the reader can then truly be blessed by being able to fully understand it. For the first century audience, understanding John's warnings and predictions meant that the reader (or hearer) could truly be blessed by keeping what it was saying.

George Eldon Ladd makes the following insight concerning the genre of Revelation:

> "The book of Revelation belongs to the genre of literature called apocalyptic. The first apocalyptic book was the canonical Daniel. This was followed by a large group of imitative apocalypses between 200 B.C. and A.D. 100 such as Enoch, Assumption of Moses, 4 Ezra, and the Apocalypse of Baruch. Two facts emerge from the study of apocalyptic: The apocalypses use highly symbolic

---

[9] See "Glossary" at the end of this book for a definition of the term "apocalyptic."

language to describe a series of events in history; and the main concern of apocalyptic is the end of the age and the establishment of God's kingdom."[10]

In the book, "Apocalypse Code," Hank Hanegraaff makes the following observations:

"In terms of a proper end-times paradigm, this principle [typology] is of paramount importance. Persons, places, events, or things in redemptive history serve as types of Christ or spiritual realities pertaining to Christ. Palestine is typological of paradise. As Joshua led the people of Israel into the Promised Land, so too Jesus will lead his people into paradise…the principle of scriptural synergy [the analogy of Scripture] means that the whole of Scripture is greater than the sum of its individual passages. You cannot comprehend the Bible as a whole without comprehending its individual parts, and you cannot comprehend its individual parts without comprehending the Bible as a whole…Nor may we assign arbitrary meanings to words or phrases that have their referen[ce] in biblical history." (pgs. 9-11)

"Over the last hundred years biblical scholars have come to understand the importance of apocalyptic as a special category or genre of writing. Although its roots lay earlier in Old Testament history, this style flourished between 200B.C. and A.D.100 among Jewish and Jewish-Christian circles. Most of the apocalyptic writings were not included in either the Hebrew or the Christian canons. Nevertheless, the genre is represented to some extent in the biblical books of Daniel and Revelation, and possibly in sections of other canonical writings, including Isaiah, Zechariah and the synoptic Gospels.
"Biblical scholars have pinpointed several characteristics typical of apocalyptic writings. Central to this literary style is the use of visions as a means whereby a heavenly messenger reveals to the seer knowledge concerning decisively important

[10] Ladd, George Eldon, *The Meaning of the Millennium.* (Downers Grove, IL: InterVarsity Press, 1977). 33.

aspects of the human destiny that had to this point been hidden in heaven but would soon transpire on earth. The seer often describes the spiritual turmoil these visions produced in the visionary's own countenance and then draws conclusions from the visions for the faithful to endure under persecution. The visionary generally employs rich, at times even bizarre, symbols to convey the heavenly message to the faithful community. The use of symbols is advantageous, as they serve to hide the meaning of the vision from the uninitiated eye while communicating clearly to members of the seer's own community."[11]

In other words, many scholars today seem ready to make up new methods of Biblical interpretation to fit what they believe is supposed to occur in the future. They do so rather than using known methods of interpretation based on the literary genre[12] and grammar in which the specific passages were written. They ignore the historical audience to whom the texts were originally written, the typological[13] significance of passages that were fulfilled in Christ in the first century, and the synergy or analogy of scripture that allows the reader to know how to interpret hard to understand passages by looking at other ones that are not so hard to understand.

So as you continue in your journey with me through this difficult subject matter on the millennium, please remember these principles of interpretation, also known as "hermeneutics." When we learn and read about the thousand years in the Bible, we need to ask ourselves several questions. Do we believe that the Apostles and disciples were teaching some new doctrine, or were they describing something that the first-century Christians developed and wrote about using known ideas from sources outside the Bible, or from the Old Testament texts? Were they describing events using language from Old Testament passages that use the same idea of

---

[11] Grenz, Stanley J., *The Millennial Maze: Sorting out Evangelical Options.* (Downers Grove, IL: InterVarsity Press, 1992). 29.
[12] See "Glossary" at the end of this book for a definition of the term "literary genre."
[13] See "Glossary" at the end of this book for a definition of the term "typological or typology."

"thousand"? And we need to ask if John's doctrine of the millennium in Revelation 20 and the other ideas contained in this book (resurrection, judgment, etc.) were based on other known sources in Scripture? For example, was the "binding of Satan" that John spoke of in Revelation 20 the same as the "binding of the strong man" written about earlier in Matthew 12:29 and Mark 3:27? I hope to answer these questions and more as we continue in this study.

In providing the answer to these questions, we will be using a hermeneutical approach to Scripture known as the "Preterist"[14] method, or what some may call Realized Eschatology[15], or Fulfilled Eschatology, or even Covenant Eschatology. This method has led us to conclude that the millennium properly fits within a transmillennial model, system, or framework. Preterist or Preterism is a view in Christian eschatology[16] which holds that some or all of the biblical prophecies concerning the *Last Days* refer to events which took place in the first century after Christ's birth, especially associated with the destruction of Jerusalem in AD70. The term preterism comes from the Latin *praeter*, meaning *past*, since this view deems certain biblical prophecies as *past*, or already fulfilled.

"The strength of realized eschatology is its tenet that much of the eschatology of which Jesus spoke was already fulfilled or being fulfilled within His time. In Christ the future had come, or at least it had begun. The tendency of some Christians to understand Scriptural eschatology in purely futuristic terms must therefore be regarded as a mistaken, perverted view of Scriptural teaching. These people miss

---

[14] See "Glossary" at the end of this book for a definition of the term "Preterist or Preterism."

[15] While the term "Realized Eschatology" was first defined by C.H. Dodd (1884-1973), it has been more strictly adapted by preterists to refer to fulfilled prophecy, with little import given to future events for us today in the realm of eschatology.

[16] See "Glossary" at the end of this book for a definition of the term "eschatology."

much of the significance of the text because they are looking forward when they should be looking backward."[17]

---

[17] Erickson, Millard J., *A Basic Guide to Eschatology. Making Sense of the Millennium.* (Grand Rapids, MI: Baker Book House Co., 1999), 34.

—————— *1* ——————

HISTORICAL CONTEXT

The Early Church and the Millennium

Before any serious inquiry can begin on this issue, a brief look at the history of thought on the millennium in the Church is in order. How did we arrive where we are today on this issue, and why is there so much diversity and opinion on such an important theological doctrine? I am inclined to argue that the "thousand year period" or the "millennium" is not a period of time that is to span an exact one thousand year period, nor is it a long period of time which spiritually or supernaturally speaking may last many thousands, or hundreds of thousands, or even millions of years. But the fact is that many people do hold to various opinions such as these. Why then do so many people today in the mainstream "orthodox" Church hold to so many vastly different and varying views about the millennium?

Various opinions of not only "how long" this period of time is to last, but also "when it is or was to inaugurate or begin" in the first place are only a few of the questions that are typically considered. There is also much debate as to what exactly takes place within the millennial period, or in the exact nature of the millennium. The question must be asked, is the "thousand year period" a past event, or is it an event currently in our midst and underway, or is it still a future event for us today that we look forward to?

I think that it's necessary to look back on a brief history of the interpretation of the millennium within the church, in addition to briefly comparing and contrasting the different views and to point out some of the major books or commentaries that have existed more recently. I think that most people will be shocked and surprised at the lack of extensive work that has been done on this very important and critical topic throughout the history of the church. Much more attention has been given to this study in recent generations, but historically, the study of eschatology and the millennium in general has been one of the most neglected theological subjects in the church, a point we will demonstrate throughout this book. Yet, for many pastors, theologians, and commentators who teach on Revelation, they seem quite sure of their position on the matter, whichever it may be.

For various reasons, of which there are far too many to indulge or discuss here, the Church has at various times and ways and throughout its history held to many different views on this subject, and this fact is also true of the very early Church. With this in mind we must then understand "why" so many people have such a hard time understanding the "correct" view about this subject. You see, if the early Church fathers disagreed about the millennium in its' infancy, then it would reasonably follow with clear logic that most, if not all Christians after the fact would likewise blunder or have a difficult time understanding the "true" or "correct" nature of understanding a proper interpretation of the "thousand years." And so it is that we come to a basic background on the history of teachings within the church concerning the doctrine of the millennium.

Before we begin this historical investigation, it must be clearly stated how significant, or insignificant church tradition really is. "While I concede that history is important, it is not authorative. In terms of sola Scriptura[1], it does not matter what these men believed. The Bible is the standard.[2] The clear fact that the New Testament writers continually had to correct errors in the Church is without question (cf. Romans 16:17; Galatians 1:8, 3:1; Ephesians 2:16-19; 2 Thessalonians 2:2; 1 Timothy 1:3; 2 Timothy 2:16-18; etc.)."[3] In light of this problem even in the times of the Apostles, each of us ought to consider the fact that even the very first Christians had a hard time understanding bible prophecy, or as with an issue like the

---

[1] See "Glossary" at the end of this book for a definition of the term "Sola Scriptura."
[2] DeMar, Gary, *The Early Church and the End of the World.* (Powder Springs, GA: American Vision, Inc., 2006), 39.
[3] Ibid., 39-40 (Paragraph adapted from DeMar).

millennium, and given the state of the early church problems, it's no wonder why we have ended up with so many versions of end times and millennial opinions.

"What makes us think that those a hundred years removed [from the Apostles and Jesus] could not also be in error on a complicated topic like bible prophecy? The history of prophetic speculation has been a persistent embarrassment to the Church. From the first century to the present, writers of theology have been wrong in their interpretation and application of prophetic texts. Proximity to an event does not assure future generations that past events have been reported or remembered accurately."[4]

There is only one conclusive truth that any astute reader of Church history might truly discover about the early church beliefs and their millennial views prior to the time of Constantine and the Council of Nicaea (AD325). That truth is that "[a]nyone studying [the early church] Fathers…will come to the conclusion that there is no prophetic consensus and no universal belief in premillennialism…The best that can be said is that there were some premillennialists in the period prior to Nicaea. In the earliest decades of the second century…there were only two early Church Fathers who could be classified as premillennial [Justin Martyr and Papias]."[5]

"During the first three centuries of the Christian era, premillennialism *appears* to have been the dominant eschatological interpretation. Among its adherents were Papias, Irenaeus, Justin Martyr, Tertullian, Hippolytus, Methodius, Commodianus, and Lactantius. During the fourth century when the Christian church was given a favored status under the emperor Constantine, [a version of] the amillennial position was accepted. The millennium was reinterpreted to refer to the church, and the thousand-year reign of Christ and his saints was equated with the whole history of the church on earth, thus making for the denial of a future millennium. The famous church father, Augustine, articulated this position, and it became the dominant interpretation in medieval times. His teaching was so fully accepted that at the Council of Ephesus

---

[4] Ibid., 40.
[5] Ibid., 42-44.

in 431AD, belief in the millennium was condemned as superstitious."[6]

"In the second century the church dealt especially with apologetics and the fundamental ideas of Christianity; in the third and fourth centuries, with the doctrine of God; in the early fifth century, with man and sin; in the fifth to seventh centuries, with the person of Christ; in the eleventh to sixteenth centuries, with the atonement; and in the sixteenth century, with the application of redemption (justification, etc.). There had been doctrinal convictions, either implicit or explicit, on these subjects previously, but it was as crises arose in these areas at these particular periods that the positions were more precisely articulated. Orr suggest[s] that the peculiar interest of the modern age is eschatology, the one remaining undeveloped topic of theology."[7]

The issues of end-times and eschatology have really never been a central theme of importance in the church at all. While it has primarily always been a visible part of the futurist, Christian hope and understanding, few Christians throughout the last two thousand years have actually undertaken a thorough examination of bible prophecy until some of the most recent scholarship beginning with the time of the Reformation. "Up until the time of the Reformation, the Bible had been a book for priests only. It was written in Latin, and the Roman Church refused to allow it to be translated into the language of the common people."[8] However, "The Reform[ers] adopted what the early Church taught respecting the return of Christ, the resurrection, the…judgment, and eternal life…It can hardly be said that the Churches of the Reformation did much for the development of eschatology…There has never been a period in

---

[6] Clouse, Robert G., *The Meaning of the Millennium*. (Downers Grove, IL: InterVarsity Press, 1977). 9.
[7] Erickson, Millard J., *A Basic Guide to Eschatology. Making Sense of the Millennium*. (Grand Rapids, MI: Baker Book House Co., 1999), 11.
[8] Ibid., 127, from Loraine Boettner.

the history of the Christian Church, in which eschatology was the center of Christian thought."[9]

"Traditionally eschatology has been one of the loci of systematic theology. It has generally been the last of the topics, so that the last things were literally the last things treated. They often were handled as a sort of appendix to Christian theology—virtually dispensable, as it were. Since theology professors have often found themselves behind schedule in their lecturing, they have often given eschatology rather scanty treatment. The impression has been conveyed, almost subliminally: eschatology is unimportant. In contrast to this, Moltmann regards eschatology as a spirit, an outlook, a framework within which all of theology is to be conducted."[10]

The Reformers of the 16th and 17th Centuries essentially focused on Soteriological (salvation and redemption) matters while essentially treating eschatology as a secondary aspect of all other essential doctrines. "In general it may be said that eschatology is even now the least developed of all the [subjects within] dogmatics.[11] Moreover, it was often given a very subordinate place in the systematic treatment of theology. ...Reformed theologians on the whole saw this point very clearly, and therefore [they] discussed the last things in a systematic way. However, they did not always do justice to it as one of the main divisions of dogmatics, but gave it a subordinate place [as] one of the other [subject matters]. Several of them conceived of it merely as dealing with the glorification of the saints or the consummation of the rule of Christ, and introduced it at the conclusion of their discussion of objective and subjective soteriology. The result was that some parts of eschatology received due emphasis, while other

---

[9] Louis Berkhof, *Systematic Theology* (Grand Rapids, MI: Wm. B. Eerdmans Publishing Company, 1996), 663.

[10] Erickson, Millard J., *A Basic Guide to Eschatology. Making Sense of the Millennium.* (Grand Rapids, MI: Baker Book House Co., 1999), 47.

[11] See "Glossary" at the end of this book for a definition of the term "dogmatics."

parts were all but neglected. In some cases the subject-matter of eschatology was divided among different [subjects]."[12]

The Apostles' Generation

But what did the Apostles teach or think about the millennium, the resurrection, the judgment, and the coming of the Lord? Despite the false doctrines they continually fought against, it's not very hard to ascertain what they actually taught, and that's because we have the Scriptures in no small number at our disposal. Any serious discussion about end times, or issues within the field such as the millennium, should begin with the period of Jesus and the Apostles. What did they teach, and what did they expect would occur in their own future? Few scholars deny that Jesus predicted, and had the Apostles believe that he would return at any moment and within their own first century generation.

However, it is and has been commonly assumed throughout church history that Jesus did not return within that first century generation, or at least, his "final" coming at the end of time did not take place. Therefore, there are a few problems that have to be addressed such as, why did Jesus tell them that his coming would take place before all of them died, and that it would take place within that generation (cf. Matthew 16:28 & 24:34, Mark 9:1 & 13:10, Luke 9:27 & 21:32)? In fact, Jesus told them in Luke 21 not to follow anyone who said that the time was near, when it really wasn't. Yet, 25-30 years later, nearly all of the Apostles and disciples began saying exactly that! Were the Apostles wrong or deceived? Surely they couldn't be! Yet, many Christians fall for this sort of argument, and attempt to explain passages that speak of a "near" and "soon" coming of the Lord by saying that time in God's eyes could mean anything. We'll address this issue later in this book.

To see the common understanding among many Christians in the mainstream Church today regarding the Apostles' and disciples' expectations of a soon and near return of the Lord in the first century, I will provide a quote that should shock any

---

[12] Ibid., from Louis Berkhof, 664-665.

Christian today. C. S. Lewis is one of the most admired Christians of our day, beloved by most evangelical scholars and lay Christians in the Church, spanning many different denominations. But what does C. S. Lewis think about the inspiration of the Apostles and even Jesus himself?

"'Say what you like,' we shall be told, 'the apocalyptic beliefs of the first Christians have been proved to be false. It is clear from the New Testament that they all expected the Second Coming in their own lifetime. And, worse still, they had a reason, and one which you will find very embarrassing. Their Master had told them so. He shared, and indeed created, their delusion.' He said in so many words, 'this generation shall not pass till all these things be done.' And He was wrong. He clearly knew no more about the end of the world than anyone else.' It is certainly the most embarrassing verse in the Bible."[13]

Scholars and critics have attacked the inspiration of the Bible on the grounds that Jesus failed when he predicted his return in the Apostle's first century generation. Not only did he fail, but the Apostles believed him, and also predicted that his return was imminent, and that it would take place at any time in the near future for them. Either Jesus came in the first century generation, and therefore, the millennium had to be fulfilled prior to that coming, or Jesus and the Apostles taught and believed a lie, or they were extremely confused or mislead. If there is any doubt that Jesus and the Apostles expected these events to take place within their own lifetimes, consider the following evidence.

"Moving from the gospels to the epistles, we find the disciples were unanimous in holding to the imminence of Christ's coming and kingdom. Paul said the 'time is short' (cf. 1 Corinthians 7:29); the night of sin and death was 'far spent;' the eschatological day 'was at hand' (cf. Romans 13:11, 12); God would 'finish the work and cut it short in righteousness: because a short work will the Lord make upon the earth' (cf.

---

[13] C.S. Lewis, *The World's Last Night* (1960), The Essential C.S. Lewis, 385.

Romans 9:28); he would bruise Satan under their feet 'shortly' (cf. Romans 16:20); the Hebrew writer urged his readers to exhort one another as they saw the eschatological day approaching, for it was a 'very, very little while' (Grk. micron hoson, hoson - μικρὸν ὅσον ὅσον) and he that was to come would come and would not delay (cf. Hebrews 10:37); James said the coming of the Lord 'draweth nigh' (Grk. eggiken), it was at the very door (cf. James 5:8, 9); Peter said the end of all things was 'at hand' (cf. 1 Peter 4:7); John said that it was the 'last hour' (cf. 1 John 2:18); [In the book of Revelation, written prior to AD70] Jesus told the churches of Asia 'behold, I come quickly;' the time is 'at hand' (cf. Revelation 1:1, 3, 22:10, 12, 20)."[14]

Is there any doubt that Jesus and the Apostles taught the imminence or nearness of his return in relation to those people who where then alive 2,000 years ago who would have heard and read all of those statements? Yet, because so many Christians today believe that events such as the millennium, the resurrection, and the Lord's Second Coming are still future or unfilled, critics and skeptics have rightfully attacked the Christian faith on grounds that Jesus and the Apostles were not only mistaken; they were uninspired or even liars! But were they?

"The confusion that existed during the lives of Christ and the Apostles was compounded after their deaths. The almost universal martyrdom of the disciples under Nero and the Jews left the church with few mature teachers or leaders capable of correctly expounding or explaining the eschatology or end-times views of the kingdom and the coming of Christ. The picture that emerges in the centuries following the [A]postolic age is one of great confusion: There is a great diversity of opinion concerning the nature and timing of end-times views among the patristic [early church] writers; their writings betray a fundamental lack of comprehension; they are as men groping in darkness after something they cannot see. Indeed, many of these men were not even certain which books ought to be received as canonical [divine and inspired from God] and

---

[14] Simmons, Kurt, *The Road Back to Preterism (Carlsbad, N.M.: Bimillennial Preterist Association, 2006), 2.*

which were not. Irenaeus thought there would be three levels of resurrection corresponding to individual worthiness; Tertullian thought there would be a millennial reign of Christ on earth"; Lactantius thought the earth would be wondrously regenerated during the millennium, and all creatures restored to their primal state in the garden. Notwithstanding these rather obvious errors, strands of Christ's and the Apostles' original end-times views were either preserved or recovered, and may be clearly identified in the vast array of the various writings of early church eschatology [end-times]."[15]

Although finding the true teachings of the Apostles and Jesus in the Patristic writings is easier said than done, it can be done. While easy to identify, a person wanting to find valid explanations of end-times issues would have to spend ages searching the available documents to sift through the muddy waters and varying ideas that accompanied the writers of the early church. So divergent and different was one writer from another on the subject of end-times and eschatology that it is any wonder that the Church ever developed any consistent views at all. Some might argue that even 2,000 years later, they still haven't.

The Post Apostolic Era

In the first few centuries following the time of the Apostles and the destruction of the Jewish Temple in AD70 during the Roman/Jewish Wars, the primary emphasis of the church writings turned from the predominant New Testament theme of eschatology and exhortation in the midst of suffering, to that of apologetics and polemic literature. With so many surrounding Greco/Roman and Eastern religious influences during this period of time, the Church was primarily concerned with defending the nature of Christ, and the truth of the doctrines of Scripture such as redemption, salvation, and the validity of Scripture itself. It was during this era that the development of the Canon[16] itself began to take shape.

---

[15] Ibid., (Paragraph adapted from Simmons).
[16] See "Glossary" at the end of this book for a definition of the term "Canon."

With the Jewish nation all but gone, "the result was that men's understanding of eschatology and *their comprehension of the prophetic method and language grew weak and attenuated.* 'Chiliasm' grew up (from 'chilia,' Greek for 'a thousand' - χίλια), which placed a literal construction upon the language of the prophets, asserting that the earth would be wondrously regenerated and that Christ would reign for a thousand years."[17] There truly was no consistent hermeneutical method of interpreting doctrines of eschatology, such as the millennium. The lack of early church writings on the subject compared to other apologetical writings and literature attest to the fact that the issue of eschatology and end-times was one of the least developed and understood Biblical subjects of that era.

But it wasn't completely absent. "Bishop Melito of Sardis, writing in the second century, presented a remarkably fulfilled eschatology along these lines. In the Homily of the Pascha, he wrote, 'It is I, says Christ, who destroyed death. It is I who triumphed over the enemy, and have trod down Hades, and bound the Strong Man, and have snatched mankind up to the heights of heaven," and "Who will contend against me? Let him stand before me. It is I who delivered the condemned. It is I who gave life to the dead. It is I who raised up the buried.".…Origen wrote, 'I challenge anyone to prove my statement untrue if I say that the entire Jewish nation was destroyed less than one whole generation later on account of these sufferings which they inflicted on Jesus. For it was, I believe, forty-two years from the time when they crucified Jesus to the destruction of Jerusalem.' (A.D.250: Origenes, Contra Celsum, 198-199)"[18]

The Epistle of Barnabas also found a great deal of allegorical expressions and interpretations of the millennium and eschatological fulfillment. "Barnabas unhesitatingly applied to the church Old Testament promises originally given to Israel. On the basis of their preference for allegorical rather

---

[17] Ibid., emphasis added.
[18] Simmons, Kurt M. *The Consumation of the Ages: A.D. 70 and the Second Coming in the Book of Revelation.* (Carlsbad, N.M.: Bimillennial Preterist Association, 2003), xvi.

than literal exegesis, the Alexandrian church fathers had no place for any variety of millenarianism. Nor did a strong premillennial tradition develop in Rome. There were exceptions however...[t]he most outstanding exception was Lactantius, tutor to Constantine's son, Crispus [who]...moved beyond the tradition in linking the thousand years to anticipation of a golden age articulated by pagan thinkers who, he declared, had obtained some inklings of true doctrine: 'In short, those things shall then come to pass which the poets spoke of as being done in the reign of Saturnus.'"[19]

The Era of Constantine

"By the fourth century, it [was] commonplace to present the preterist view of the Bible. In fact, we are told that the majority of writers found prophetic fulfillment in the Fall of Jerusalem. In A.D. 375, John Chrysostom of Antioch wrote, 'Was their house left desolate? Did all the vengeance come upon that generation? It is quite plain that it was so, and no man gainsays it.' (A.D.375: St. Chrysostom, Homily LXXIV) Though an early form of preterism was exhibited in his day, it is still quite significant that Chrysostom regarded this view as the unanimous opinion among his peers. Meandering through the centuries, the preterist view of first century fulfillment was generally assumed, and therefore, not explicitly defended. For [the first few] hundred...years, the Church ha[d] generally been engaged in defending more critical aspects of Christian doctrine."[20]

Even among those who did hold to a futuristic eschatology, there was a consistent belief among may Christians by the end of the fourth century that the millennium was something quite different, both in nature and duration, than some who viewed it as a very long period of time, and as a future, literal earthly Kingdom Age of perfection, with Christ on His throne.

---

[19] Grenz, Stanley J., *The Millennial Maze: Sorting out Evangelical Options.* (Downers Grove, IL: InterVarsity Press, 1992). 41-42.
[20] Ibid., xvi-xvii.

"Tyconius (an African Donatist writing around 390AD) rejected the strictly eschatological view of Revelation 20 according to which it describes a purely future reign of Christ...He expected the end to come, and in the year 380...if Christ was to come in 380, then the millennium would precede it...In Tyconius' understanding the first resurrection of Revelation 20, which introduces the millennium, is from the death of sin to the life of righteousness. Those who participate in the first resurrection are those who have been born again, and this new birth takes place through baptism. The first resurrection is therefore a spiritual resurrection: it is the new birth...Tyconius did not interpret the word millennium literally, seeing the rule of Christ only as an extended period of time."[21]

In the age of Constantine and the advancing, Christianized Roman Empire (from approximately AD250-450), a radical change began to take place concerning the teaching of the thousand year millennium and the Kingdom reign of Jesus. Now only two centuries removed from the time of Christ and the complete destruction of Jerusalem, the Roman Empire was beginning to reach not only the poor and oppressed, it was now also reaching the wealthy and those in power and with authority. Contrary to all expectation, Christianity triumphed in the Roman Empire and was embraced by the Caesars themselves by the early part of the fourth century.

The millennial reign, instead of being anxiously awaited and prayed for as had been the case by so many Christians in the previous two centuries (for various reasons), began to either be dated back to the first appearance of Christ or to the conversion of Constantine himself. It was generally regarded as a current reality in the glory of the dominant, imperial state-church of Rome; thus, we have an early form of millennial thought which placed the reality of the millennial age as a present and current one as early as the fourth century. This view was widespread as it began to dominate the church through the rise of the new, Christianized Roman Empire.

---

[21] Erickson, Millard J., *A Basic Guide to Eschatology. Making Sense of the Millennium.* (Grand Rapids, MI: Baker Book House Co., 1999), 59.

Some may even describe this era as the precursor to modern amillennial or postmillennial thought. However, as Grenz points out in his book "The Millennial Maze," "the Greek philosophical tradition, which dominated the theology of Alexandria, gained increasing influence on Christianity as a whole...By the time of Augustine's death, the nonmillenarian theology of Alexandria and Rome had engulfed the millennialism of Antioch and Ephesus. As a result, at the Council of Ephesus, A.D. 431 the church condemned as superstition the belief in a literal, future thousand-year reign on the earth" (pp. 42, 44).

"From that time on the doctrine of chiliasm [the view of a literal, physical one thousand year period on the earth, with Christ spiritually reigning on His throne through the Roman Empire] came to be defined as the hope of a golden age of the church on the earth, and of a great Sabbath or peace of the world after the hard labor of the world's history, but in its distorted Ebionistic[22] form took its place among the heresies, and was rejected subsequently even by the Protestant reformers more than a thousand years later as a Jewish dream."[23]

And so Christians began holding to forms of premillennialism (much different than today's versions), subsequently followed by the historic amillennial beliefs, then much later followed by Protestant reformed views of historicism and postmillennialism, which completely rejected all the former views before them. "W. G. T. Shedd observes that 'early millennialism was held mostly among Jewish converts. A few Apostolic Fathers held it as individuals, but those who do not mention the millennium had greater weight of authority and influence: [such as] Clement, Ignatius, [and] Polycarp' (History of Christian Doctrine, 2:390–391). In fact,

---

[22] The beliefs of a Judaistic Christian Gnostic sect of the second century, especially partial observation of the Jewish law, the rejection of St. Paul and gentile Christianity, acceptance of only one gospel – Matthew – and an early adoptionist Christology.
[23] Philip Schaff and David Schley Schaff, *History of the Christian Church, Volume 1*, 3rd ed. (New York: Hendrickson Publishers, Inc., 2006), 299-301.

according to church historian Jaroslav Pelikan: 'It would seem
that very early in the post-apostolic era millenarianism was
regarded as a mark neither of orthodoxy nor of heresy, but as
one permissible opinion among others within the range of
permissible opinions' (*The Christian Traditions*, 1:125)."[24]

The following early church writers are a historical proof
that there were many aberrant, diverse, and various Christian
teachings as early as the second century regarding the
millennium. The fourth century writer Epiphanes (AD315-
403), in his work against heresies said:

"There is indeed a millennium mentioned by St. John; but
the most, and those pious men, look upon those words as
true indeed, but to be taken in a spiritual sense." *(Heresies,
77:26)*

Eusebius (AD325) writes several opinions concerning this
matter.

"This same historian (Papias) also gives other accounts,
which he says he adds as received by him from unwritten
tradition, likewise certain strange parables of our Lord, and
of His doctrine and some other matters rather too fabulous.
In these, he says, there would be a certain millennium after
the resurrection, and that there would be a corporeal reign
of Christ on this very earth; which things he appears to
have imagined, as if they were authorized by the apostolic
narrations, not understanding correctly those matters
which they propounded mystically in their representations.
For he was very limited in his comprehension, as is
evident from his discourses; yet he was the cause why
most of the ecclesiastical writers (up to this point), urging
the antiquity of man, were carried away by a similar
opinion; as, for instance, Irenaeus, or any other that
adopted such sentiments. (Book III, Ch. 39)

---

[24] Kenneth Gentry, "Premillennialism and the Early Church," *Against
Dispensationalism* (June 9, 2009): under "6th Paragraph,"
http://againstdispensationalism.blogspot.com/2009/06/premillennialis
m-and-early-church.html (accessed January 5, 2011).

From this work Eusebius clearly states that he believed that the primary root cause of an "earth based literal one thousand year millennial reign" doctrine was that of Papias, and that it influenced Irenaeus, as well as MOST other early church writers. He argued that the views of Papias and Irenaeus primarily impacted all future ecclesiastical writings on this issue. Additionally, many scholars admit that Papias' view of the "future, literal millennium" was that it was to take place AFTER the resurrection. This was and still is a view rejected by most scholars and Biblical commentaries today.

Papias' view of the millennium contained a spiritual period which had already been fulfilled, or which they believed they already lived in, however, it included a future, literal millennial period which would follow Papias' Greco/Roman fantasized view of corpse or bodily resurrection. Prior to Papias, even this spiritual millennium view was believed to have already found its fulfillment in Christ and in the first century. It is no doubt that Epiphanes agreed with it during this same time period. Continuing his critique against the literal, physical earthly millennium view, Eusebius further states:

> "But Cerinthus, too, through revelations written, as he would have us believe, by a great apostle, brings before us marvelous things, which he pretends were shown him by angels; alleging that after the resurrection the kingdom of Christ is to be on earth, and that the flesh dwelling in Jerusalem is again to be subject to desires and pleasures. And being an enemy to the scriptures of God, wishing to deceive men, he says that there is to be space of a thousand (literal) years for marriage festivities...One of the doctrines he taught was that Christ would have an earthly kingdom." *(Eusebius's Ecclesiastical History, Book III, Chapter 28)*

He then states in this same work in Book V, Chapter 24, that while John was at Ephesus, he entered a bath to wash and found that Cerinthus was within, and refused to bathe in the same bath house, but left the building, and exhorted those with him to do the same, saying, "Let us flee, lest the bath fall in, as long as Cerinthus, that enemy of the truth, is within." Also speaking about Cerinthus, Eusebius further states:

"Cerinthus required his followers to retain part of the Mosaic Law, but to also regulate their lives by the example of Christ: and taught that after the resurrection Christ would reign upon earth, with his faithful disciples, a thousand years, which would be spent in the highest sensual indulgences."

Regarding the early church chiliast view of a literal thousand year millennium, it was no doubt that "[a] mixture of Judaism, [Greco/Roman], and Oriental philosophy [which] was calculated in order to make many converts, and this sect soon became very numerous. They admitted a part of St. Matthew's Gospel but rejected the rest, and held the epistles of St. Paul in great abhorrence."[25]

The fact that early forms of premillennialism were in no way approaching "universal" is evident also in that Dionysius (AD190–264) successfully dealt with "this doctrine" in a certain area where it prevailed and split "entire churches." He eventually disputed the doctrine of chiliasm in the Egyptian district and ultimately turned the majority of Christians in that area away from premillennialism (Ecclesiastical History 7:24).

In speaking of the Kingdom of God, Justin Martyr (d. AD165) said:

"And when you hear that we look for a kingdom, you suppose, without making any inquiry, that we speak of a human kingdom; whereas we speak of that which is with God, as appears also from the confession of their faith made by those who are charged with being Christians, though they know that death is the punishment awarded to him who so confesses. For if we looked for a human kingdom, we should also deny our Christ, that we might

---

[25] George Gregory, *A Concise History of the Christian Church: From Its First Establishment to the Present Time* (n.p.: Kessinger Publishing, LLC, 2007). 30.

not be slain; and we should strive to escape detection, that we might obtain what we expect. But since our thoughts are not fixed on the present, we are not concerned when men cut us off; since also death is a debt which must at all events be paid." *(First Apology of Justin Martyr, Chapter 11)*

Justin continued to state that:

"Chiliasm found no favor with the best of the Apostolic Fathers...the support from the Apologists too, is extremely meager, only one from among their number can with reasonable fairness be claimed." (Dialogue with Trypho the Jew, v. 25-36)

And what about Justin Martyr's response to Trypho regarding the hope of "a thousand years in Jerusalem, which will then be built"? Justin replied:

"I admitted to you formerly, that I and many others are of this opinion, and [believe] that such will take place, as you assuredly are aware; but, on the other hand, I signified to you that many who belong to the pure and pious faith, and are true Christians, think otherwise." (*Dialogue with Trypho the Jew,* 80)

Note the reference to "many" who "think otherwise." Thus, anyone claiming that there was anything remotely close to uniform opinions about the millennium in the early church is simply not being intellectually honest about the facts. The truth of the matter is that there was no unanimity regarding the millennium which existed in the early church.

Victorinus, a third century Christian writer, stated:

"Even though the floods of the nations and the vain superstitions of heretics should revolt against their true faith, they are overcome, and shall be dissolved as the foam, because Christ is the rock by which, and on which, the church is founded. And thus it is overcome by no traces of maddened men.   Therefore they are not to be heard who assure themselves that there is to be an earthly reign of a thousand years; who think, that is to say, with the heretic Cerinthus.   For the kingdom of Christ is now eternal in his saints." *(Commentary on the Apocalypse)*

Beyond the Early Church

Later doctrines of the millennium were no doubt influenced either negatively, or in response to earlier errors on this subject.   They ranged from allegorical methods of interpretation, today known as idealist or spiritual models, to historicist methods of interpretation which see the millennium as a future event, or an event inaugurated in recent history. Reformed schools of scholarship ultimately rose when the lack of chiliast fulfillment became a predominant problem in the Church by the end of the first millennia.   Trying to explain how and why the thousand year period suddenly appeared to be lasting much longer than a literal one thousand years was definitely a problem that had to be dealt with.   From the age of Constantine and moving forward a thousand years, the rise of the middle ages and the 14th to 15th centuries predominantly gave way to an age of universities, reformed thought, new scholarship and education, math, science, and a truly "enlightened" age known as the renaissance period.   "As the Middle-Ages developed, it seemed increasingly that only fringe groups and cranks viewed the millennium as a future event.   What we know today as premillennialism came more and more under the suspicion of heresy."[26]

The enlightenment period saw the rebirth of apocalyptic literature, the likes of which had not been seen before.   New interpretations of the book of Revelation saw applications to modern day events during the Middle Ages, and specifically to the Catholic Church and Rome.   Kurt Simmons described the period this way:

[26] MacCulloch, J. A., "Eschatology," in *Encyclopedia of Religion and Ethics*, ed. James Hastings (New York, N.Y.: Charles Scribner's Sons, 1914). 388.

"The history of apocalyptic frenzy among the Franciscans reache[d] unto the latter half of the fifteenth century. The Great Schism (AD1378-1418) witnessed three popes reigning simultaneously, one from Avignon, one from Rome, and a third from Pisa. The schism was healed by the Council of Constance, which deposed the Avignonese and Pisan popes, allowed the Roman pope to resign, and elected a new pope, Martin V (AD1417-1431). As a necessary condition to reform the church, the Council declared its supremacy to the pope and established a timetable for future reform councils, which Martin and his successor preceded to undercut. Thus died hopes for reform of the medieval church. However, the fact of the schism fueled apocalyptic expectations. Dissident off-shoot groups of Franciscans called 'Fratricelli' (Little Brothers) circulated a new generation of private revelations. The reformation and perfection of the church continued to be a recurring theme; the carnal church was [identified as] the whore of Babylon; the coming perfected church of the third status/seventh age was identified with the New Jerusalem. More and more the papacy was interpreted as the actual or mystical antichrist. The drama finally drew to a close when, after nearly three hundred years of spurious claims of new revelations and irresponsible exegesis of biblical texts, the Franciscan order was reined in following a period of inquisition and executions by papal authorities on the one hand, and determined resistance and assassinations on the other."[27]

The Reformation period sparked a new trend in the Church which saw the book of Revelation as a continuous unfolding scheme of the apocalyptic plan of God in the history of the Church, which would culminate in the rise and eventual destruction of the Roman Catholic Church, and it's Pope. Martin Luther and other popular reformers saw the millennial period as a time just on the horizon, where God would come to establish a new age of peace and prosperity following the

---

[27] Simmons, Kurt, *The Road Back to Preterism (Carlsbad, N.M.: Bimillennial Preterist Association, 2006). 15.*

demise and destruction of the Catholic Church and the Pope. "Luther came to speak of the papal institution itself as antichrist. This view became standard fare in Protestant writings...Luther altered his interpretation of Revelation, as he came to see in it a prophecy of the history of the Church...This historicist reading of the book of Revelation remained the standard means of exegesis in Protestant circles well into the seventeenth century."[28]

However, this interpretation too passed with time, and as the Reformation Era waned, new models of interpretation gave rise in conjunction with advancements in scholarship, technology, new academic discoveries, and other sciences and advancements which aided students of the Bible in properly understanding many of the foreign ideas contained within The Apocalypse (The Book of Revelation). "[T]he early English Puritans followed the historical interpretation of the book of Revelation and viewed the millennium of Revelation 20 as having occurred in the past—roughly between the years A.D. 300 and 1300. Yet other ideas were also at work, and these brought a rebirth on English soil of a futuristic understanding of the millennial era,"[29] along with others who sought historical fulfillment of the book in the early church, even within the first century.

Of the many academic achievements of the Reformation era, there is one in particular that is often missed, primarily because it was achieved not by a Protestant Reformer, but rather, because it was achieved by a Catholic Reformer. A doctrine knows as Preterism experienced a brief rebirth in the midst of the Reformation when a Spanish Jesuit Priest named Luis De Alcazar (AD1554-1613) published his commentary called *Investigation of the Hidden Sense of the Apocalypse.* Alcazar proposed that the book of Revelation applied to Christianity's triumph over Judaism and pagan Rome. According to Alcazar Revelation chapters 1-11 described the rejection of the Jews and the destruction of Jerusalem by the Romans in AD70. Chapters 12 - 19 described the overthrow

---

[28] Grenz, Stanley J., *The Millennial Maze: Sorting out Evangelical Options.* (Downers Grove, IL: InterVarsity Press, 1992). 50-51.
[29] Ibid., 52.

of Roman paganism (the great harlot) and the conversion of the empire to the church during the time of the Apostles and the Great Commission. Chapter 20 described the persecution from, and judgment upon the antichrist, identified by Alcazar as Nero Cæsar (AD54-68). Revelation 21 -22 described the triumph of the New Jerusalem, the establishment of the Roman Catholic Church and the continual and perpetual Kingdom which had expanded and continued to grow since the time of the first century.

In attempting to understand the book of Revelation in terms of the historical circumstances of the first century audience to whom it was written, Alcazar relied on the scientific books of interpretation and of literary criticism available to him in the university libraries of the Catholic Church, and thus, he came very close to a first century fulfilled understanding of nearly the entire book. He identified aspects of every chapter of Revelation to the first century, which included the millennium. Thus, if Alcazar applied Revelation 20 to a first century fulfillment, there is additional reason to believe that it was at least a plausible alternative to the other diverse millennial views.

However, in ascribing his explanation of Revelations' conclusion and climax to the final victory of the Roman Catholic Church, Alcazar struck a sour note at a time when Europe and the world was committed to breaking ties with Papal Rome. Preterism's rebirth was thus aborted in favor of anything opposed to something which had originated from the Catholic Church, and ultimately Preterist understandings of Revelation would have to wait almost another three hundred years before it received serious academic attention again.

"In seventeenth century England...an important theological line divided those thinkers who anticipated a future millennial era from other visionaries who believed that the thousand-year period lay in the past. The millenarians, in turn, disagreed among themselves concerning the actual nature of the imminent millennial reign of Christ. Some believed that Christ would reign spiritually from heaven through his saints...Yet others anticipated his literal presence on the earth...The closing decades of the seventeenth century saw the demise of the...theologically based political struggle of the

Monarchists and...[t]hey exchanged the millenarian hope of a future temporal kingdom on earth for the presence of a spiritual kingdom within the individual."[30] In the mid to latter eighteen hundreds, scholars began to realize the preterist context of Revelation and related eschatological events. Some of the preterist titles of this period include:

- Moses Stuart, *Commentary on the Apocalypse* (1845);
- J. Stuart Russell, *The Parousia* (1887);
- F.W. Farrar, the late canon of Westminster, *The Early Days of Christianity* (1891);
- Milton S. Terry, *Biblical Hermeneutics* (1890) and *Biblical Apocalyptics* (1898).

With the exception of Russell's *Parousia,* the above titles were primarily "partial preterist," which assumed that at least *some* of Revelation's imagery remained to be fulfilled in our future. At this stage, Preterism was merely academic, existing almost entirely in scholarly circles. It would be another hundred years before Preterism would become a grass roots movement. Ultimately, the understanding of the nature and timing of the millennium would naturally coincide with the advancements in academic and scholarly approaches to Biblical interpretation. As the old adage goes, "you can't place the cart before the horse." Thus, as the history of the Church continued to develop, change, and mold its end-times' beliefs, so too did the view of the millennium change with it.

With the passing of Historicist thought from the mainstream church, new interpretations developed which saw the millennial period in a manner that combined the chiliast views of earthly reconstruction and Church dominion with the spiritualization of the thousand year period. The idea that Christ reigned and ruled through the Church on the earth gained enormous popularity during the 16th and 17th centuries, and eventually gave way to the Puritan expansion and the foundation of America. The view that the Church was God's tool for bringing prosperity to the world during the millennial

---

[30] Ibid., 53, 55.

period gave rise to most of the modern advancements over the last 200 years. This view quickly became known as the postmillennial interpretation, defined as such because the primary belief was that Jesus would return after (post) the glorious and wonderful millennial period of the Church Age. But the puritan fervor still primarily served the scholarly masses, and eventually dispensational premillennialism became the predominant view of the mainstream church.

Modern Interpretations

To this day dispensationalism is probably the dominate approach to eschatology in the Westernized Church, particularly in the United States. This view sees the Church Age as a time in between the Old Covenant and the millennial period, and also has multiple dispensations of God's plan for redemption throughout the history of humanity. According to this view the Church Age will come to an end just prior to a terrible seven year tribulation period, typically preceded by the rapture of the Church, and then followed by the return of Jesus to reign on the earth for a literal one thousand years. Thus, the early church doctrine of premillennialism was once again revitalized in a new rendition of dispensational theology.

John Nelson Darby of the Plymouth Brethren is typically given credit for the popularization of this view. Darby and the writings of the Plymouth Brethren influenced protestant ministers all over America, including D.L. Moody, James Brookes, J.R. Graves, A.J. Gordon, and C.I. Scofield. Despite the optimistic view of postmillennial theology offered up by the Puritans, dispensationalism gained grass roots enthusiasm largely through the bible conference and the bible institute movements in America.

Beginning in the 1870's, various bible conferences sprang up all around the U.S. These conferences were not started to promote dispensationalism, but proponents of this new theological system promoted their program at the conferences and gained widespread popularity. The primary cause of this was because of the advancements in the printing press and the fact that their views were widely published and publicized in popular writings for the first time in the history of humanity.

In time, conferences like the American Bible and Prophetic Conferences (AD1878—1914) would actively promote dispensational methods of interpretation. In the late 1800's several bible institutes were founded that taught dispensational theology. These included The Nyack Bible Institute (1882), The Boston Missionary Training School (1889), The Moody Bible Institute (1889), the Bible Institute of Los Angeles (1907), and the Philadelphia College of the Bible (1914). However, dispensationalism received its greatest promotion by Cyrus (C.I.) Scofield. The publication of Scofield's Reference Bible by Oxford University Press in 1909 was a wind-fall for advocates of dispensationalism. *The Scofield Reference Bible* became the leading Bible used by American Evangelicals and Fundamentalists for the next sixty years, essentially limiting the advancement of any other view of eschatology or the millennium by any substantial amount.

These movements "founded several schools as a means of preserving orthodoxy, as the major church seminaries were taken over by modernists. T[hey] focused on mission rather than academic pursuits, and they fostered the training of lay Christian leaders. Nearly all of the new schools were doctrinally committed to dispensationalism. Consequently, they produced a large group of eager Christians committed to both traditional orthodox doctrine and the newer premillennialism...[D]ispensationalism [became] the dominant eschatology of fundamentalism and evangelicalism in America by the middle of the twentieth century. Large numbers of conservative Christians came to equate any denial of the tenets of this system with the denial of the faith of the Bible itself."[31] Unfortunately, this attitude still permeates the minds and beliefs of many Christians today.

Following World War I many dispensational bible colleges were formed. The foremost of these was Dallas Theological Seminary (1924). Dispensationalism thus began to be taught in an academic setting for the first time, influencing generations of college students. With the establishment of Israel as a nation in 1948, dispensational theology again emerged to the forefront of popular Christian thought. With

---

[31] Ibid., 62-63.

the mainstream books and preachers that would follow, the dispensational premillennial movement would have an impact on millennial thought for an entire generation of Christians that even today are influenced by it.

However, failed prediction after failed prediction quickly drowned out the message of a "soon" return of Jesus within the modern generation of Christians, and as the year 2,000 came and went Y2K fever dissipated and Christians were once again left with a desire to return to scholarly approaches to understanding the book of Revelation in light of the events in history, and especially the first century church. Thus, new scholarship today primarily sees preterist interpretations of the book of Revelation, although the final few chapters of the book are still a matter of great debate among many scholars who study the doctrines of eschatology.

And while some Christians may cry-a-foul that preterist interpretations are "unorthodox" (something we have clearly shown to be false), "the preterist viewpoint has been held, for instance, by the ancient church father Eusebius, seventeenth century Puritan Talmudic scholar John Lightfoot, nineteenth-century Methodist theologian and hermeneutics authority Milton S. Terry, and modern Reformed writers, J. Marcellus Kik, and Jay E. Adams."[32] There are a myriad of scholars, a few of which I quote throughout this book, who attest to the varying and divergent views concerning the interpretation of the essential eschatological views (resurrection, judgment, Second Coming, the millennium, etc.), and the passages to which these doctrines are assigned. This fact alone should give pause to anyone claiming to hold to any "orthodox" position on the matter.

Therefore, while there is certainly no conclusive or established view within the Church today and among its thousands of denominations, there are more and more people who are approaching the study of end-times and doctrines such as the millennium with a much more academic approach. Less and less people see the merits of having an apocalyptic zeal for end-times to happen at any point in the near future, or at all.

---

[32] Gentry, Kenneth L. Jr., Three Views on the Millennium and Beyond, (Grand Rapids, MI.: Zondervan, 1999). 21-22.

The doom and gloom and pessimistic approaches to dispensational, Zionistic, premillennial theology, while still the popular layman's view held by the majority of Christians today, is no longer the popular view held among serious scholars of the Word of God and within the field of eschatology.

Based on the clear evidence that the early Church was not able to agree on one of the most essential "end-times" or "eschatological" issues in the Bible, how is it then not possible that most people today do not have it right, or at least do not have a very good grasp of what this issue is really supposed to be all about? I would charge that, in fact, the vast majority of Christians today are in about the same category as the early Church and that so little consistency has ever been achieved on the issue of the thousand year period that one can only imagine if the Church will ever truly figure it out. However, times are changing! "How marvelous [it] is compared with the very limited proclamation that prevailed for so many centuries [that] that the overall result is that for the first time in history the people of the entire world have the evangelical Christian message made available to them...Statistics indicate that the world over, Christianity has grown more in the last one hundred years than in the preceding eighteen hundred."[33]

I believe that the Word of God is very clear on this matter, and that a consistent and accurate view can be found within this great collection of books we call "The Bible." The Bible is not too out of reach for common understanding in today's world. The problem arises when too many people allow traditional interpretations, creeds, or doctrines of fallible men to interpret these issues for them, rather than simply attempting to understand the proper meaning and context of passages in light of the rest of Scripture and new advancements in research, literary sciences, new historical data, and other areas. When we allow the historical events surrounding the book of Revelation to help in understanding the events contained within it, and when we consider the occasional circumstances of the first century, in addition to the genre in which the

---

[33] Boettner, Loraine, *The Meaning of the Millennium.* (Downers Grove, IL: InterVarsity Press, 1977). 128.

language of the thousand year period is found (apocalyptic literature), the doctrine of the millennium can then, and only then, be more clearly understood.

The great progress that has occurred in recent generations has now given us the ability to interpret Scripture more accurately than at any other time before until now. "What marvels must lie ahead when nations the world over are Christian—when [properly understanding the doctrine of] the millennium becomes a reality!"[34]

---

[34] Ibid, 132.

— 2 —

THE THOUSAND YEARS

Psalms 90:4 – "⁴For a thousand years in your sight are but as yesterday when it is past, or as a watch in the night."

2 Peter 3:8 – "⁸But do not overlook this one fact, beloved, that with the Lord one day is as a thousand years, and a thousand years as one day."

Revelation 20 – Describes the thousand year reign of Christ, the binding of Satan, the resurrection, and the judgment.

Popular Views of The Millennium

When studying the issue of the millennium, that is, what the Bible describes as the thousand year reign of Christ and the binding of Satan, it is often accompanied by numerous and perplexing ideas with various opinions in the popular church today. Opinions held by Christians in the Church today regarding what this period of time is remains at the forefront of numerous end-times books, radio broadcasts, and commentaries, and is one of the most widely debated topics in eschatology (the study of last things). Although sadly, it is also one of the most neglected subjects in eschatology having been seriously shortchanged in scholarly circles. For every book on end times or eschatology, and for every commentary on Revelation that exists, the millennium is a fan favorite to speculate about, but is often the most glossed over subject without extensive research performed. Is the thousand year period a period of time in our past, in our present, or is it yet to come in our future? Is it a period of an exact one thousand years, or is it figurative, and if figurative, is it to be interpreted as a period that is to last very long, very short, or does it even deal with a specific length of time at all?

The Pessimistic Millennial Views

At the very heart of this discussion is the relevance of understanding why it is even important to know what the millennium is referring to. Depending on the pastor, theologian, or commentator you read or listen to, you might get the impression that we are living in a Church Age, still waiting for the millennium to take place. In this view, Christ reigns in heaven, but he must still return back to earth to set up a physical Kingdom, a temple, and on and on this interpretation goes. Of course, this view is known as the Pre-millennial view (often associated with the Dispensational view), in which Christians today are waiting for the imminent return of Jesus to take place at any moment, accompanied by the rapture of all Christians. But when Jesus returns, he remains on the earth to rule over the nation of Israel. Of course, this doesn't happen until two thirds of all Jews are slaughtered in a world war III during the Great Tribulation, after which Jesus sets up his earthly throne to rule for a thousand years, followed by another final battle at the end of time.

Now, all of this sounds sort of sci-fi, like something you might watch on a blockbuster movie, but seriously, how a person views the millennium does and can impact their life. Having a view that Christians will escape planet earth at any moment so that Jesus can set up a thousand year Kingdom on planet earth changes how people live their lives today. Millions of Christians are affected by these types of doctrines, many of whom don't realize how it has truly changed their behavior until it's too late. One of the mainstream, popular Christian writers today, Hal Lindsey, made a startling, but all too often common statement in his book "Planet Earth – 2000 A.D." In the "Afterword" of his book, in the section titled "What to Look For in the Days Head," Lindsey spoke about a grand party being held at the Great Pyramid of Cheops in Giza, Egypt, gearing up for the Y2K event. Concerning Y2K and the parties leading up to it, Lindsey said this:

"Just for the record: I'm not planning to attend. In fact, looking at the state of the world today, I wouldn't make any long-term earthly plans." (pg. 305)

Then, Lindsey makes another statement that seems to contradict his former one:

> "As Christians, we should not be pessimistic and drop out of the world out of despair for its travails. We should be rejoicing in the knowledge that Jesus could return at any moment…Even though He may come today or tomorrow, we should plan our lives as though we will be here on Earth for our full life expectancy. Don't drop out of the world." (pg. 312)

Then Lindsey gets right to the point in describing how his millennial view directly shapes what he thinks his purpose is in the world today:

> "It's late, but there's still time to bring many others to salvation. And that is our final mission." (pg. 312)

I hope that in reading the last few quotes from Hal Lindsey that you get an idea of what many Christians, in fact most Christians today have bought into. They have developed a doctrine of the millennium that places the Kingdom of Jesus into a future, physical reality, and they say in one breath that they expect to be transported out of the world at any moment, and therefore, don't see any reason to make future plans for their life or to really be involved in changing society, yet, in the next breath they claim that it's vitally important to live "as if" they will be around for years to come. This sort of bi-polar attitude is at the heart of what I would call "Dysfunctional Christianity."

The main goal of many Christians today is to try and save as many people as possible by preaching a doctrine that judgment and doom is right around the corner, and that the world is going to hell in a hand basket, and that no matter what we do, it's not going to get better. It's only going to get worse and worse. This is hardly the message that will cause real change in the world today, and what's even worse, is if this doctrine is theologically incorrect the people who adhere to these types of teachings will be responsible for the utter chaos and dysfunction that resulted from their actions, or inaction.

The Optimistic Millennial Views

But not all millennial views have this pessimistic, doom and gloom teaching. In the minority of Christian churches today there are scholarly approaches to the millennial view that have a much more optimistic view of the world, the future, and the result is a much different attitude about life and how a person lives and works out their faith. These alternative millennial views primarily include the postmillennial view, the amillennial view, and the transmillennial view. The primary purpose of this book is to argue for the transmillennial view of the millennium; however, it is my belief that both alternative views of the millennium (postmil and amil) provide many wonderful benefits to the Christian as opposed to the mainstream, popular view of premillennialism held by most Christians today.

To my knowledge, the term "transmillennial" was primarily first used around 1999 by early modern preterists such as Max King of Presence Ministries, however, I have defined the term somewhat differently than they might have used it. According to their official website, Presence Ministries defines transmillennialism as follows:

"As a prefix to millennialism, "Trans" means "across" or "over" or "on the other side of." It also means "above and beyond, transcending" such as "transatlantic." The "trans" part of Transmillennialism™ stands for moving through or beyond what has gone before. In light of this, Transmillennialism™ is prepared to biblically challenge the other three mainline millennial views. Through the first-century reign of Christ, God's creation was transformed – people were transformed. Humanity's relationship with God moved "through" or "past" the Mosaic system of death and into the New Creation of the resurrected Christ. Through this, the kingdom has come." (cf. www.presence.tv/cms/transmillennial_view.php)

While I would certainly agree that the millennial period was the transformation from the Old Covenant to the New Covenant, I have primarily defined the transmillennial period as a transition period, where "trans-"stands for "transitional." And so, the millennium was a transitional period from the Old Covenant to the New Covenant.

It is my belief, and I will attempt to demonstrate my views here, that the "thousand year reign of Christ," also known as the "thousand year binding of Satan," or more commonly referred to as "the millennium," is a generational period which took place during the time of Christ and the Apostles. That is, in the Jewish concept, it is a generational period that is a length of time which lasts approximately forty years. This was the approximate time from the life of an adult to their offspring, or their children's children. This period of time was to begin during the ministry of Christ prior to the cross event and was to culminate in the events leading up to the destruction of Jerusalem and the Jewish War with the Romans in AD70.

The significance of the number forty (40) in the Biblical record is astounding. It is one of the most significant numbers used in the entire Bible, and a short survey of its usage reveals how Jewish and Christian writers of the Bible primarily used this number:

Forty (40) in the Old Testament

- Rain fell for "forty days and forty nights" during the flood.
- Spies explored the land of Israel for "forty days." (Numbers 13)
- The Hebrew people lived in the Sinai desert for "forty years." This period of years represents the time it takes for a new generation to arise.
- Moses' life is divided into three 40-year segments, separated by his fleeing from Egypt, and his return to lead his people out.
- Several Jewish leaders and kings are said to have ruled for "forty years", that is, a generation. (Examples: Eli, Saul, David, Solomon)
- Moses spent three consecutive periods of "forty days and forty nights" on Mount Sinai:
  1. He went up on the seventh day of Sivan, after God gave the Torah to the Jewish people, in order to

learn the Torah from God, and came down on the seventeenth day of Tammuz, when he saw the Jews worshiping the Golden Calf and broke the tablets.

2. He went up on the eighteenth day of Tammuz to beg forgiveness for the people's sin and came down without God's atonement on the twenty-ninth day of Av.

3. He went up on the first day of Elul and came down on the tenth day of Tishrei, the first Yom Kippur, with God's atonement.

- A mikvah consists of 40 *se'ah* (approximately 200 gallons) of water.

- 40 lashes is one of the punishments meted out by the Sanhedrin (*though in actual practice only a maximum of 39 lashes were administered, since it was believed that 40 would bring certain death*).

- One of the prerequisites for a man to study Kabbalah is that he be forty years old.

Forty (40) after the Old Testament

- Jesus was presented at the Temple in Jerusalem forty days after his birth.

- Before the temptation of Christ, Jesus fasted "Forty days and forty nights" in the Judean desert.

- Forty days was the period from the resurrection of Jesus to the ascension of Jesus.

- In modern Christian practice, Lent consists of the 40 days preceding Easter. (*In much of Western Christianity Sundays are excluded from the count; in Eastern Christianity Sundays are included*).

Thus, we have a very significant reason to believe that the number forty (40) is used extensively in the Bible for landmark periods of time or for major laws and measurements, whether it is used for 40 days, 40 years, 40 lashes, measurements, or in other ways. But the primary significance of the number forty (40) in this study is the Hebrew understanding of a "generation," which was approximately 40 years.

Understanding how a "generation" relates to the "millennium" is critical to properly understanding what the Bible is speaking about when it refers to this period of time.

Since it is my belief that the thousand year period is a direct reference to the "generation" to which Jesus predicted all the events of Matthew 23:36 and 24:34, and the same generation in which Jesus began to "bind the strong man" as recorded in Matthew 12:28-29 and Luke 10:17-20, it follows therefore that it must also precede or take place before the events of the great tribulation and the Resurrection and glory of the Saints at the coming of the Lord.

In addition to providing arguments for the nature and meaning of the thousand year period, I will also attempt to demonstrate the connection between the events near the end of the millennium with the great tribulation, the judgment of Revelation 20, and the Resurrection at the Lord's coming. Again, my entire argument is that the millennial period took place during the time beginning with the ministry of Jesus in or around AD27-30 and concluded at some point prior to the dissolution of the Jewish Temple and the Old Covenant Jewish system in or around AD67-70 at the Parousia[1], or the coming (*lit. Gr. "Presence"*) of Jesus.

Old Fashioned Arguments and Presuppositions

Now, the argument might be made by some people that, since we "already know" that Jesus has not yet returned, then we must either be living in the millennial period now, or it must still be in our future. It cannot have taken place in the past. However, this is the assumption made by people who "first" read Scripture with the view that Jesus is "yet to come" in our future, and then attempt to interpret all other passages and issues such as the millennium within that system or framework.

But if Jesus did in fact "already come," then it is not necessary to make the case that we must be in the millennium now, or that it must still be future. While it is not my primary

---

[1] See "Glossary" at the end of this book for a definition of the term "parousia."

purpose here to demonstrate that Jesus has already come in His glory in the first century, it is important to understand that before making the case for "when" Jesus did or did not come, it is more critical to first understand the rest of what Scripture says about the events leading up to and including His coming. In other words, if you "first" believe that Jesus still must come in the future then no matter what you read in Scripture everything will be interpreted based on your belief before you have actually read the Scriptures. However, if you first read Scripture without having an opinion on the matter, and then work out all of the details of what the Bible says about when, how, and what is to occur regarding the millennium, the resurrection, the judgment, and the coming of Jesus, then you just might arrive at a different conclusion than what you might have had before actually reading the Bible.

The Transmillennial View *(a transitional millennium)*

Therefore, I will attempt to prove the case for the transmillennial view of the millennium by first allowing the Bible to interpret itself. I will attempt to demonstrate that the Bible describes what this period of time is with respect to the forty (40) year period, which was the generation Jesus said would experience all of the prophecies and other things related to and leading up to his coming in THAT generation.

With reference to the binding of the strong man mentioned in Matthew 12 and Luke 10, it is my opinion that this is the same binding that is recorded in Revelation 20 with the "binding of Satan," using John's infamous apocalyptic imagery. It is also a period of time in which the "night" would be in the world and where Jesus would not be with His people anymore, though they would long for him to be with them, marked by the statements in John 13 where we are told by Jesus Himself that the hour had come for Him to leave the world to be glorified at once.

When He left the room we are told that "it was night." The "night" motif and other references throughout the Bible to this idea is a direct allusion to a period of time when Jesus is not with his people. It is also a period of time describing the conditions leading up to some expected event. For example, when it is night people sleep or stay indoors, and thieves steal and kill and destroy under the cover of darkness. When the day arrives people wake up and go about their normal business and the evening crime scene is utterly gone. In the same way, the Bible uses the imagery of the "night" and "day" to describe the conditions beginning with the crucifixion of Jesus (the night), and leading up to the coming of the Lord (the day, or the dawn). The Apostles were to be a "light" in the world and in a dark place, bearing good news of the Gospel and the "near" return of the Lord. The reason they were considered a "light" in the world was because they lived during the "night."

Now, it's possible that John was writing an obscure, pointless statement about the time of the day in which Jesus left the upper room to depart from them, but I think that any reasonable person will see that it is much more likely and reasonable to conclude that John intentionally placed this statement within the text to declare that Jesus was leaving the world and that His presence (parousia) would not be with them until a later period of time. Thus, the idea that is being expressed is that the absence of Jesus from His people or in the world is known as a time of "darkness" or "night."

The binding or millennial period would mark the beginning of the re-gathering of God's people, or the great commission. This is the very binding which allowed the Gospel to be spread over the whole world during the Apostles' ministry to establish the Church until nearly 34 years later when the first fruits church (first-century Christians) would then be persecuted or even put to death under the reign of the Roman Emperor Nero in cohorts with those Jews already persecuting and attempting to kill and capture them. Remember, throughout Paul's ministry he was persecuted and chased from city to city by the Jewish leaders.

Only his Roman citizenship protected him while he was imprisoned and as Paul stated in Acts 28, he was able to boldly proclaim the Kingdom of God without hindrance. Because of this protection and because of the power and authority Jesus had given to the first-century Apostles, their efforts would not be overcome, and their ministry would not be defeated or stopped. In fact, the Apostles and Christians during this period were given power and authority to bind, loose, and do anything they thought necessary in order to bring about the fulfillment of the Great Commission to the ends of the earth and to establish the church forevermore (cf. Matthew 16:19, 18:18).

In Acts 28:30 Luke recorded that near the end of Paul's ministry, he was able to preach the Gospel to all who came to him with boldness, and without hindrance. The miracles, signs, and wonders described in the book of Acts and in many of the other books of the New Testament show us in great detail that the Apostles were able to fulfill the Great Commission with authority and power, and this ability was the means which allowed them to spread the Gospel everywhere. The end of the Great Commission would also mark the beginning of the Great Tribulation period in which "the nations" (unbelieving gentiles, the Diaspora Jews scattered abroad, and unbelieving Israel) were deceived when Satan was to be loosed for a short time to cause them to fight against the Saints until his final destruction when the entire system of Old Covenant Judaism came to its utter destruction in AD70.

The primary difference between transmillennialism and postmillennialism is that the transmillennial view places the end of the millennium at the coming of the Lord in AD66-70, where the Kingdom Age, or Church Age, or New Covenant Age is consummated and fully established forever, never to end, and that the Church, or Christians everywhere for all time live within the Kingdom mandates to have dominion in the world and to bring healing to all nations, forevermore (cf. Revelation 22:1-5).

In the postmillennial scheme, the millennium generally or typically begins at the same time as in the transmillennial scheme, however, while the postmillennial view also teaches "a" coming of the Lord in AD70, they do not see this coming as the final coming of Jesus, and therefore, the postmillennial view maintains that the millennial period did not end, but continued beyond the AD70 coming of Jesus, and that it continues on, exists now for us today, and that we will continue in this millennial reign with Christ until his final coming at the end of time. Thus, in this scheme Christians are also to have dominion in the world making it a better place and preparing the world for the ultimate reign of Jesus back on earth with the Saints.

So the primary differences between these two views is that one maintains a future expectation of another coming of Jesus at the end of time (historic or traditional postmillennialism), whereas the other sees no additional coming at an end of time (transmillennialism); however, BOTH views see Christians having dominion in the world, bringing about change, healing, and the advance of the Gospel message throughout the world. Thus, there are differences in the "outworking" of these two views as it relates to Biblical dominion and bringing healing to the nations through love and the Gospel. The primary differences exist in the semantics of "how" the millennium and reign of Christ is carried out, and whether or not Christians ought to expect or even demand that there shall ever be a future "end of time" or final coming of the Lord beyond AD70, including whether or not the "Great Commission" still applies today, or whether it applies in the same way that it did 2,000 years ago.

—————— *3* ——————

THE MILLENNIUM AND CREATION

The Creation Account

One of the least understood aspects of the millennium doctrine has to do with its relationship to the Creation, the Fall and the Flood stories in the book of Genesis. Missing in most commentaries regarding the millennium is that nearly every millennial passage includes a reference back to one of these accounts. Did you ever notice what I'm talking about before? Could this be mere coincidence? Psalm 90 refers to Genesis extensively in its earlier context. 2 Peter 3 and Revelation 20 likewise do the same. Yet, why is there so little mention of the book of Genesis in so many commentaries on the millennium? The Creation, the Fall, and/or the Flood appear at every reference in the Bible to the millennium.

The same could also be said of nearly every resurrection passage in the Old Testament. In Acts 28, Paul said that *he taught nothing but what was taught in the Law and the Prophets of the Old Testament* (cf. Acts 23:6, 24:14, 28:20-23; Romans 3:21). When you go back and read the Old Testament texts on the Resurrection, it is always joined with some reference to Genesis and the Creation, the Fall, and/or the Flood. Adam is always a central figure in nearly every resurrection and millennium passage.

Likewise, whenever Paul talks about the Resurrection he almost always goes back to the last Adam (Jesus) reversing what was lost in the garden (cf. Romans 5ff). He always talks about "the sting of death," and being restored "back to life" from "the death." Yet, every time Paul talks about "the life" that he and his audience was currently receiving, or the blessed hope that they looked forward to, it NEVER speaks of physical life or resurrection from physical death. Why is this so? It is always with reference to life in Christ and the hope of Israel.

Our brief overview yields another observation. Practically every time the millennium is mentioned it is directly connected to the Resurrection and the appointed time for judgment (cf. Daniel 12; Revelation 20). This is no mistake! The time of fulfillment for all of these events is to take place together, simultaneously or concurrently, and thus, if any of these events has taken place in the past, then they must have all taken place in the past. If the millennium, the Resurrection, and the judgment takes place at the same time, or in concurrent and chronological order, and if any one of these events were fulfilled at or prior to AD70, then all of them were fulfilled in the past at or prior to AD70.

We learned the nature of the death and resurrection from Genesis 3. This is where we first read and learn of the hope of Israel! The hope of Israel was that they would stand again and be clothed once more forever! Notice what Paul said about the Resurrection in 2 Corinthians 5:

> 2 Corinthians 5:1-3, "[1]For we know that if the tent that is our earthly home is destroyed, we have a building from God, a house not made with hands, eternal in the heavens. [2]For in this tent we groan, longing to put on our heavenly dwelling, [3]if indeed by putting it on we may not be found naked."

Notice what Paul said in reference to being naked. It is an allusion back to the garden scene. "Genesis 2:25 tells us that Adam and Eve were 'both naked, and they felt no shame' when God created them. The Hebrew word for 'naked' in Genesis 2:25 is a different Hebrew word for the 'naked' condition Adam and Eve experienced after the fall [in Genesis 3:7]. John Sailhamer, a prominent Hebrew scholar, offers this explanation:

> "[T]here is a difference in meaning between ['naked'] in 2:25 and ['naked'] in 3:7. Although both terms are infrequent in the Pentateuch, the latter is distinguished by its use in Deuteronomy 28:48, where it depicts the state of

Israel's exiles who have been punished for their failure to trust God's Word...In distinguishing the first state of human nakedness from the second, the author has introduced a subtle yet perceptible clue to the story's meaning. The effect of the Fall was not simply that the man and the woman came to know that they were ('naked') [according to the use in 2:7]. Specifically, they came to know that they were ('naked') in the sense of being 'under God's judgment,' as in Deuteronomy 28:48" (cf. – Ezekiel 16:39; 23:29)."[1]

Thus, the clothing that Paul is referring to in 2 Corinthians 5 was a covering for their naked condition in Genesis 3:7. Sin brought shame and judgment to humanity once they were aware of the Law of God. However, as Paul states in his letter, he longed to put on a heavenly dwelling, a covering that would deal with the shame of being naked before God, in sin, and under the Old Covenant Law which produced covenant or relational death between man and God. In Genesis 3:7 Adam had sinned, and was found naked before God. God clothed them with animal skins (animal sacrifice) as a covering. This covering mirrored the exact same Law followed by Abraham as well as Noah, who sacrificed animals to God after the flood, and it mirrored the same Law followed by Moses when he spoke the Law again to Israel at Sinai.

But a better covering was promised in the future which would not be made or consist of fleshly ordinances or laws or sacrifices. That covering was the Holy Spirit, and the sacrifice of Jesus, once and for all. This covering would remove the nakedness of shame and guilt among God's people and would restore them to a proper relationship with Him. Paul did not wish to put off his physical body; his wish was to put off the Old Covenant sacrifices and that fleshly system of ordinances and rituals which was a noose around their necks, a burden no one could bare, and was only temporary. Those things could not properly deal with sin or the death of Adam (Covenant

---

[1] Timothy P. Martin and Jeff L. Vaughn, PhD., *Beyond Creation Science*, 3rd ed. (Whitehall, MT: Apocalyptic Vision Press, 2007), 348-349.

Death), and that is why it was necessary for Christ to come as He did in the first century. Thus, as Paul discussed the Resurrection, his doctrine came straight out of the garden scene, and of the promises of resurrection in the Old Testament going all the way back to Adam. Resurrection was the renewal of what was lost in the garden, and a restoration of people created by God back to Himself.

What was lost in the garden was the ability to continually fellowship in the presence of God because of sin. It was a covenantal relationship that was lost, and God established new covenant stipulations in the garden to deal with sin until Jesus would come once and for all to deal with sin forever. "The Death" that took place in the garden was not a physical death; it was a covenantal death and separation from God in his continual presence and fellowship. God promised Adam that "in the day" that they ate of the forbidden fruit they would surely die.

Did Adam and Eve physically die the exact same day that they ate from the fruit? No! Adam and Eve ate in a single day, and they died in a single day. Certain people argue that Adam only "began" dying in the day that he ate, and they make this argument in order to show that Adam's curse was "physical death," or that it at least "included" physical death. If Adam only "began to die" in the day that he ate of the fruit, then did he also only "begin to eat the forbidden fruit" in the same day? The logical dilemma here is unavoidable. If you argue that "dying" *only began* with Adam's sin, then "eating the fruit" only began as well.

While the 930 years of Adam's physical death does have significant meaning to this discussion, it is only representative of "the death" of mankind due to sin. We'll get to the relevance of Adam's life of 930 years in a moment. But for now, it is clear that Adam's death "in the day" that he ate was not related to biological decay or his physical death 930 years later. Indeed, Adam was created with a sin nature. If he had not been created this way, then there would have been nothing within Adam that would have caused him to sin in the first place.

Adam's physical death was not the curse of his sin. God created Adam from the dust of the ground, and all life in the cosmos for that matter contained the natural design of decay, and physical death and entropy. In Genesis 3, God said that from the dust Adam had been created and to the dust he would return at the end of his life. If we are going to say that returning to the dust was a curse then being created by it was also a curse. Physical dust (dirt) is not eternal, and therefore, to create Adam using it would mean that his physical body was also not eternal, naturally speaking. The curse in the garden scene for Adam and Eve is expressly indicated, and it was not physical death. Adam's problem was not dying of physical death and returning to the dust. His problem became a life cursed with unfruitfulness and hard labor until he died, and it was that after returning to the dust he was given no hope of life with God beyond the grave. While there was a promise of redemption in the future given to Adam and Eve, there was also a sense of finality in "returning to the dust" from where he had been created, since after this, there was nothing!

Prior to the Fall in the Garden, Adam and Eve lived and walked with God, and were allowed to eat from the "Tree of Life" which sustained them forever. However, after the Fall, they would return to the dust with no continued sustenance. They would die and then there would be nothing. This is the cry throughout the Old Testament. The fear of dying and going to the grave brought tears and sorrow because it was empty, void, and lacked any life with God.

Likewise, when Paul talks about what was lost in the garden due to Adam's sin (cf. Romans 5ff), he says NOTHING about physical death! Remember, what did God say to Adam about what would happen if he ate of the fruit? God told them that they would die in the day they ate of it. Did Adam physically die in the same day that he also ate? No! They did die in that very day, but it was not a physical death. It was a covenantal or relational death. All of the elements of the curse pronounced on Adam and Eve provided a fuller description of what covenant death entailed as God evicted them from the Garden. In other words, the curse in Genesis 3 is expounding on this "death sentence" understood in covenant context.

The purpose of Jesus coming to earth was to deal with sin, and to restore humanity back to their original condition before the Fall, not to bring an end of the world or human history, or and end of physical death and decay. God certainly was going to deal with "the death" which is spoken of in the New Testament. But this death was not talking about the natural and normal reality of physically dying. It was with regard to what had cursed humanity since the very beginning. It was "the death" which separated mankind from God. Again, this was covenantal death. Jesus told his disciples that whoever believed in his name had passed from this death to life already, even though they might physically die (cf. John 5:24, 8:52; Romans 6:4, 13-14, 8:2; 1 John 3:14). And so, if physical death had nothing to do with receiving eternal life in Christ, then why must we argue that physical resurrection is required to reverse the curse of the garden?

Why do so many Christians ignore this? While many Christians are focused on current events and the end of the world, many overlook that the central redemptive purpose for Jesus coming again was to complete his restoration and bring completed salvation (cf. Hebrews 9:28). Being sinful creatures, God had to deal with sin, and this required a redemptive plan, and that is the whole story of the Bible. It is a story of God dealing with humanity from the garden scene in Genesis all the way until we complete the redemptive process in the book of Revelation.

But this is not the end of history, or of humanity! This is the beginning of the story of humanity and our new opportunity to have a relationship with God *after receiving redemption despite our sins, which have been removed from us as far as the East is from the West*! The book of Revelation is not the story of the final events of the world; it is the story of the final events of the Old Covenant Age, and the end of the story of humanity prior to receiving the opportunity for the fullness of redemption in Christ. It is the end of the story of mankind outside of the presence of God, where the veil has been lifted, and the wall of separation between God and his people has been removed.

The Old Covenant Law was the veil, and it was what kept humanity separated from the opportunity to have a full and continual relationship with God. The Law was needed because of sin until a final sacrifice and covering was given by Jesus.

Now that Jesus has come, that wall and veil is gone, and we are now in the presence of the Lord. Thus, Revelation is the story of placing humanity back in the garden, restoring His people to a right relationship with God, where mankind may now have the opportunity to belong to the heavenly city, a city not made with hands, where God dwells within every believer (his New Covenant tabernacle and temple).

And so when we discuss the resurrection, we are also discussing the millennium, because the resurrection takes place during and immediately after the millennial period. Both the resurrection and the millennium are dealing with restoring humanity back to the Garden. Again, the writers of the Bible mention the idea of the Creation, the Fall, and/or the Flood stories every time the millennium and the resurrection are mentioned or alluded to. Plus, Paul said clearly and adamantly that *his doctrine of the Resurrection was nothing but the hope of Israel*, which we have already defined as the hope first introduced in Genesis 3:15 after the Fall of Adam and Eve.

Therefore, if the resurrection and the millennium have not yet occurred, and if the judgment has not taken place, then Israel has not yet received her hope of redemption, and we are all still under the Law of Moses and the Old Covenant Law of death going all the way back to Adam (cf. Romans 5:14), and it has not yet passed away. If that is true, then we have not yet received redemption. You cannot say that Jesus came and gave us redemption and then say that Israel has not received redemption because God has not dealt with her yet. That is the core of Dispensational Theology, and that is the primary reason so many Christians today are either rejecting this theology, or they are living a dysfunctional Christian life, and a lie.

Many Christians still do not see the simple connection with the redemptive plan of God from the story of creation, and the plan of His Son with the texts that deal with the resurrection and the millennium. If redemption is completed, and if Israel has already received her blessed hope in Christ, then the resurrection has already taken place and is already fulfilled. If that is true, then the millennium has also been fulfilled, and was completed in the past.

Romans 11:15 – "[15]For if their [Israel's] rejection means the reconciliation of the world [all nations], what will their [Israel's] acceptance mean but life from the dead?"

Romans 5:11 – "[11]More than that, we also rejoice in God through our Lord Jesus Christ, through whom we have now received reconciliation."

Therefore, if Paul could say that they "have now received reconciliation," and that this reconciliation was "passing from death to life," then Israel has already received her blessed hope of receiving life from the dead, and this means that the resurrection and the millennium MUST be placed in the past as fulfilled events in history.

Revelation and Creation[2]

Another idea that is often missed when trying to interpret the millennium is the fact that the language used to express the millennium is found in the most symbolic and cryptic book of the Bible, Revelation. But Revelation is not the only text that uses highly symbolic figures and language. While Genesis is not generally regarded as apocalyptic genre of literature, certain aspects of Genesis use language that other portions of Scripture draw from in describing apocalyptic events, or events that are described using apocalyptic literature. Numbers are often used in this manner throughout Scripture, although not always. However, it is generally easy to see when a figure is given in some way that is symbolic or apocalyptic. For example, Tim Martin and Jeff Vaughn describe the Biblical use of numbers with symbolism this way:

"The fact that the early chapters of Genesis are apocalyptic and prophetic is the key which unlocks the meaning of the long life-spans [recorded in the book]. Apocalyptic genre is known for its use of symbolic numerology as Terry notes:

---

[2] Much of the information provided in this section was taken from Martin and Vaughn in "Beyond Creation Science," which has been cited in every case I quote from that book.

'That certain numbers are symbolically used in the prophetical books is conceded by all interpreters.'

There are a couple of obvious examples in Revelation which utilize symbolic numerology. The 144,000 (Rev. 7:4-8) is a symbolic number (12 x 12 x 1000) related to the 12 tribes of Israel, God's holy remnant. The millennium (Rev. 20:4) is another symbolic number (10 x 10 x 10) which symbolizes perfection and completeness. If there is a literary connection between Genesis and Revelation, then we have good reason to believe these long ages are symbolic and serve numerological purposes. They are not given as a scientific or mathematical record of biological age. Some young-earth creationists note the presence of numerology in ancient texts. [James] Jordan writes:

'Ancient and medieval literature abounds in numerical symbolism, large parallel structures, intricate chiastic devices, astral allusions, sweeping metaphors, typological parallels, and symbolism in general.'"[3]

Martin and Vaughn continue to discuss the relevance of numerology in ancient Mesopotamian documents contemporary with the Genesis account, and suggest the following:

"Another relevant point to consider is that ancient Mesopotamian documents contemporary with Genesis also include a record of extremely long life-spans of Sumerian kings. One author explains:

'The Sumerian antediluvian king list includes eight kings who reigned, according to that list, for a total of 241,200

---

[3] Timothy P. Martin and Jeff L. Vaughn, PhD., *Beyond Creation Science*, 3rd ed. (Whitehall, MT: Apocalyptic Vision Press, 2007), 307-308.

years. That document dates from the third dynasty of Ur or earlier.'

[Christians] seldom mention this type of ancient literature from Mesopotamia. But this is important to consider for those who value the cultural context and original audience expectations surrounding biblical texts. The fact [that] these Sumerian lists are related to kings may provide an important original cultural context for the apocalyptic life-spans in Genesis. Perhaps the obstacle to understanding the long life-spans in Genesis is the common assumption that [they] must refer to biological life and death.

If 'the death' Adam and Eve experienced when they sinned was covenant death, [rather than] biological death, then we have good reason to consider the possibility that these long life-spans make a covenant statement rather than a biological statement. Why would the writer of Genesis switch from an account dealing with [covenantal] death in Genesis 3 to an account of biological life-spans in the following chapters? Where does this supposed shift in the definition from "the death" [covenantal] to some other kind of death [physical] take place?"[4]

No one is denying the fact that the genealogical records of Genesis included real people, with historical records of the fact that they lived and died. However, is it possible that the historian who recorded those events had much more in mind than simply the length of time that they lived when he recorded the number of years of their lives? Most scholars recognize the highly significant aspect of each of the names given for nearly every person mentioned in the genealogical record of Genesis. Whether their names were chosen because their parents had something specific in mind, or whether the writer chose those names to provide the readers with detailed information about the life of those individuals is arguable. However, one way or the other, their names were highly

---

[4] Ibid., 308.

symbolic and represented something very significant about their life and Israel's history.

This same idea must also be true of the number of years that these men and women lived, and how they were recorded for us in the Biblical account. Now, how and why this all relates to the millennium will be pointed out shortly. But for now I will attempt to further bolster the case for the symbolic method of interpretation regarding the numerologies used in dating the ages of men in the Genesis account. Martin and Vaughn make a very strong case as they continue their argument which I am happy to reiterate here:

"What evidence do we find in Genesis that these long life-spans are symbolic, in keeping with apocalyptic [and symbolic] literature?

We should first point out that the genealogies in Genesis 4 (related to Cain) and Genesis 5 (related to Seth) present another double picture common to apocalyptic form. Cain symbolizes the faithless and wicked line which lived 'shut out' from the Lord's presence. Seth embodies God's righteous covenant seed line which ultimately brings the Messiah into the world.

In the case of these parallel genealogies, it seems curious that only one genealogy records long life-spans. The long ages appear only within the godly line related to the Messiah (Gen. 5). They do not appear in relationship to Cain's line (Gen. 4). The same is true of the genealogies which are listed after the flood (Gen. 11). By placing Seth's genealogy in Genesis 5 together with Shem's genealogy in Genesis 11, we find that Adam's line to Abraham through Seth, Noah, and Shem is communicated with long life-spans and no one else. *Only the Messianic line is described with these extremely long ages!* Only God's covenant line is recorded with these life-spans, for they are the offspring of Eve rather than the serpent.

The reason Cain's line has no life-spans recorded was because his line was dead [even though they were physically alive]. Remember, Cain was driven out from the presence of God (Gen. 4:13-16). This was his death sentence for killing his brother. The result of Cain's wickedness was that he and his offspring would have no life in them. That is why there are no life-spans listed in the line of Cain.

[Some Christians] assume that the long life-spans in Genesis were universal, meaning they applied to all people living on planet Earth at the time. However, a careful reading shows that Genesis does not say that all people referenced in Genesis lived to these ages – only those within the faithful covenant line. There is a clear covenant context in which the long life-spans appear. They are not universal. They apply only to God's covenant line [the line of Adam and through his son Seth].

The apocalyptic, symbolic interpretation of the long life-spans relies on three points thus far: (1) ancient literature and apocalyptic is known to contain numerological symbolism, (2) Mesopotamian records contemporary with Genesis used extremely long life-spans in ancient Sumerian king lists, and (3) only the covenant line from Adam to Abraham are referenced with such life-spans. These facts combine to make a numerological, symbolic reading of these life-spans reasonable.

It is also important to recognize the remarkable patterns in the listing of numbers in the genealogy of long life-spans in Genesis 5:

'These numbers are not only excessively large but also seem to fall into a discernible pattern... All of the numbers in Genesis 5, along with those for Noah that appear in Genesis 7:11; 9:28-29, are either exact multiples of five, or else multiples of five with the addition of seven (one number, the years of Methuselah's life, was twice augmented by seven).'

That is a remarkable coincidence. What are the chances of that happening in any given group of individuals of this size in any historical setting? Realize the pattern must be maintained not only in the total years lived, but the timing of the births as well!

Key individuals are associated with highly significant biblical numbers. Lamech, the father of Noah, lived 777 years (Gen. 5:31). Might this be an obvious case of symbolism? Noah lived 500 years (a nice round number) and became the father of his three sons (Gen. 5:32). The flood began when Noah was 600 years old (Gen. 7:11).

The apocalyptic interpretation becomes stronger as we continue to examine key individuals. Genesis emphasizes that Enoch, the seventh from Adam who "walked with God," lived 365 years (Gen. 5:23-24). [Milton] Terry notes the symbolic meaning of this life-span by saying:

'The number of 'all the days of Enoch'... is symbolic of an ideal cycle of perfect human life, a full year of years; and men who attained such perfection of fellowship with the Elohim are apocalyptically styled sons of the Elohim (comp. Gen vi, 2).'

This is one additional item that lends support to the conclusion that the long life-spans in Genesis communicate through prophetic numerology and are not intended to be taken as a 'literal' statement of biological age."[5]

Martin and Vaughn make many compelling arguments for the idea that long life spans in the Bible represented blessings and those who followed God, and that short life spans represented those who were cursed and did not follow God, or that the life spans represented degrees of blessing and cursing given by God. Isaiah 65 uses similar language in speaking of those who are cursed who live short lives (less than a hundred

---

[5] Ibid., 312-314.

years, doubtful that it is a coincidence that Isaiah uses this exact figure) verses those who are blessed and live very long lives. It is hardly an accident that Isaiah uses the idea of a very long life beyond one hundred in describing his vision of the "New Heaven and Earth," since Genesis gives the original story of the first "Heaven and Earth" and also describes those men who lived very long lives, who were only those men who were born of the line of Seth, God's covenantal lineage and chosen people! From Martin and Vaughn's arguments, it can also be seen that a long life span for someone from the line of Seth also seems to parallel the Sumerian idea that these people were "priests and kings." We'll touch on this idea later as we ponder over Revelation 20 with regard to those who would reign with Christ as Kings for a thousand years.

Extra Biblical Texts

While it's not my intent to make primary arguments based on conjecture, hypothetical theories, or extra-biblical sources (writings outside of the Bible), it is still quite helpful to know what the people who lived 2,000 years ago thought, read, and knew about this important subject; that is the thousand years. If we go back to the time of the Apostles and first-century Christians, what would they have thought about John's doctrine of the millennium? After all, the Apostle John did not stop and explain a new concept of the millennium to the readers of his new book of Revelation. The book itself certainly doesn't expound on its own meaning. This means that his readers would have probably already been familiar with the literature that John used to write the book, or that there would have been other messengers who could relay the message and explain what John was talking about.

Apocalyptic language was very common in John's day 2,000 years ago, and anyone who had received a copy of John's book (or more properly referred at that time as John's Letter), or who had listened to one of the messengers reading from it, would have easily recognized the meaning of the majority of the symbols and images contained within the book if they had any knowledge of Old Testament imagery and contemporary apocalyptic literature, or even Greco/Roman mythology. The same cannot be said for most people today! This implies that we will need to look into the Jewish literature that was readily available and floating around during the first century, and the ancient Jewish and Greco/Roman culture of that period of time, in order to get a glimpse at how John's first-century audience would have understood what he meant when he spoke about the millennium.

One of the best ways to understand the literature of the Bible in the first century is to read the contemporary literature of the same period in order to pick up on the meanings and nuances of how people in that time and culture would have understood what the writers of the New Testament were talking about. Not that everything can be understood this way, but many wonderful facts and ideas can be obtained simply by looking at writings outside of the Bible which were written around the same period of time that different portions of the Bible were written.

There are many writings from practically all periods and ages of the books of the Bible, and it's hard to take the time to focus on every one of them. However, since our study is only primarily concerned with understanding the concept of the thousand years, we can narrow down our search to a few important pieces of literature relevant to this discussion. Some of the ideas about the thousand years are reflected in the Jewish Talmud, the Midrash, and the Kabbalah, or the Zohar. Most of these ancient Jewish writings indicate that a Messiah would come and inaugurate a time of great peace and rest, and that each day of creation symbolized a thousand years of human history. They believed that each millennial period reflected the seven days of creation, and that the seventh day (seventh millennial period) would be the time of the great reign of the Messiah, their King.[6]

Elaborating on the theme of the seventh millennium representing the Messianic Age are numerous early and late Jewish scholars, including the Ramban, Isaac Abrabanel, Abraham Ibn Ezra, Rabbeinu Bachya, the Vilna Gaon, the Lubavitcher Rebbe, the Ramchal, and Aryeh Kaplan. The

---

[6] Babylonian Talmud, Rosh Hashanah 31a and Sanhedrin 97a, Zohar 1:117a and Zohar Vayera 119a.

acceptance of the idea of the seventh millennium representing the Messianic Age across the Ashkenazi – Sephardi divide, the Chassidim – Misnagdim divide, and across the rational Talmud and mystical Kabbalah perspectives, shows how central the idea of the seventh millennial period was and is within traditional and ancient Judaism.

While the Jewish traditions did view each millennial period as a literal thousand year period, what is significant about their beliefs is two-fold.

1. The Jews applied the seventh millennial period to the Messianic Age, which began with the ministry of the Messiah, which most Christians would agree began with the birth of Christ, or at least with the beginning of his ministry. If their (Jews) traditional understanding is at least somewhat true, then the beginning of the millennial period began with Jesus in the Christian framework.

2. While the Jews applied a "literal" understanding to the first six periods of millennial days, the seventh period or Messianic millennial age typically would have no end within the vast majority of Jewish writings, and so, even in the Jewish tradition, the millennial period was not a period of an exact number of years. It simply represented a final age in which their Messiah would reign with them, and which never came to an end, and was not necessarily restricted to a literal thousand year interpretation.

Other ancient ideas surrounding the thousand years can be found in some of the Greco/Roman literature before the time of Christ, and include Plato, Virgil, Homer, and Justin Martyr among others.[7] Generally speaking, beliefs about the Hadean realm (Hades, or the realm of the dead) were current among the Greeks and Romans, as we see from Justin Martyr's writings, and other Christian works of the early and later historical church periods. Some of those writings are also reflected in Dante's "Divine Comedy," better known as

---

[7] Plato, Republic, Bk. X; Virgil, Aeneid, B. VI; cf. Justin Martyr, 1st Apology, VIII.

"Dante's Inferno." Common among the Greco/Roman beliefs was that when a Greek or Roman Hero died, they would enter the underworld and live for a thousand years until they would be raised to life, either reincarnated into their previous body, or given a new life altogether.

And so we can already begin to see aspects of Greco/Roman ideas found in New Testament resurrection and millennial language and literature. Of course, the New Testament writers were more concerned with Jewish understandings, as we will see shortly, however, they were quite familiar with and keen to address their gentile contemporary audiences, and thus, they would have definitely had those views in mind when expressing the doctrines of the resurrection, the millennium, and the judgment.

More relevant to this discussion are the writings of Enoch, Jubilees, and the Christian commentary called Barnabas. Now, none of these or the other Greco/Roman, or Jewish writings outside of the Old Testament are considered inspired or canonical to most Christians today, but they do provide a frame of reference that a Biblical writer would have had and used when writing the Word of God. Surely a New Testament writer wouldn't have referred to something such as the thousand years completely out of the literary or cultural context in which his audience would have been familiar, unless he wanted to specifically explain that he was giving an interpretation altogether different. But since no explanation or alternative meaning was given when the millennial passages were written, we must conclude that the writer had his culture in mind, and the literature that his audience would have had available to them and would have been familiar with.

When you study these writings and begin absorbing literary genre and their manner of storytelling, then things start to pop out at you in the extra biblical writings (writings outside the Bible). In reading these documents you could swear that they were saying many of the same things that you read right there in the Bible. The reason that this happens is because these types of literature were actually some of the most influential and common pieces of writing available during the time of the first century when our New Testament was written. Believe it or not you can find quotes and numerous allusions to

Enoch and Jubilees throughout the New Testament alone, very similar to how our New Testament quotes from the Old Testament texts.

The implications for this are huge when it comes to the book of Revelation for those who have studied Enoch in much detail, and there is certainly much to be gleaned from Jubilees as well. Again, these other writings are not used as God inspired works of literature by most Christian scholars today, but how they impacted the writers of the New Testament is very significant and without question. Below I will attempt to quote from some of Barnabas and Jubilees in an attempt to demonstrate how they are tied together to drive home the similarities between those writings and John's language, and his use of the phrase, "the thousand years" in the book of Revelation.

Later in this book, I will take a very close look at 2 Peter 3 and how this chapter ties into the idea of the millennium, however, for now notice that in 2 Peter 3:8, Peter quotes from the book of Jubilees which was written 200 years earlier. Remember, here is what Peter said:

> "But do not forget this one thing, dear friends: With the Lord a day is like a thousand years, and a thousand years are like a day."

Now notice what Jubilees says (nearly 200 years earlier):

> Jubilees 4:29 – "...thereof, Adam died...And he lacked seventy years of one thousand years; for one thousand years are as one day in the testimony of the heavens and therefore was it written concerning the tree of knowledge: 'On the day that ye eat thereof ye shall die.' For this reason he did not complete the years of this day; for he died during it."

Shockingly, most scholars have either ignored, or been unaware of this significant parallel statement. Not only was Peter alluding to Old Testament ideas and passages like Psalm 90:4, Peter was quoting nearly verbatim from the book of Jubilees written 200 years prior to his own letter! And what was the context of this statement in Jubilees? What did the "thousand years" refer to in that book? Adam physically died before obtaining to the "thousand years." He was sinful, and he was a mere mortal who did not obtain eternal life. Adam was unable to complete the promise given to him to be able to eat from the tree of life and live forever. To live a thousand years was to obtain eternal life! Remember earlier in this chapter as I spoke about the significance of the genealogies and age numerology in the book of Genesis?

Now, again, let me be clear that I am not preaching Jubilee doctrine here, but I am making a startling comparison between the way in which the book of Jubilee would have been understood and with the purpose of Peter quoting from it. Why would Peter quote from this uninspired source to refer to the "day" that was supposedly going to come at any moment according to Peter, since God was not slack concerning His promises? Peter believed that Jesus would return at any moment, and the evidence he provides was that the Jews were mocking him and the other Christians and asking why the predictions of Jesus hadn't yet come true as he said they would (within THAT generation). Peter responded by telling his audience to be patient, because God was not going to forego his promise to return in that generation, but that He wanted to wait until the very last minute. So Peter exhorted them to patiently endure further persecution and mocking, because the day of the Lord was right around the corner.[8] But why does Peter quote from a non-Biblical source to speak of the "thousand years" as a day he has in view?

Before I answer that, let's take a look at the Epistle of Barnabas for a moment. Notice that the literature of Barnabas, a Christian commentary, also quotes from Jubilee:

> Barnabas 15 – "… for a day with him means a thousand years. And he himself is my witness when he says, 'Lo, the day of the Lord shall be as a thousand years.'"

---

[8] For a full explanation defending this position, read chapter 6, *Establishing Some Parameters, The Prophetic Context of the "Thousand Years,"* in addition to Chapter 7, *The Day of the Lord, A Day as a Thousand Years.*

The truth of the matter is that it was a common saying during the time of the first-century writers concerning Adam and the "Day of the Lord," and it was also applied to the Hebrew understanding of the word day (In Hebrew the word Yom is used in Genesis in reference to a "day" which CAN pertain to a period of time, or something other than a literal 24 hour period of time) as well, which is how Peter and Barnabas applied it in the first century. In fact, even Augustine, an early church historian, applied the one thousand year metaphor to the Days of Genesis 1 as most other Jewish writers and commentaries did as well. And so we can clearly see that this language was well established and was often used in ancient times to describe "eternal life" and "the Day of the Lord." The language of a thousand years has certainly been lost over time as it was understood in ancient times and many historians and wonderful, devout men of God have been unable to learn of these things, or they have completely ignored their relevance to this important study.

Other important ideas we should consider within the book of Jubilees is that it is also attempting to reiterate the incompletion of Adam having attained to one thousand years of life. It is my opinion that this was the primary reason Peter quoted from Jubilees. Adam did not live to a thousand years because he had eaten from the tree of knowledge and disobeyed God's Law. We know from Paul that Adam's sin was what brought covenantal death to Adam because it was bound up in the commandment or "Law" which produced "sin" in Adam, and for the rest of humanity for that matter. And while Adam did "die in the day that he ate," the writer in Genesis has given us a literary device to describe the incomplete nature of Adam's life of 930 years, in that he does not have eternal life beyond the grave and died short of obtaining it. For Adam to have lived a thousand years would have meant that he obtained eternal life, and that he would have been in a covenant, eternal relationship with God.

Thus, while we, or Peter, or any New Testament writer would certainly not form a doctrine out of the application that Jubilees might have used, Peter certainly understood the Jewish hermeneutic of Adam's age and not living to a thousand years. Did Adam die in the day he ate the fruit? Yes! However, Adam's natural life and the 930 years described is representative of what he lacked. Adam lacked life with God, and that life was more than physical; it was Covenantal Life, and it was life with God forever. That Adam died at 930 years was not a physical curse. Adam may well have died at 80 years, or 358 years, or 672 years, or whatever we might ascribe to him arbitrarily and in physical terms. But the writer intentionally chose 930 as a literary device to explain something much deeper, something we have and will continue to touch on here.

According to Jubilees, Barnabas, and other early church writers, a thousand years then is a metaphorical age to demonstrate Adam's lack of attaining to perfection, or eternal life. In fact, his inability to ever attain to that goal, and his spiritual relationship with God was completely subjected to futility and bondage, and being separated from his Creator. And so this language serves more than one purpose as a metaphor for the Jews. One purpose of expressing "thousand years" language was to denote or describe the "day" [the heavenly works of God being completed and perfect] and another purpose was to denote or describe "eternal life" [spiritual completion and a covenant relationship with God]. It was used to describe Adam's mortal status, and thus, his lack of immortality since he could not live to a thousand years. If Adam had reached a thousand years of age, would he have physically lived forever? Probably not. Physical death was not part of the curse. However, the length of Adam's age was certainly used as a literary explanation to describe something missing in Adam. It is in essence a literary metaphorical tool.

Take a look at how Jubilees used the language of a thousand years later on in its writings. The same idea expressed in Jubilees is found somewhat similarly in Isaiah 65:20 discussing the New Heavens and Earth. In Jubilees we are reminded that the ancients lived to nearly one thousand years [but they could never quite attain it] because God's chosen people [which is "Adam" in Hebrew] became progressively more evil as the Garden scene had become a distant reality. Thus, the flood story describes God dealing with the problem of progressive evil coming into the world.

Genesis 8 says that mankind is evil from his youth, and thus, without redemption mankind was without hope of ever receiving eternal life and a renewed covenant relationship with God.

Every successive generation after the flood saw the line of Seth (God's chosen people) beginning to live shorter lifespans, and thus, as we see the Law of Moses given some time later at Sinai, we also see God's chosen people living lives much shorter than described prior to the flood. The progression seems obvious. The further humanity gets from the garden, the more God reveals sin within us all, and our reprobate condition as sinful human beings. The Law was more pronounced and was made more predominant as the Old Testament story unfolded. And so we see that as sin is made more known, life becomes shorter and shorter. Only when Jesus arrives on the scene is eternal life once again extended to humanity.

In Jubilees 23:28 we see that there is a new period of time that will bring back the path of righteousness and the life of the faithful people of God who will once again grow to be a thousand years old (as Isaiah 65 alludes to), even beyond the ancients who did not reach the thousand year life span. All of this language is highly charged symbolic literature, and it is talking about the conditions of the New Heavens and Earth, and life "back in the Garden." The scene in Isaiah 65 was the reversal of what was lost in Genesis 2-3 and Jubilees helps us to confirm this idea, and it uses language of a "thousand years" to describe the "Day of the Lord" and "eternal life." This is what John alludes to in Revelation 20 when he discusses the thousand year reign of the saints and it is also how he uses a thousand years to denote the time of the Last Days of the Old Covenant, or the "end of the age" (cf. Matthew 24:1-3) and the "day of the Lord."

A thousand years according to Barnabas and Augustine was how they interpreted the Days of Genesis 1. According to Jewish literature, both recent and ancient, the days of Genesis were used in establishing one thousand year periods as well. According to Augustine, the millennium or thousand years referred to each "day" in the book of Genesis, with the sixth Day being the period when mankind received the Image of

God through Christ in the first century. Augustine believed that the sixth day (the end of the six thousand years leading up to Christ) was nearing when he wrote, and that the seventh day (thousand year age) was fast approaching. He believed that very near in his future he and the rest of humanity would have the opportunity to enter into God's full rest and peace, and that it would be a period of a thousand years.

While I wouldn't agree with Augustine's entire application of the thousand year motif or metaphor, nor with the Jewish application of this idea, it is enough for me to see that it was common knowledge among the first century Christian audience and that the idea of a thousand years was typically and regularly applied to the "Day of the Lord" and to the time of receiving "eternal life" and "restoration" back to God. It was seen as a time where life, peace, and prosperity with God would be restored, and where "the death" in the garden would be reversed, and that it would give God's chosen people the opportunity to be brought back into a right relationship with Him. It was seen as a covenantal period where God renewed humanity back to their original condition before the sin of Adam in the garden. In the pre-Fall condition Adam and Eve ate from the "Tree of Life," and thus, they had eternal life as long as they ate from that tree. However, when sin came through Adam humanity was separated from that life, and it would not return until the "Tree of Life" (Jesus) once again sustained the people of God. This is the picture in Revelation 21-22. It is Christ once again dwelling with his people, sustaining them forevermore.

Thus, when Peter, John, or any other New Testament writer spoke of our life in Christ, or entering into his rest, or receiving eternal life, or when we read of the New Covenant poured out in Jesus' blood for us (cf. Luke 22:20; 1 Corinthians 11:25; Hebrews 12:24), or when we see any references to a "thousand years" regarding the millennium of Revelation 20, what we are reading about is not some new literary device, nor is it something completely foreign to the first-century audience in that they couldn't have understood what Jesus, Peter, or John were trying to convey. What we are reading about is the time of redemption, the time of salvation, the time of healing and being brought back to a relationship with God, and we are reading about the ministry of Christ and the Great Commission of the Apostles to establish the Church and to bring about an end to the Old Covenant system that brought only death, tears, pain, and bondage under The Law.

Additionally, many people of the first century Biblical audience more than likely would have also been familiar with the ancient Mesopotamian literature which presented their kings as having lived thousands of years. Never did this language apply to normal subjects of a kingdom, but only to Lords and Kings of the ancient Near Eastern world. With this in mind, it is important to note how John ties this into his idea of "reigning and ruling" for "a thousand years" with Christ in Revelation 20. The millennial life-span and reigning period is a reflection of the Kingly office of believers who are sons of "the King of kings." Christians were to reign with Christ in God's Kingdom during this period (cf. Isaiah 32:1; Matthew 19:28; Luke 22:30; Ephesians 1:20, 2:6; Revelation 4:4, 11:16, 20:4).

God's day for Adam lasted 930 years; but God's day for Jesus would fulfill what Adam could not. Paul refers to Jesus as the last Adam, and surely Paul would have had this in mind when he spoke about gaining in Christ what had been lost in Adam! Well, what did Adam lose? Covenant Life with God! How long did Adam have left to live to attain it when he died at 930 years old? Seventy years! From the birth of Jesus until AD70 (the coming of the Lord in the Preterist framework), how long did Jesus remain on the scene (as incarnate man, Holy Spirit, and at the consummation or coming in AD70)? Seventy years! In Matthew 28:20, Jesus told his disciples that He would be "with them until the end of the age," and so, while he was physically gone, he was still with them (the Helper was given to them, which was the Holy Spirit of God)! The time of the Messiah was seventy years; it began with the birth of Jesus, it continued with the presence of the Holy Spirit, and it was completed with his coming in judgment and salvation in AD70. The time of the Messiah completed the seventy years which Adam could not, and thus, the millennium (the 930 year life of Adam combined with the 70 year span of the life and ministry of Jesus till His return in AD70) was fulfilled in every way, and Covenant Life was restored to God's people!

Martin and Vaughn finish the argument very nicely:

"The patriarchs were greatly blessed because of their friendship and communion with God [provided by the provisional covenants and the Law given to them by God]. But they lived in anticipation of the coming Messiah. Their long (symbolic) life-spans could never reach the blessedness attained through the accomplished redemption of Jesus Christ, the Messiah and last Adam. Every one of them died before reaching the (symbolic) age of 1000 years.

When Jesus came to earth, he removed the Adamic curse, which was 'the death,' for all those who live in the Holy City. Believers have access to the tree of life forever and ever. Every generation of God's faithful people live (symbolically) a thousand years, because they live 'in Christ.' They [and we] have eternal life.

[The] millennial life-span [described by John in Revelation] is a historical reference directly to that first generation of Christians who lived during the 40 years between the ministry and coming of Christ in AD70 [many of whom suffered and died as martyrs as John described in chapter 20].[9] That was when the true light came into the world. However, every redeemed life since then (together with the Old Testament saints in glory, see Heb. 11:39-40) is a new millennial life-span, for God's people continue to reign with the King of kings in the glorious Kingdom of God. This is a symbolic life-span however, because the physical length of [a person's] life is not relevant to the eternal life which all of God's people have in Christ. The millennial life-spans, like the long life-spans in the early chapters of Genesis, are symbolic of covenant life [with

---

[9] For more evidence for this argument, see Martin and Vaughn's book, Beyond Creation Science, chapter 20, beginning on page 411.

God]. None of these long life-spans describe biological life [or] death in any way."[10]

Chapter Observations

From what we have discovered so far in this section, a few things can be ascertained:

1. The Jews understood the millennium or transition period into Messiah's days to fulfill what Adam could not. Adam lived 930 years, and the days of Jesus were to last 70 years in order to reach the full 1000 years (Jubilees 4:29-30 - to fulfill the "probationary period") and were to be a literal second exodus or "generational" period. From the time of Jesus' birth (around BC4) to AD66 (the beginning of the great tribulation and the Jewish war with Rome) was roughly seventy years. This would have fulfilled the 1000 year period, the Day of the Lord, and it would have inaugurated the "little while" loosing of Satan for 3 ½ years, from the middle of the year in AD66 leading up to and including AD70 with the destruction and end of the Temple, the nation of Israel, and the Old Covenant system.

2. Greco/Roman mythology literature taught that the 1000 year period represented the time in Sheol/Ghehena, which they called "Hades," in which they waited for resurrection or reincarnation back to life from the dead.

3. With the Jewish understanding of the incompleteness of Adam's life, some Jewish traditions believed that their Messiah would return and rule and complete what Adam could not, and that its completion (1000 years) would usher in a new age, a new Kingdom reign. They also expected that their coming Messiah would take the throne of David over a 40 year period,

---

[10] Ibid., 317-318.

a Jewish generation, just as David, Solomon, and others Hebrew Kings did, prior to establishing his rule forever at the end of that generation.

4. Given the dynamic of "both" Greco/Roman and Jewish literature in play here, I believe it is quite possible that the New Testament writers drew from both of the ideas of the thousand years, and developed a Christianized adaptation that we find in our Bibles. This would have included the ushering in of the 40 year period of "reigning and ruling" with Christ the King, which was also the time of the "Resurrection" of life back from the dead! Thus, we have very neatly combined the Greco/Roman view of 1000 years with the ancient Jewish understanding and hope of their returning Messiah and the restoration of Israel, who was dead, and was brought back to life.

5. Adam is the likely source or is at least alluded to in Psalm 90:3 (connected to the 1,000 years in vs. 4) as well as many other millennial and resurrection texts.

6. The Church being united to Christ in the first century was fulfilling what had been lacking in the first Adam. The Church was putting on Christ and thus was being clothed with immortality and in the process was being raised (i.e. – from "the death" in Adam) and was receiving eternal life, which is what the thousand years represented all along. It was the period of time to fulfill all that had been promised in the Old Testament in order to receive eternal life and a covenant relationship back with God. It was the period of time in which the veil was being fully removed, and the dividing wall of hostility between God and His people was being fully destroyed.

7. Isaiah 65 reminds us of the later writings of Jubilees and Barnabas, and it refers to what life will be like when all things are restored in Christ. The language is highly symbolic, and is charged with all sorts of

metaphors and Jewish motifs, such as similar motifs like the "lion lying down with the lamb" (peace and safety is the idea), or "beating our weapons into pruning hooks" (again, peace and safety), and humans symbolically living very long lives (less than 100 being considered a curse). Thus, in the "New Heavens and Earth" those who live a thousand years have eternal life, and those who live a short life-span, do not.

8. The understanding of the millennium in the first century is not concerned at all with a very long period of time which might last thousands or millions of years or more; that would have been completely foreign to them to say the least. Even in the Jewish understanding at that time, a thousand years could have only lasted a maximum of exactly one thousand years, or it might have referred to the symbolic time of the Messianic reign during the final, endless age. Many scholars today reject that Revelation 20 and the millennial language is referring to a literal one thousand year period (see any of the myriad of academic scholars or theologians who hold to amillennialism, historicism, idealism, or postmillennialism), and thus, we are left to discern and figure out for ourselves exactly what the imagery of Revelation actually refers to in light of the literature, and culture of the day. Given the weight of the Scriptural evidence, and the cultural context, and the literary genres of the ancient world more than two thousand years ago, I believe the weight of the evidence is heavily in favor a forty year period culminating in the events of AD70.

9. The millennium is only concerned with fulfilling the appointed time of the "Day of the Lord" to complete what could not be finished in the garden. Adam lived to be 930 years old. Thus, the work of Jesus, from his birth to his coming in AD70 to fulfill all of the Old Testament prophecies and to complete the entire story

of redemption for God's people, was completed in the first century and by AD70. In doing so, Jesus finished the millennial period and redeemed His people back to a right standing before God, lifting the yoke of bondage, the veil that covered their eyes, and united Himself to His new bride, true Israel, the Church!

10. I have shown how the long life-spans mark covenant life related to the lineage of Seth (God's holy and chosen people). The thousand years is a life-span signifying the eternal life that an individual receives once redeemed to God. John's millennium (the fulfillment of Isaiah 65:20) is ultimately rooted in the symbolic life-spans described in the genealogical records of Genesis, proven by the fact that Isaiah mentions that people who live fewer than one hundred years are cursed. The only people we ever find living more than this long can be found only in the Genesis genealogical records and in the Ancient Near East Sumerian King texts outside of the Bible.

11. The Old Testament patriarchs, while being blessed and given a Covenant covering by God, never lived one thousand years. All those who receive redemption from the Adamic curse (i.e. - the death) are raised and live symbolically for one thousand years (cf. Revelation 20), which Adam and the patriarchs could not do under the Law, outside of redemption.

12. Just as the symbolic life-spans in Genesis refer to single lives of individual patriarchs, so it is with the millennial life-span of New Covenant Christians. While a typical life-span of an ancient patriarch might have symbolically been hundreds of years long, their actual life-span would have been between forty and seventy years on average, just as anyone living today. The millennium refers to a full generation (in the Jewish world that was forty years). Jesus predicted that he would return within a single generation, and so, it would have been within his contemporary generation

that he would have returned to fulfill the millennial period.

13. Though many scholars and lay students have seen that the number thousand is a symbolic number representing fullness and completeness, most have not seen the source of the millennial language referring to the long life-spans referenced in early Genesis and Isaiah 65:20, in addition to the myriad of extra-Biblical ancient and traditional sources.

14. The millennium is certainly symbolic, but it is important to recognize exactly what John's symbolism represents.   John's imagery (written in the most symbolic and apocalyptic book of the Bible) refers to the eternal life that the first Christians received through faith in Jesus Christ where they would have passed from death to life (as in the Greco/Roman myths) and also where they would receive resurrection and obtain eternal life (as in the Jewish and ancient Hebrew literature).   If this is correct, then John's millennium can only be applied to the forty years of the first century generation, since the millennium of Revelation 20 only refers to a specific group of people during the time which John is speaking about in this chapter.   Furthermore, as a literary device communicating eternal life, the application can also be made to a person's life who has been redeemed beyond AD70.   Remember, the millennium DOES NOT refer to the literal length of years of an individual; it refers to the quality of existence during their normal human life span and beyond (a millennium is the "fullness" of life, or for someone who is able to "live out their days," cf. Isaiah 65, and who is redeemed by God).

15. Therefore, the "fullness" of the life of any believer of the first century (this is the context of the people mentioned in Revelation 20) would have been approximately forty years, since that is the period of

time they eagerly waited for and expected which would bring about their glorious hope, and the fullness of the redemption of Christ, and which was also the period in which the first century saints experienced their martyrdom. Since few people lived beyond an average of forty years in the times of ancient antiquity, the millennial period is restricted to the life of a first century redeemed individual; approximately forty years (from the time of Christ's ministry until his return in AD70; an exact Jewish generation, or the average lifespan of a person who would have lived 2,000 years ago). Beyond AD70, the millennial idea or application can also be made to all believers in Christ. While "the millennium" in Revelation 20 is a specific reference to the first century audience, and that period of time, the millennial idea can be expressly applied to all believers beyond this point. It applies to the entire Church who continues to reign in the kingdom of God through the power of the gospel and for anyone who is in Christ; they shall have eternal life whether they live or whether they die, and in Christ every Christian shall live and reign for a thousand years (symbolically speaking).

—— *4* ——

INTO ALL THE WORLD

Has The Gospel Gone Everywhere?

The argument is often made by ardent futurists (those who believe that Jesus must return soon in our future) that the Gospel must be preached into "all the world" before the millennium begins, or they might argue that the Gospel must be preached to the whole world before the end of the millennium can come. They argue that, "since this has obviously not happened yet, we can know that Jesus has not yet returned, and the millennium is either future for us still, or we are living in it now." But is this a valid argument?

It is my belief that the Gospel did indeed go into "all of the world" within the first century prior to AD70, and therefore, the millennium did in fact already "come to an end," or that at least there is little reason to extend the millennial period beyond AD70. Since the "end" was to arrive immediately after the Gospel had gone out to the whole world, whatever that encompasses, then if the Gospel had been preached everywhere the end would have taken place immediately following the completion of the Great Commission. Here is what Matthew's Gospel says:

> Matthew 24:14 – "And this gospel of the kingdom will be proclaimed throughout the world as a testimony to all nations, and then the end will come." (ESV)

I intend to demonstrate and prove that this "great commission" was in fact fulfilled during the period of the forty year transition from the Old Covenant Age to the New Covenant Age (also known as the "millennium," the "binding of Satan," or the "millennial reign of Christ"). What did the "world" mean to first-century Christians? Whatever Jesus was talking about in Matthew 24:4, later statements in the New

Testament teach that this was already accomplished prior to the end of the Apostles' ministry, and prior to AD70. Was the Gospel to go out to the entire planet earth, and every single person alive living at a single moment in the future, or was the great commission speaking of something altogether different? First, I'll provide Old and New Testament predictions of the Gospel going forth to the whole world (whatever that means). Then I'll provide passages in the New Testament that validate and confirm that those predictions were fulfilled already. Thirdly, I'll provide some extra-Biblical evidence which shows that early church Christians and historians applied the statements of the Gospel going to the whole world as having been accomplished prior to AD70. And lastly, I'll perform a word study which shows that all of the words Jesus used to command that the Gospel must go out to the whole world before the end were in fact used in exactly the same way by the Apostles to show that it had already been accomplished prior to the end of their ministries.

Old Testament Predictions

• "Then the iron, the clay, the bronze, the silver, and the gold, all together were broken in pieces, and became like the chaff of the summer threshing floors; and the wind carried them away, so that not a trace of them could be found. But the stone that struck the image became a great mountain and **filled the whole earth**" – Daniel 2:35

• "And in the days of those kings the God of heaven will set up a kingdom that shall never be destroyed, nor shall the kingdom be left to another people. It shall break in pieces all these kingdoms and bring them to an end, and it shall stand forever" – Daniel 2:44

• "But you, Daniel, shut up the words and seal the book, until the time of the end. **Many shall run to and fro, and knowledge shall increase**" – Daniel 12:4

• "...for **the earth shall be full of the knowledge of the LORD as the waters cover the sea**. In that day the root of

Jesse, who shall stand as a signal for the peoples—**of him shall the nations inquire**" – Isaiah 11:9-10

New Testament Predictions

• "...you shall not finish going through **the cities of Israel**, until the Son of Man comes" – Matt. 10:23

• "you will be hated by **all nations** for my name's sake" – Matt. 24:9

• "And this gospel of the kingdom shall be preached **in all the land for a witness unto all nations**; and then shall the end come" – Matt. 24:14

• "Go therefore and make disciples of **all nations**" – Matthew 28:19 (The Great Commission)

• "But you will receive power when the Holy Spirit has come upon you, and you will be my witnesses **in Jerusalem and in all Judea and Samaria, and to the end of the earth**" – Acts 1:8

Biblical Fulfillments

• "Now there were dwelling in Jerusalem Jews, devout men **from every nation under heaven**" who heard the Gospel **in every language** that was spoken – Acts 2:5-11

• "...and they were all scattered **throughout the regions of Judea and Samaria**...Now those who were scattered went about preaching the word" – Acts 8:1, 4

• Philip preaches in **the African desert** and to all the towns **from Azotus until he came to Caesarea**" – Acts 8:1-40 (Historical Note – It is believed that all of Africa was witnessed to from this high ranking official's conversion)

• **Peter took the message to the Gentiles** at the house of Cornelius, an event that was a turning point in the missionary activities of the church (Acts 10, 11). The book of Acts gives a sketch of the mighty missionary work that advanced rapidly throughout the known world.

• "These men who **have turned the world upside down** have come here also" – Acts 17:6

• "For we have found this man a plague, one who stirs up riots among all the Jews **throughout the world** and is a ringleader of the sect of the Nazarenes" – Acts 24:5

• "Your faith is spoken of throughout **the whole world**" – Romans 1:8

• "…from Jerusalem and all the way around to Illyricum **I have fulfilled the ministry of the gospel** of Christ" – Romans 15:19

• Historical Fact: We know that Paul traveled through Asia Minor, Greece, and Crete; and that he was in Italy, and probably in Spain and Gaul – (cf. Romans 15:24-28)

• "…the preaching of Jesus Christ…**has been made known to all nations**, according to the command of the eternal God" – Romans 16:25-26

• "the gospel, which has come to you, as indeed **in the whole world it is bearing fruit and growing**" – Colossians 1:5-6

• "…the gospel that you heard, which **has been proclaimed in all creation under heaven**" – Colossians 1:23

• "For not only has the word of the Lord sounded forth from you in Macedonia and Achaia, but **your faith in God has gone forth everywhere**, so that we need not say anything" – 1 Thessalonians 1:8

• "He was manifested in the flesh, vindicated by the Spirit, seen by angels, **proclaimed among the nations, believed on in the world**, taken up in glory" – 1 Timothy 3:16

Extra Biblical Statements

• Crysostom (AD375) – "Therefore **He [Paul] added** moreover, 'And this gospel shall be preached in the whole world for a witness to all nations, and **then shall the end come,' of the downfall of Jerusalem**. For in proof that He meant this, and that **before the taking of Jerusalem the gospel was preached**, hear what Paul saith, '**Their sound went into all the earth**;' and again, '**The gospel which was preached to every creature which is under Heaven**.' Which also is a very great sign of Christ's power, that **in twenty or at most thirty years the word had reached the ends of the world**. 'After this therefore,' saith He, 'shall come the end of Jerusalem.' For that He intimates this was manifested by what follows."

• Eusebius (AD325) – "Thus, under the influence of heavenly power, and with the divine co-operation, **the doctrine of the Saviour**, like the rays of the sun, **quickly illumined the whole world; and straightway**, in accordance with the divine Scriptures, the voice of the inspired evangelists and apostles **went forth through all the earth, and their words to the end of the world**." (Book II, Ch.III.).

• "Tradition assigns the following fields to the various apostles and evangelists: Andrew is said to have labored in Scythia; hence the Russians worship him as their apostle. Philip spent his last years in Hierapolis in Phyrgia. Bartholomew is said to have brought the gospel according to Matthew into India. The tradition concerning Matthew is rather confused. He is said to have preached to his own people, and afterward in foreign lands. James Alphaeus is said to have worked in Egypt. Thaddeus is said to have been the missionary to Persia. Simon Zelotes is said to have worked in Egypt and in Britain; while another report connects him with Persia and Babylonia. The evangelist John Mark is said to have founded the church in Alexandria."[1]

Gospel Preached Word Study

"And this gospel of the kingdom shall be preached in all the _world_ (Greek _oikumene_) for a witness unto all nations; and then shall the end come" (Matthew 24:14)	"But I say, have they not heard? Yes indeed: 'Their sound has gone out to _all the earth_, and their words to the ends of the _world_ (Greek _oikumene_)" (Romans 10:18)
"And the gospel must first be preached among _all_ _nations_ (Greek _ethnos_)" (Mark 13:10)	"...My gospel... has been made manifest, and by the prophetic Scriptures _has been made known_ to _all nations_ (Greek _ethnos_)..." (Romans 16:25-26)
"And He said to them, 'Go into _all the world_ (Greek _kosmos_) and preach the gospel to every creature" (Mark 16:15)	"...of the gospel, which _has come to you_, as it has also in _all the world_ (Greek _kosmos_), as is bringing forth fruit...," (Colossians 1:5-6).
And he said unto them 'Go into all the world and preach the gospel to _every creature_ (Greek _kitisis_) " (Mark 16:15)	"...from the gospel which you heard, which _was preached_ to _every creature_ (Greek _kitisis_) under heaven, of which I, Paul became a minister" (Colossians 1:23)
"But you shall receive power when the Holy Spirit	"But I say, have they not heard? Yes indeed:

[1] Lars P. Qualben, _A History of the Christian Church_ (New York, NY: T. Nelson, 1936).

has come upon you; and you shall be witnesses to Me in Jerusalem, and in all Judea and Samaria, and to the *end of the earth* (Greek *ge*)" (Acts 1:8).	'Their sound has gone out to *all the earth* (Greek *ge*), and their words to the ends of the world" (Romans 10:18)

• The Kosmos (world) and the Ktisis (creation)

"And he said to them, 'Go into **all the world [kosmos]** and proclaim the gospel to **the whole creation [ktisis]**" – Mark 16:15

Here Mark records Jesus using two different words to define the scope of his command concerning the gospel being preached to the "kosmos" (world) and the "ktisis" (creation). These two words are the exact same words used by Paul in his letter to the Colossians to show that Jesus' command and predictions about what would happened before the end were indeed already fulfilled:

"...in the **whole world [kosmos]** it is bearing fruit and growing" – Colossians 1:6

"...which has been proclaimed in **all creation [ktisis] under heaven**" – Colossians 1:23

• The Ethnos (nations)

"And the gospel must first be proclaimed to **all nations [ethnos]**" – Mark 13:10

"And this gospel of the kingdom will be proclaimed...as a testimony to **all nations [ethnos]**" – Matthew 24:14

"Go therefore and make disciples of **all nations [ethnos]**" – Matthew 28:19 (The Great Commission)

Here Mark and Matthew use another word to define the scope of Jesus' command concerning the great commission. And once again this word [ethnos] is used by Paul in his letter to the Romans to show that it had also been fulfilled already:

"...the preaching of Jesus Christ...has been made known to **all nations [ethnos]**, according to the command of the eternal God" – Romans 16:25-26

• **The Oikumene (world)**

"And this gospel of the kingdom will be proclaimed throughout **the whole world [oikumene]**" – Matthew 24:14

Interestingly, while Mark uses the word "kosmos" in describing the scope of the "world," Matthew here uses the Greek word "oikumene." Paul is obviously not ignorant of this fact and in his forward thinking he uses this same Greek word to show complete fulfillment so as not to leave any doubt as to whether or not the gospel had indeed been spread throughout the entire scope of what the great commission intended:

"...their words [have gone out] to the ends of **the world [oikumene]**" – Romans 10:18

• **The Ge (earth or land)**

"But you will receive power when the Holy Spirit has come upon you, and you will be my witnesses in Jerusalem and in all Judea and Samaria, and to **the end of the earth [ge]**" – Acts 1:8

While it has been Paul's main priority to show complete fulfillment of the total spread of the gospel according to Jesus' command, Luke also takes liberty in the book of Acts to record how this will take place, and he uses the word "ge" for "earth." Paul reiterates the same word in Romans 10 to show that even Luke's usage and intent was indeed fulfilled:

"Their voice has gone out to **all the earth [ge]**, and their words to **the ends of the world [oikumene]**" – Romans 10:18

The "End" of What?

In the final analysis concerning the spread of the gospel, the fulfillment of the prophecies of both the Old Testament and the New Testament on the matter are very complete, comprehensive, and surely historical. The fact that Paul goes out of his way to record every word penned by Matthew, Mark, and Luke (3 of the 4 Gospel writers) with regard to the scope of the great commission leaves us with little doubt that he intentionally did so in order to show his readers that in every way the gospel command of Jesus (the Great Commission) had been fulfilled prior to the end of his [Paul's] ministry.

This fact, along with the historical evidence provided above, should be substantial enough to convince any honest historian and student of the Scriptures that everything needed to bring about the predicted "end" spoken of by Jesus in Matthew 24:14 was indeed already fulfilled prior to the destruction of the Jewish Temple in AD70.

To this end it is therefore substantial evidence against any argument which states that the end has not yet come because the Gospel has not yet been preached into the "whole world" as we know it today. The Gospels know of no such thing! The Gospels don't speak of a world "as we know it today." The gospel world was a very different world 2,000 years ago, and the language employed by its writers in no way intended for its readers today to think that the fulfillment of the Great Commission was a far distant future event that would put a long tenured hold on the fulfillment of the passage at hand (i.e. - Matthew 24:14).

If the Great Commission has not been fulfilled then the "end" has not come. If the Great Commission has been fulfilled, then the "end" had to have come already! Based on the evidence provided above, I can see no consistent manner in which a person can apply the Gospel going to the whole world as having to do with anything other than the completed fulfillment of what Paul and Luke spoke about in their letters.

The application of a future fulfillment for us today of the Great Commission is a stark misapplication of the Scriptures and its original intended audience. The readers of these commands and predictions, and Paul's words of fulfillment in his day were in no way intended to be understood as events that would occur far off into the distant future (some 2,000 or more years later). The end of the "age" that was near to the Apostles and that was predicted by Jesus Christ in Matthew 24:1-4 was no more an "end of the world" event as was the great commission to be spread "over every inch of soil" on the literal, physical planet.

World language for the Apostles and readers 2,000 years ago was political language; language that employed the reader to think of the world as they knew it, and the world in which they lived. It was their "known world," and more specifically, it was the world that was relevant to the covenant dealing of God with the nation of Israel, however far her people extended. The "end" spoken of in Matthew 24:14 was the end of the Jewish world; that was a world system or order, a world government, and it was the end of the Old Covenant "Age" and the Jewish Theocratic National system to be exact.

The temple that was to be destroyed at this "end of the age" judgment was not some distant rebuilt temple. How could the predicted temple that was to be destroyed at the "end of the age" refer to a rebuilt temple in the distant future, when the Herodian Temple of the first century was still standing in all its glory? The end of the age would bring about an end to the whole Jewish theocratic system, and the temple that was to be destroyed was the same temple the disciples witnessed and pondered some 2,000 years ago which was still standing before them when this prediction was made.

It was this temple that the disciples and Jesus had in mind when he predicted its demise and utter destruction where every stone would be thrown down. It was the same temple that was surely destroyed in AD70 approximately forty years later, and it was a judgment that took place within the generation and lifetime of Jesus and his disciples who had survived long enough to see it.

Indeed, Jesus had told them that "some of them standing there would not taste death" before the end had come and the Kingdom had come with Power (cf. Matthew 16:28; Mark 9:1). Along with the old Herodian temple, the entire Old Covenant system and its aging skin was passing away 2,000 years ago as well. Paul said in 1 Corinthians 7:31 that "this world in its present form is passing away." So what is "this world" that was coming to an end and passing away according to Paul?

Has "it" been passing away now for over 2,000 years? If the "present form" of the world that is passing away is the world as we know it today, then it has been slowly passing away now for the last 2,000 years since Paul made this statement. That is an uneducated statement to say the least, and anyone interpreting this passage in such a way clearly shows little understanding of the original context, or the Jewish "world" and language that was employed in these passages. The writer of Hebrews spells it out very simply and defines for us what the world (also called, "heavens and earth" in other passages) being spoken of refers to:

Hebrews 8:8-13 – "Behold, **the days are coming**, declares the Lord, **when I will establish a new covenant** with the house of Israel and with the house of Judah, **not like the covenant that I made with their fathers** on the day when I took them by the hand to bring them out of the land of Egypt. For they did not continue in my covenant, and so I showed no concern for them, declares the Lord. For **this is the covenant that I will make with the house of Israel after those days**, declares the Lord: I will put my laws into their minds, and write them on their hearts, and I will be their God, and they shall be my people. And they shall not teach, each one his neighbor and each one his brother, saying, 'Know the Lord', for they shall all know me, from the least of them to the greatest. For **I will be merciful toward their iniquities, and I will remember their sins no more. In speaking of a new covenant, he makes the first one obsolete. And what is becoming obsolete and growing old is ready to vanish away.**" (cf. Hosea 2;

Jeremiah 31:31; Luke 22:20; 1 Corinthians 11:25; 2 Corinthians 3; Hebrews 9:15, 12:24)

Notice in the very last verse (vs. 13) that the writer of Hebrews said that in his day (2,000 years ago) that the first covenant was "becoming obsolete" and was "growing old" and was "ready to vanish away"! This means that the "world" being spoken of here was the Old Covenant world. Everything the Jews knew for hundreds and even thousands of years was a world under the Old Covenant, including the sacrificial system, the Law, and the Temple; all of which were established in stone at Sinai. God declared in the Old Testament that just as He had created the heavens and earth in Genesis 1, so too had he created His holy people to be His New Creation (New Heavens and Earth). In Isaiah 1 God gave a decree to the "Heavens and Earth" to hear and give ear to his words.

In the same manner, Lamentations 2:1 describes God's anger towards the "daughter of Zion" and says that she has come under the "cloud" of judgment and that God would bring low "the splendor of Israel" from Heaven to the Earth, and that "His footstool" would no longer be remembered. This language of "Heaven and Earth" and God's "footstool" is also used for God's dwelling place (cf. Isaiah 66:1; Acts 7:49). God's holy people, that is the nation of "Israel," was His dwelling place and He had made His abode with them, and He had created them just as He had created the cosmos.

This is the world (the Old or First Heavens and Earth) that was coming to an end; not the physical cosmos and the physical heavens and earth and all that is in it. The new world order or the New Covenant Age was set into action at the beginning of Jesus' ministry. This period of time, a period where both the New Covenant and the Old Covenant coexisted was the most climactic point in the history of humanity! This was a transitional period of time in which something old was waxing away and in which something new was being established and brought to its fullness. The one would not be complete until the other had been dissolved. In the same way that Isaac and Ishmael coexisted for a short time, so too did these two covenants. One covenant was of the flesh or the natural (the body of death), and was physical, while the other covenant was of the spirit (cf. Romans 9; Galatians 4). Galatians 4 clearly describes the conditions of the first century where both covenants coexisted simultaneously:

> Galatians 4:24-31 – "[24]Now this may be interpreted allegorically: these women are two covenants. One is from Mount Sinai, bearing children for slavery; she is Hagar. [25]Now Hagar is Mount Sinai in Arabia; she corresponds to the present Jerusalem, for she is in slavery with her children. [26]But the Jerusalem above is free, and she is our mother…[28]Now you, brothers, like Isaac, are children of promise. **[29]But just as at that time he who was born according to the flesh persecuted him who was born according to the Spirit, so also it is now.** [30]But what does the Scripture say? "Cast out the slave woman and her son, for the son of the slave woman shall not inherit with the son of the free woman." [31]So, brothers, we are not children of the slave but of the free woman."

Notice clearly what Paul says about the two covenants. They existed together when Paul wrote, and he clearly says that the "old woman" (national Israel) was persecuting them, and that the "new woman" (true Israel) would CAST OUT the old! Then he says that the children of the old woman (National Jews who followed the Law) would NOT inherit with the children of the new woman.

Are there still Jews persecuting Christians today? Is the old Law still active and relevant today, needing to be "cast out"? Too many Christians claim that we have not yet received our "inheritance," yet, to most of those same Christians they would also argue that the Old Covenant Law has been abolished or fulfilled, or somehow postponed. Which is it? The inheritance is not received until the Old Covenant is cast out! If the inheritance has not yet been received, then we are still under the Law and legal ramifications of the Old Covenant.

This was the "generation" spoken of by Jesus. It was the millennial period (representing a complete generation, or a full period of time) spoken of by John in the book of Revelation. It was the time for fulfillment of all things spoken of by the prophets (cf. Luke 21:22), and for the establishment of the Kingdom of God and Jesus Christ for all time (cf. Isaiah 9:7; Daniel 7:13-14, 18, 22, 27; 9:24). This transitional period is known as the second Exodus, primarily because of its typological fulfillment of the first Exodus (a forty year period of wandering, miracles, manna, and seeking/entering the Promised Land).

During this second Exodus there would also be a "wandering" of God's people during the great commission. There would be manna from Heaven (heavenly food, The Word of God going to all God's people) and miracles being performed. It would also be a time that would usher in the Heavenly Promised Land; i.e. – The New Jerusalem, or the Heavenly City of God and His Eternal Kingdom (cf. Ephesians 2:6; Hebrews 11:16, 12:22; Revelation 3:12, 21:2, 9).

The word study chart and passages on pages 82-85 and the explanation that follows it should clearly show the reader the direct parallel of the passages which indicate a prophecy or command given by Jesus using the exact Greek words he used, along with the fulfillment of those passages where the New Testament writer expresses the exact same Greek words to show a direct fulfillment of the Great Commission without leaving any wiggle room for interpretation by the reader. If Jesus' words to his disciples to carry out the Great Commission to the "end of the earth" have in fact NOT yet been fulfilled, then surely the New Testament writers were quite confused or intentionally misleading to their audience by going out of their way to use identical words and language used by Jesus to show a complete fulfillment of Jesus' command to them to complete the Great Commission to all the world, and within their generation.

And lastly, if the Great Commission has in fact been completely fulfilled as Jesus predicted, and as Paul and Luke recorded, then the end came immediately following its completion. If that has taken place already, then the millennium has already been fulfilled, since it must take place "prior to the end."

————— 5 —————

ESTABLISHING SOME PARAMETERS

What Did John Say?

In the book of Revelation, John establishes some very important parameters for us in the very first chapter which helps us to define the period of time in which the millennium, or the thousand year period, ought to fit. In Revelation 1:19 John was told to write the things that he had seen, the things that were currently taking place, and the things that were about to take place.

The literal Greek phrase for "about to take place" is "...mellei genesqai meta tauta - μέλλει γενέσθαι μετὰ ταῦτα." The Greek word "mello" here is without exception used for an eager expectation of something that is about to take place. This word is a strengthened form of "mello" which means to "defer" or to "put something off for a later date." Of the 110 times this word is used in the New Testament, it almost always refers to something that will soon take place.

Some theologians have attempted to show that the word "mello" can simply mean "a sure expectation" or a "certain expectation." By doing this they have attempted to remove the "soon" element from John's words in Revelation 1:19 (and in other passages) because in their view, some of the events contained within the book of Revelation surely could not have occurred "soon" in John's lifetime, or future. However, few scholars will make this argument, and a very quick look at how the word "mello" is used in other passages of the Bible will put the argument to rest.[1]

---

[1] While some futurist Christian theologians argue for "certainty" regarding "mello", there is "near consensus" among Historical Jesus Scholarship, Historical-Critical Scholarship, Liberal Scholarship, Historians, etc., that the word "mello" is defined as "near

In Matthew 2:13 an angel appeared to Joseph and told them to "flee" because Herod would come to destroy their child MELLO. Now, did this mean that Joseph and Mary could wait a long time before they needed to flee, as long as when they did, it was "quickly" or "suddenly"? No! The strength of the word is that they should leave "soon" to avoid Herod's plot. In Luke 7:2 a certain centurions' servant, who was dear to him, was sick, and ready (mello) to die. Now, does mean that the servant would live a long time further, but when he died it would take place "suddenly" or "quickly"? No! The servant was "ready" to die any moment. In Acts 3:3 a lame man saw Peter and John who were about (mello) to enter the temple gates before he stopped them to ask for alms.

Now, were Peter and John simply going to take a while, but when they went through the gate they would enter "quickly" or "suddenly"? No! They were so near they had almost walked through the gate when they had been stopped. In Acts 20:7 Luke records that upon the first day of the week, when the disciples came together to fellowship and eat, Paul preached to them, ready (mello) to depart the next day; and that he would continue his teaching until midnight. Are we to believe that Paul was simply going to wait a very long time before he would leave, but that when he finally decided to, it would be "quickly" or "suddenly"? No! The writer says that Paul was going to leave the "next day."

I could literally go on and on throughout the New Testament to show that the word "mello" is used as an eager expectation of something that is about to take place, or that it will take place soon in the near future. The word certainly does carry with it a "certain" or "sure" expectation and it implies that the event being spoken of will surely take place, without fail, or that it is at least the intent of the writer to show that what is being spoken of is intended to be fulfilled without any doubt. However, to disregard the "time element" of the

---

imminence." The only scholars to my knowledge who don't recognize this clear definition are theologians with a futurist axe to grind who deny a first-century coming of the Lord, and who are then forced to re-define the word in order to substantiate their view of a future coming of Jesus.

word, and the strength of "certain expectation" within the parameters of an event which would "soon" take place "very near" in the future is to entirely miss the true meaning and strength of the word and the context of nearly every passage in which the word "mello" is used in the New Testament.

Now, the reason this is so significant for our study here is because EVERYTHING contained within the contents of the book of Revelation either must have already occurred when John wrote it, or the events must have been occurring during the time in which he wrote it, or they would have required that the events which are predicted in it were about to begin to take place very soon after John had written the book (again, see Revelation 1:19). So in short, we have some of the events of the book of Revelation past for John when he wrote it, some events concurrent with the time when he was writing it, and some events (arguably the latter ones near the end of the book) still yet to take place in the near future for he and his contemporary audience. According to John some of the events were about to take place, or were ready to be fulfilled shortly after he had written the book.

Our amillennial and postmillennial friends would have us believe that we are currently living in the millennial period, however they would define it. Our premillennial friends would have us believe that the millennium has not even begun yet and that it is still to take place sometime in our future (they will typically say that this will occur "soon" in OUR near future).

However, if the book of Revelation contains events which include the judgment, and the creation of the New Heavens and Earth, and the New Jerusalem (whatever the identity of those things might be), and if the millennial period takes place prior these events, yet John tells us that EVERYTHING in his book has either already happened, was currently happening when he wrote the book, or was about to take place shortly in his future, how then can the millennial period be a period of time that hasn't even begun when John wrote the book? If this period of time (the millennium) is supposed to last for a very long period of time (thousands of years or longer), yet all of the things in the book were to be fulfilled soon (including the judgment and new creation), how could the millennium extend beyond John's day or his immediate future?

Again, if the judgment and New Heavens and Earth were about to take place according to John's own parameters of the book in Revelation 1:19, then certainly the millennial period must have either already taken place when John wrote the book, or it must have been the period of time in which John was living and writing just prior to the time of the judgment and the New Heavens and Earth which were to immediately follow the millennium.   John limits the time frame of fulfillment for the entire book of Revelation to having its consummation or completion in his near future.   Many of the events spoken of in the book had already happened, or they were already happening for John, or they were about to happen to John's future contemporary audience, and in his own lifetime and generation.

Thus, the millennial period could not have been a period of time far off or distant for John, nor could it have been a period of time that lasted for hundreds, or even thousands of years.   It must be confined to John's contemporary generation, having started some time before he wrote the book and having its completion shortly after or at the completion of having written the book prior to the fulfillment of the judgment and the coming of the New Heavens and Earth of Revelation 20-22.

In his book, "Who is This Babylon," Dr. Don K. Preston makes the following observation concerning the parameters and timing of the book in relationship to the time of the millennium. He says the following:

> "This is evident…[T]he coming of Jesus as foretold in Revelation was at hand (Revelation 22:6, 10-12, 20). The coming of Jesus as foretold in Revelation was to come at the end of the millennium.   Therefore, the end of the millennium was at hand…John said that the coming of the Lord was at hand.   This is…evidence that it was the consummation, not the inauguration, of the millennium that was at hand."[2]

---

[2] Preston, Don K. *Who is This Babylon?* 2nd ed. (Ardmore, OK: JaDon Productions, 2011). 260.

Since John's vision predicted that everything in it would "shortly come to pass," there is absolutely no way that anything in his book could be fulfilled or completed thousands of years beyond the time that he wrote the book. In both the amillennial and postmillennial views of prophecy, John was writing during, or just prior to the beginning of the millennial period. According to them, we are currently living within the time of the millennium today (a period that has so far lasted over 2,000 years).

But how is that possible when John said that everything in his book was about to be fulfilled, shortly, and that Jesus was going to "come quickly"? If John wrote the book only a few years prior to AD70, doesn't it make perfect sense that he was writing near the end of the period of the millennium, since all that remained was the judgment and resurrection? If everything was truly near to an end for John, then surely he was living and writing the book near the very end of the millennial period.

The Language of a "Thousand Years"

To properly understand the idea of the "thousand year" generational period, we need to understand where the writers of the New Testament, and specifically John, got this language, and we need to understand why they chose to use this imagery to describe a forty (40) year period of time, or the events contained within it, if indeed my proposition is correct.

Something to always keep in the back of your mind concerning this period is that it is nowhere mentioned specifically in the New Testament anywhere else until we read about it in the book of Revelation. This is very critical since "all" of the things that Jesus spoke about during His ministry, such as ALL the events He said would occur before His coming in Matthew 24-25 and Luke 21, "should" have included everything up to and including His final return for judgment and the full establishment of His Kingdom.

For Jesus to speak of ALL the events in Matthew 24 or Luke 21 (which include His coming and judgment), and for the Apostles to repeatedly describe those events as a current reality in their lifetime, or as events which would "soon" take place in their future, but to intentionally leave out the "millennial period" as though it was an afterthought, is quite revealing about the nature or actual interpretation of the thousand year period to the Apostles. "I can find no trace of the idea of either an interim earthly kingdom or of a millennium in the Gospels...The New Testament nowhere expounds the theology of the millennium, that is, its purpose in God's redemptive plan."[3] "Nowhere in any formal sense does the New Testament expound the theology of the millennium...[indeed] there are serious theological problems with the doctrine of the millennium. The student of Scripture is confined to revelation, and not all the problems are resolved there."[4]

Think of it this way: The Apostles believed that Jesus would come "soon" in their very near future. They believed they were living in the generation which would see and were seeing all the signs of His eminent coming, and they even said so. This is undeniable, and only conservative Christian theologians deny this. However, many scholars admit that the "millennium" is an event that is to occur BEFORE the coming of Jesus in judgment at the end of the age. Therefore, what does this mean about the Apostles' view and belief of the "millennium"?

Whatever the "millennium" actually is or was, is it possible that the Apostles could have viewed the "millennium" as a very long period of time, or a literal period of exactly one thousand years or longer? Either the Apostles were mistaken, and thus, they were not inspired of God, or they did not view the millennium as a period of time to last beyond their own generation. Right or wrong, this simple fact cannot be avoided.

While it is not specifically addressed by name, I believe the primary reason for the lack of detailed references by both Jesus and the Apostles' in their letters is because John the Revelator simply expounded on and took from what he already knew to be a theological fact (the binding of the strong man by

---

[3] Ladd, George Eldon, *The Meaning of the Millennium.* (Downers Grove, IL: InterVarsity Press, 1977). 38-39.
[4] Ibid., 45-46, from Herman A. Hoyt.

Jesus). It is argued by many scholars that the book of Revelation is John's version of the Olivet Discourse. John's Gospel is the only synoptic Gospel to omit this part of Jesus' earthly ministry and teachings. However, given the content and parallel themes found within the book of Revelation compared to the Olivet Discourse material, it's practically undeniable that John's Olivet Discourse was in fact a synopsis of the book of Revelation, stated in apocalyptic terms.

John took what he already understood about the timing and nature of this period and he used the apocalyptic imagery of a thousand years, along with other apocalyptic or eschatological images and numbers, to describe something that his first-century audience would have quite readily understood and applied in a correct manner without requiring a detailed explanation or commentary on the matter. While the symbolism throughout the book would have certainly confused a Roman soldier who may have intercepted one of these "Revelation" letters, it would have been undeniably clear to a Christian with a Jewish background or understanding.

We must remember that of the 404 passages in the book of Revelation, 278 of them are direct quotes, allusions, or references to the Old Testament literature. Many of the remaining passages are similar or even identical to other statements made in extra Biblical apocalyptic literature. It's quite clear that John had as his primary audience readers who would have been very familiar with Old Testament imagery and symbolism, and the apocalyptic literature (genre) of their day.

The fact that the book of Revelation is one of the most Jewish New Testament books of the Bible is not disputed among any scholar that I am aware of. This being the case, it would seem quite appropriate that the writer would then use known language, ideas, imagery, Jewish idioms, and motifs that his readers would not have had to spend a great deal of time figuring out.

Indeed, John even told his audience in Revelation 1:3 that his readers would be blessed by the book if they would read, understand, and keep its teachings or commands. The contents of the book of Revelation were not meant to be hidden, unknowable, confusing, or incomprehensible to the audience to whom it was written; that is, a pre-AD70 audience.[5]

A question that any reader should ask concerning the thousand year period is this: "Is it likely that John revealed something entirely new which no other Gospel writer or Old Testament Saint or Prophet ever knew or spoke about, including Jesus Himself, or is it more likely that John was using imagery and language to describe and depict those things already taught and shown to us in the Old Testament, in the Apostle's letters and the rest of the New Testament, and in Jesus' own teachings?"

Keep that question in the back of your mind as you continue to read and ponder this presentation of the millennial period. Again, the lack of identical millennial language in every other portion of Scripture from that of the book of Revelation should be quite revealing about its timing and nature of fulfillment. The disciples understood that it was to be fulfilled in their own lifetime; they expected it. Why shouldn't we expect that it was fulfilled in their lifetime as well?

The Grammar and Language of "One Thousand"

At this point it would be a good idea to take just a few moments to comment concerning the number and definition of the word "thousand," both as it relates to its use in Revelation 20, and also as this idea, number, or word is used throughout the rest of the Bible and in extra Biblical literature. In Revelation 20, the words used for "thousand years" are "xilia eth", or transliterated they are CHILIOI ETOS - χίλια ἔτη. Now the word "chilioi" is used once each in Revelation 11, 12, and 14, and in Revelation 20 it's used six times.

It's also used in 2 Peter 3 when Peter says that to God a day is as a thousand years, and a thousand years is as a day. However, surely Peter was not intending to say that a day equals exactly a thousand years to God, nor did he mean to say

---

[5] See Kenneth Gentry's book "Before Jerusalem Fell" for a complete discourse on the arguments for a Pre-AD70 dating of the book of Revelation.

that an exact thousand years equals a physical 24 hour day to God. It's obvious that Peter was using a "period of uncertain affinity" (or an unknown period of time) to express that God does not live within the parameters of time and space as we do. We will get to this passage a little later for more clarity here. The basic meaning of the word "chilioi - χίλια" in the Greek is "a plural number of uncertain affinity."[6] What that basically means is that it is a number of multitudes or more than one, typically a great number, in which it has no specific quantity or amount, unless accompanied by other numbers, or context for clarity, which would then specify an exact amount, or the exact meaning. The word can be used properly (or in a straight forward manner), or it can be used figuratively, depending on the context.

Does any serious scholar really think that the context of the word "thousand" in Revelation 20 is to be properly understood as an exact or literal idea of 1,000? The vast majority of instances in which this word is used in the New Testament are nearly always as a conjunction with a pre-fixed number attached to it, when an actual numerical idea is being expressed. The vast majority of instances in which the Old Testament uses the number one thousand, it does so in a figurative manner, or it simply represents the completeness of something in context. But which is it? "[T]he number 'thousand' which is used here must not be interpreted in a literal [straight forward] sense. Since the number ten signifies completeness, and since a thousand is ten to the third power, we may think of the expression 'a thousand years' as standing for a complete period...of indeterminate length...we may conclude that this thousand-year period extends from Christ's first coming to just before his Second Coming."[7]

[6] Strongs Concordance and HELPS Word-studies, 2011: **5507** *xílioi* – properly, a *thousand*; the product of 10 x 10 x 10 (10^3, ten *cubed*); (figuratively) *emphatic*, *total inclusiveness*, showing no one (*nothing*) is left out. A plural of uncertain affinity; a thousand -- thousand.
[7] Hoekema, Anthony A., *The Meaning of the Millennium*. (Downers Grove, IL.: InterVarsity Press, 1977). 161.

While I would agree with Hoekema's statement above, our primary difference exists in the timing of his defined "Second Coming." We both agree that the millennium does indeed exist during the period in which he defined. But if a person believes that the millennial period has been fulfilled in the past, they will arrive at a much different conclusion as to the nature and length of the millennium, as opposed to someone who believes that the Second Coming is still future and that we are in the millennium now (and have been for nearly 2,000 years).

For example, if the number "12" comes before "thousand" (chilioi), it is very specific as to what is being expressed (12 is a number often used within the Bible; when attached to "thousand" and in reference to people, it usually indicates the fullness or completion of whatever the number "12" is representative of, and could represent a great number of people in this instance. However, it may not literally be 12,000 people, or even a number close to this amount. It could also be speaking of many more than 12,000 people, or far fewer than 12,000 people. The exact number is not what is at issue; rather, it is the complete number of the context in question, whether people, items, animals, places, or other things.[8]

"The 'thousand years' is quite clearly not to be understood as an exact measure of time but rather as a symbolical number. Strict arithmetic has no place here. The term is a figurative expression, indicating a…complete, perfect number of years…It is…a definitely limited period, during which certain events happen, and after which certain other events are to follow."[9] "It is quite certain that the number 1000 represents in Biblical symbolism absolute perfection and completeness; and that the symbolism of the Bible includes also the use of a period of time in order to express the idea of greatness, in connection with thoroughness and completeness…When the seer [John] says seven or four or three or ten, he does not name

---

[8] Many historical Jesus scholars (Wessinger, Ariel, Tabor) believe that the Millennium is not to be taken as a specific period of time (an exact number), but that it is used to refer to a time of transition to a collective salvation.

[9] Boettner, Loraine, *The Millennium.* (Phillipsburg, N.J.: Presbyterian and Reformed Publishing Company, 1957). 64.

these numbers at random but expresses by each a specific notion. The sacred number seven in combination with the equally sacred number three forms the number of holy perfection, ten, and when this ten is cubed into a thousand the seer has said all he could say to convey to our minds the idea of absolute completeness."[10]

In the case of Revelation 7 and 14 for example, the numerical use of 144,000 is used. However, if one understands the numerology at play here, you would find that John is using the numerical values of 12 x 12 x 1,000 (or 10 cubed). Why is that so significant? Because it is essentially the same description John gives in Revelation 21:9ff. In Revelation 21:9ff, John describes the New Jerusalem with 12 gates, 12 foundations, and a perfectly square length, width, and height.

This is the description of the Church, perfect and purified, and equal in every way. It is the fullness of the Bride made ready for her Lord to dwell in Him. The significance of the number 12 in these instances is that they describe the 12 Apostles and the 12 Tribes of Israel. The number 1,000 is used to describe the perfect quality and fullness of the Church, equal in every way. Thus, when we come to numbers like 7, 10 (or 7 + 3), 12, 40, 144, or even 1,000, we must be aware of how those numbers are used elsewhere throughout the Bible to gain proper insight into what the writer is trying to convey or express by using those numbers.

If the New Testament writer had wanted to express a literal number of exactly "one thousand years," he could have easily placed the Greek equivalent of the number "one" before "chilioi" to designate this number as an exact figure or amount. Likewise, he surely could have expressed an explanation to ensure his audience that a literal reading was intended. But it is not done, and the vast majority of scholars today recognize that the word used in Revelation 20 does not designate a literal or exact number of one thousand years. Now, in light of this Greek definition, how did the New Testament writers apply

---

[10] Warfield, Benjamin Breckinridge. *The Millennium and the Apocalypse*. (Richmond, VA.: Presbyterian Committee of Publication, 1934). 654.

this word or idea? Again, in 2 Peter 3, Peter described this "uncertain period of duration" as a single day for God. In other words, what appears to be very long and uncertain in duration to man, is as but a single day for God. Nowhere is there a specific reference to an exact, literal, one thousand years being described by the writers of either Peter or John, or any other New Testament author anywhere.

In addition to the grammatical problems a person might face when trying to apply a proper, literal, exact interpretation to the word "chilioi," the idea of a "thousand" in the symbolic literature of the Old and New Testament is quite prevalent. In Leviticus 26:8 the number thousand is used to signify a "great number" while not being strictly literal. In Deuteronomy 1:11 it says that God shall make him a "thousand times" greater than he is. Does this mean God will not make him a thousand and one times greater? No! The language is figurative of "a lot" or "much" greater.

In Deuteronomy 7:8-9 God says that He is faithful to Israel even to "a thousand generations." Does that mean that God isn't faithful to a thousand and one generations? No! This is figurative for "all of them." In Deuteronomy 33:2 it says that the Lord came from "ten thousands" of holy ones. Does this mean that God came from literally ten thousands of holy ones? No! It means that He came out from "all of His people." In Judges 15:16, it says that Sampson killed a "thousand" men with a single jaw bone of a donkey. Did he really kill exactly 1,000 men? No! We may never know exactly how many men Sampson killed with the jawbone of a donkey. This is figurative of the "many" people that Sampson killed, however many it actually was, it was "a lot." Many people use the same sort of typological language. Have you ever heard someone say, "I've told you a thousand times," when it was really only a few times?

In 1 Chronicles 16:14-16 it says that God's Covenant would continue for a "thousand generations" forever! Is this an exact figure? No! It means "for all of them," or that His Covenant would continue for as long as it was in force, to the fullest of its time, without end. In Job 9:3 it says that a person could not contend and answer God once in a "thousand" times. Does this mean that on the one thousand and first time he could? No! This is figurative for "every time." Psalm 50:10 says that the cattle on a "thousand" hills are His. Does this mean that the cattle on the thousand and first hill is not His? No! It means that they are "all" His! Psalm 84:10 says that a day in Your courts are better than a "thousand" elsewhere. Does this mean that a thousand and one days elsewhere is better than to be with the Lord? No! It means that a single day with the Lord is better than "all days" without Him.

As you can see, the language used here is quite figurative for "all," or "complete," or "the fullness thereof" (regardless of whether it is actually speaking of many, or literally tens, hundreds, thousands, or millions). I could continue this for quite some time. However, you probably get the point by now.

Throughout the Bible the idea of a "thousand" is often used for "all" or "fullness" or "many." When it is unaccompanied by another number or specific idea, it is typically a generic word without a specific reference to time or quantity. However, the quality of the word is still in effect. That quality is the "fullness thereof" and the "entirety" of what is spoken about in context. It is in this period of time and in this manner that Revelation 20 says that the Saints of God are to reign with Jesus. It is also during this time that they would reign with Jesus without hindrance, with power, to the utter most parts of the earth, and not one day short of God's plan and scheme.

Therefore, based on the parameters of the language and the context of Revelation 20 and the word "thousand" (chilioi), it cannot be a reference to a period of an exact one thousand years. It also cannot be a reference to a period of time far removed from when John wrote the book, since all the events in the book of Revelation were said to have either already been fulfilled, or they were currently being fulfilled, or they were about to be fulfilled in the near future to John's contemporary audience. So how else can we identify when and what this period of time is to help establish additional parameters for the "thousand years"?

The Prophetic Context of the "Thousand Years"

Within most prophetic schemes both preterist and futurist, Christians believe that the thousand years will take place prior to the great tribulation, the general resurrection, and the "little season" shortly before the judgment and coming of the Lord. The great debate then is not typically in the order of things (except for some within the dispensational, pre-millennial schemes), but rather, the debate is on the nature and timing of the fulfillment of those events previously mentioned.

I have already mentioned on several occasions that it is my belief that the millennial reign of Christ, or the binding of Satan, is the forty year transition period or the generation of Jesus' and the Apostles' contemporary audience. But what was the prophetic context of Jesus' and the Apostles' generation? Understanding the "occasional context" in which our Bible was written will help us a great deal in understanding the time in which these prophecies were written, to include the prophecy of the "millennial period" which John said in the Book of Revelation was already taking place, or was about to take place or be fulfilled soon in his near future.

Practically all Hebrew scholars admit that the Jewish temple was the center of the people of Israel in the first century prior to AD70. It had been so for hundreds of years, spanning both the time of Solomon's Temple, and also the rebuilt Herodian Temple in existence during Jesus' day. Isaiah 2 describes the Temple of God as the "mountain of the Lord" which sat within the Heavens and Earth of chapter 1. The mindset of the ancient people 2,000 years ago and prior concerning "temple" life was that they identified the temple as the central identity to their very way of life and history.

This was primarily true of the people of Israel, who believed that God had created them and chosen them as His holy people, that God had given them their Law, their temple, and their customs and ordinances. With the loss of the Herodian temple in AD70, some Rabbis have said that this event was paramount to God placing an iron wall between himself and His people. It was a loss of covenant relationship with God, and God was bringing the full brunt of covenant provisions of wrath and judgment upon them, thereby also removing his elect status from them as God's chosen people. What had formerly been God's house and city and people would become an eternal desolation and rejection (cf. Jeremiah 23:43-45 describes this).

With all of this said it's important to realize that even though the Old Testament prophets recognized that an earthly temple could not house God or contain Him (cf. 1 Kings 8:27), temple imagery, ordinances, and the buildings they were instructed to create pointed to a far greater realization which was to come at some future date (at the end of the "age" or the "last days" of Israel). In the New Testament, this "temple imagery" is often employed or used to signify the true temple or dwelling place of God. In 1 Peter 1:2 Peter speaks of the "elect" people of God who are sanctified, for obedience to Jesus and for sprinkling with His blood.

This language is liturgical, temple imagery taken directly from the dedication of the tabernacle as in Exodus 40 and 1 Kings 8. In 1 Peter 2:4ff, Peter said that God was building a "Spiritual House" made of "living stones" of which Jesus was the Chief Cornerstone. They were to be a "Holy Priesthood" offering up "acceptable sacrifices" to God. Peter then goes on to describe them as a "chosen race," a "royal priesthood," a "holy nation," and a "people for His own possession." Peter says that they were called "out of darkness" and "into the light." In this passage Peter quotes directly from Hosea 1, which speaks about the divorce and eventual restoration of Israel back to God.

The imagery used by Peter is all temple dedication imagery, and it would only be used if a temple was being "rebuilt." In the Jewish mindset, the temple sacrifices could only take place within the inner most portion of the temple, and yet Peter tells his first-century audience that "they" were being built up as living stones to establish God's Holy temple once and for all, and that it is within "this temple" that they were to offer up acceptable sacrifices to God. In 1 Peter 4:7ff, Peter urges them not to engage in acts of the flesh, or as the Gentiles do because "the end of all things is at hand." He goes on to say that "it is the time for judgment to begin at the household of God," and that they shouldn't think that it is strange or odd that they would have to be insulted, tested, or even share in the sufferings of Christ.

Now, what makes this even more incredible is that Peter says that through their sufferings and trials, "...you are blessed, because the Spirit of glory and of God rests upon you." What did Peter mean by this? This was no accident folks. Peter goes right back to his temple dedication imagery, and here describes the Shekinah Glory Cloud which sat upon the tabernacle or temple at the completion of the construction of those edifices in the Old Testament.

But now Peter says that this glory cloud "rests upon you." In the Old Covenant the Shekinah Glory Cloud would descend and fill the house, which would represent the Spirit of God with His people and dwelling within the Temple (cf. Exodus 40; 1 Kings 8). Now Peter applied this event to his contemporary audience who was suffering with him because they were "being built up" as "living stones" to establish the "Spiritual Temple" of God.

It could not be stated any more clearly that the eschatological (last things) and soteriological (salvation) hopes of all the New Testament writers were to bring in, fulfill, and establish those things which were promised to Old Covenant Israel. What "they" were receiving and ushering in was exactly what had been promised by the Old Testament prophets; nothing more and nothing less. Peter makes this abundantly clear in 1 Peter 1:8ff when he states that "they" were obtaining (present tense) the outcome of their faith, which was the salvation of their souls. Concerning this salvation, Peter said:

"...the prophets who prophesied about the grace that was to be yours searched and inquired carefully, [11]inquiring what person or time the Spirit of Christ in them was indicating when he predicted the sufferings of Christ and the subsequent glories. [12]It was revealed to them that they were serving not themselves but you, in the things that have now been announced to you through those who preached the good news to you by the Holy Spirit sent from heaven, things into which angels long to look." (ESV)

Peter said that the sufferings of Christ and the subsequent glories that they would receive were revealed to "them" (Old Testament Prophets) but were not for them; rather, they were for Peter and his audience (New Testament Saints), and Peter further stated that it was "now being announced to them" (Peter's audience) by Peter and the other Apostles. What does this mean? It means that what the Old Testament Prophets had spoken about and prophesied concerning the last days and the new Messianic Kingdom was now being revealed through Peter and the other Apostles.

It was not to them (the Old Covenant Prophets), but it was to "us" Peter said (that is, the first-century audience Peter was speaking to) that all the prophecies were being revealed in and fulfilled through. Peter is also emphatic that it was through the Holy Spirit that he was giving the divine revelation to reveal those things to his audience; things that angels even long to look at and understand. The Old Testament Prophets were told that those things "were not" for their own day and time, but Peter said, "It's for us" to his audience 2,000 years ago! Peter said that the Old Covenant Prophets "didn't understand" the time or nature of those things, but that now "they do" to his audience 2,000 years ago!

In order to properly understand the prophetic context, the nature, and the timing of the millennial period, we must understand how the Old Testament prophecies were given. According to Peter and the other Apostles the Old Covenant Prophets did not understand the imagery they had been given with regard to the tabernacle, the Temple, or the ordinances and rituals, nor did they understand the prophecies they had been told about concerning the distant future and the Messianic Kingdom and Temple that was to come.

However, Peter says that those mysteries were "being fulfilled" through them, and to them, and that it was through the divine power of the Holy Spirit that all those things were being fulfilled and revealed to them; and it was "them" 2,000 years ago who were chosen to fulfill those prophecies, and who were chosen and elect or predestined to suffer with Christ to usher in the true Kingdom of God, the Spiritual Temple and the New Jerusalem not made with hands (cf. Mark 14:58; 2

Corinthians 5:1; Hebrews 9:11, 24, 11:16, 12:22; Revelation 3:12, 21:2, 9).

Through the Holy Spirit the Apostles were revealing the very nature and timing of the Messianic Temple and the Kingdom of God. Whatever they said, and however they said it, it was through the divine power and authority of God. They could not have been wrong. Thus, by understanding the prophecies of the Old Testament concerning the "time and nature" of the Messianic Temple and Kingdom, we can then pin-point the time and nature of the New Testament fulfillment of the ushering in of this Temple and Kingdom. And how do we properly understand the Old Testament prophecies concerning these things? Do we use the traditions of the church? God help us! No we don't! We use the Analogy of Scripture, that is, we let New Testament Scripture define and clarify what the Old Testament says about those things. So what do we learn from the Old Testament or Old Covenant Prophets about the Messianic Temple and Kingdom from what the New Testament writers tell us?

We learn that Israel was divorced in Old Testament times for violating the Covenant of God (cf. Isaiah 24:5; Hosea 1-2). As a result of Israel's divorce and exile, there was a promise of restoration which included the restoration of the "Temple of God with His people." This is the same language Peter uses when he writes to his audience concerning the Temple and the regathering of God's people. Peter could not have been more clear as to who his audience was when he said the following:

> "To those who are elect exiles of the dispersion in Pontus, Galatia, Cappadocia, Asia, and Bithynia, [2]according to the foreknowledge of God the Father." (cf. 1 Peter 1:1-2)

Who were the "elect exiles of the dispersion"? These were Israelites from the ten northern tribes of Israel, who had formerly been divorced by God under the Old Covenant and were comingled among the gentiles (cf. Hosea 8:8, they are vessels wherein there is no pleasure, and in Romans 9 they are referred to as vessels of God's wrath). Peter tells them in 1 Peter 1:17-20 that they were to conduct themselves in holy conduct during their "exile" since they were being ransomed from the futile ways of their forefathers by the blood of Christ who was made known "in the last times" for the sake of them, and so that "they" could receive faith and a hope in Him. Peter's focus and theme throughout his letters was on the exilic aspect of his audience, that is, that his audience consisted primarily of the dispersed Jews throughout the gentile nations who were exiled, and who were strangers and wanderers and foreigners. As Peter discussed their "suffering" in his letters, he was certainly not focused on the "general suffering" of the human experience. While we might make some applications today from Peter's occasional context (the first-century audience who was suffering), Peter's direct audience were suffering Jews who were sojourning or wandering among the nations, just as God's people had wandered in exile in the book of Exodus.

In 1 Peter 2:11 Peter again described his audience as "brethren and strangers and foreigners" who were "among the gentiles" (cf. Hosea 8:8-10). But why do I bring all of this up again? I bring it all up because behind all of this language, and imagery, and the audience of Peter's letters, lies the promises made to Israel of the regathering of God's people, and the rebuilding of the Temple, and the establishment of the Messianic Kingdom. If Peter was revealing to them (his first-century audience) that "they" were fulfilling the promises made to Old Covenant Israel, then how can we extend those promises far beyond Peter's direct audience and first-century context, and into a far distant future context which Peter wasn't addressing or talking about? Is it Scripture or tradition that is guiding our interpretation?

In Hosea 3:4 God said to Israel that she would dwell "many days" without a King or prince, without a pillar or sacrifices, and without an ephod or idol. In other words, God was going to destroy their temple and He would make them strangers to Him. But even though this was true, God told them that "in the last days" He would bring them a Messiah (a savior). The entire story of Hosea is concerned with the remarriage, the restoration, the regathering, and the resurrection of Israel, in addition to the rebuilding of Israel's temple which was all to take place during the last days when the New Covenant of the Messiah was to be established (cf. Hosea 2).

During this time Israel would receive a new Temple, a new alter, and a new priesthood. This restoration would take place during a time when Israel was called "not my people" (cf. Hosea 1:10). It also would take place during the time when Israel would again be called "the people of the living God." What God promised was that "in the last days" He would again give her a new temple, a new alter, a new priesthood, and He would call them by a new name and they would be ruled by the promised Messiah once again.

Peter explains that all of this was revealed to the Apostles, and that they were ministers of this Gospel which was being given to those first-century saints, and in Peter's letters his direct audience were the lost tribes of Israel; they were the exiled ones who lived among the Gentiles and were wanderers and strangers to God. God was regathering his people to Himself. Paul expressed the same idea when he wrote:

"[11]Therefore remember that at one time you Gentiles in the flesh, called "the uncircumcision" by what is called the circumcision, which is made in the flesh by hands— [12]remember that you were at that time separated from Christ, alienated from the commonwealth of Israel and strangers to the covenants of promise, having no hope and without God in the world. [13]But now in Christ Jesus you who once were far off have been brought near by the blood of Christ. [14]For he himself is our peace, who has made us both one and has broken down in his flesh the dividing wall of hostility [15]by abolishing the law of commandments expressed in ordinances, that he might create in himself one new man in place of the two, so making peace…" (cf. Ephesians 2:11-16)

The "strangers" and "aliens" to the covenants of promise having no hope and without God in the world was Old Covenant Israel who had been divorced by God (cf. Hosea 1). But Israel was now being brought near to God again, giving Israel peace, breaking down the veil of division and abolishing the law and its ordinances. This entire act is the "creation of one new man" in place of two. This was the "New Creation" and the "Resurrection of the body" promised to Israel. According to Peter these people would now offer up Spiritual sacrifices. As I had shown before, in 1 Peter 2:4ff, Peter quotes directly from Hosea 1 to show his audience that "they" were taking part in the fulfillment of the regathering of Israel, or the restoration of Israel back to God.

According to Hosea 5:14-15 God declared that He would "go away to His place" until His people once again sought His face and repented of their sins. In Ezekiel 10, Ezekiel saw several fascinating signs, and of those the Shekinah Glory Cloud had left the Temple. In the same way, God's presence had left His people Israel in Hosea 5. In Ezekiel 23 the Lord uses some of the most explicit language in all of the Bible to declare the desolation of his people and their temple. Israel, now referred to as "Samaria" had already been carried off into exile, and now Judah was on the verge of being judged as well for committing even worse sins than Israel had formerly committed.

In this passage, Israel and Judah are referred to as "Oholah" and "Oholibah." These Hebrew names represent two harlot sisters, and in Hebrew those names mean, "her tent is in her," and "my tent is in her." These definitions are a way of saying, "she has her own temple" and "my temple is with her." This picture story shows us the digression of Israel (Oholah) in establishing her own temple, sacrificial system, priesthood, and ordinances contrary to those God had established for her, which ultimately led to her divorcement from God. Thus, the ten northern tribes of Israel were also referred to as "Samaritans" or "among the nations." Now, God's holy House is being defiled (Oholibah), and God warns them that they too would be divorced and cast away until they return to Him and repent of their sins. Thus, the same promise existed for both Israel (the ten northern tribes) and Judah (the 2 southern tribes).

In Zachariah 1:16 and 2:10 God declares that He will return to Israel with mercy and rebuild His house and dwell in their midst. This restoration would consist of all twelve tribes of Israel (cf. – the 144,000 of Revelation) and it would take place during the New Covenant, the re-marriage by God to His people (cf. Hosea 2), the establishment of the Messianic Kingdom, and at the "last days" of the Old Covenant which according to the writer of Hebrews was "passing away" nearly 2,000 years ago (cf. Hebrews 8:13). There would once again be a new temple, a new priesthood, a new people, and a new sacrifice. Peter makes it very clear that they (Peter's first-century audience) were receiving those promises. Peter's only concerns were regarding the promises made to Israel. They had nothing to do with promises made to people at the end of time, or to our future generations, or future Israelites.

Peter was writing to the dispersed, exiled, divorced Jews among the Gentile nations. Peter was an Apostle according to the "circumcision" (that is the Jews). Thus, whatever Peter spoke about it was in direct fulfillment of what had been promised to Israel under the Old Covenant, and Peter was explaining and revealing what the true timing and nature of those fulfillments were. They were for his audience and for his generation to experience and witness, and they would usher in the fullness of the Messianic Kingdom and Temple for all time, never to be overcome or destroyed.

According to Peter, his audience was becoming a royal priesthood, receiving an inheritance and giving acceptable sacrifices to the Lord. In Numbers 18:20, as God was divvying up the land, the tribes each received their inheritance. But the tribe of Levi was given no inheritance. Why? God says that it is because "I am their inheritance." Given the statements by Peter concerning the "inheritance" which they were receiving, what was it that Peter's audience was going to receive? Was it a physical land of inheritance? Was it tangible, fleshly, physical, or something along those lines? No! The priests don't get to inherit physical property! The inheritance of the priesthood was God Himself with His people, not physical land!

Interestingly, in both the Roman and Jewish laws of the land 2,000 years ago, non-citizens and foreigners were not allowed to own property. Peter and Paul called the Diaspora Jews "strangers and foreigners" in the land, and therefore, their inheritance was not anything physical or temporal, nor would it ever be. The inheritance which was to be received by God's people was His presence dwelling within and among them!

This was a Spiritual inheritance, and it was a personal relationship with God, where there was no wall or separation from His presence any longer. Interestingly, Peter uses imagery that excluded physical ownership of land, and he then applies Israel's restoration promises to those people who could own no land (exiled strangers and foreigners).

All throughout Peter's letters, Peter quotes, utilizes, or alludes directly to the Old Testament passages found in Isaiah 2, Isaiah 28, Hosea 1-2, Ezekiel 37, Psalms 118, Zechariah 6, and Malachi chapters 3 and 4. Specifically in Malachi 3-4, God says that he is going to purify the priesthood so that they could offer sacrifices in righteousness and then the Lord would come to his temple and dwell with them. Well, what did Peter say? Malachi described a Levitical priesthood, yet, Peter described a Spiritual priesthood which was the fulfillment of those Old Testament passages. Peter and his audience were offering up their faith, their hearts, and even their lives, and this was an acceptable sacrifice to God in order to establish the Holy Temple, and the New Covenant Kingdom of God. Peter said that through their suffering they were being made more precious and were being purified as gold refined with fire (cf. 1 Peter 1:7).

According to Peter, he was writing about, commenting on, and giving the true interpretation of the promises made to Old Covenant Israel. Peter was not just drawing an analogy between the Old Temple and a new Spiritual temple, i.e. the Church. Peter said that what he spoke about was the true temple of God! Peter never used language that would indicate that his divine revelation from God was only to be interpreted as a metaphor, or a parable, or a symbol, or to simply be understood as an analogy.

Now, the question must be asked at this point; if Jesus was the true fulfillment of Psalm 118:22, which, as Peter indicates, was the "Chief corner stone" upon which the builders rejected, and if Peter quoted from this Psalm to indicate that Jesus was the literal and true fulfillment of this passage in addition to Psalm 2 (I have set my King upon my Holy Hill Zion), then the Church must also be the literal and true fulfillment of those passages as well because, as Peter illustrates, the Church was made up of the "living stones" which was capped off by the "Chief corner stone" (Christ)!

Therefore, if Jesus is the Chief Corner Stone, and the first-century people of God (the first fruits Church) are the foundation stones upon which the whole church is build or established, it must follow then that if Jesus is the literal and true fulfillment of Psalm 118:22 and Psalm 2, that the Church is also the literal and true fulfillment of those passages as well. In other words, the Church is God's true and literal temple! If the Church is only analogous to the actual rebuilt temple of God, then Jesus is only analogous to the actual messiah who is to come. Peter does not delineate between the two, and neither should we.

It is nearly unanimously accepted in the modern church today, and rightfully so, that the regathering of God's people Israel and the Messianic reign of Christ and the full establishment of the Kingdom should all occur near or at the end of the millennial period. Based on all the evidence I have presented here everything Peter says about these things indicates that his contemporary audience and generation is the only period of time that qualifies as the fulfillment of the millennium. If Peter said that the establishment of that Kingdom and of the Temple of God, and of the Messianic Reign of Jesus was happening in his own day, then the completion of the millennium must have been occurred during the generation of Jesus, Peter, Paul and their contemporaries.

If Peter argues that the Church and the saints living 2,000 years ago were fulfilling and consummating all the promises made to Old Covenant Israel, and if Peter is arguing that "they" were the true people of God being built up as a living temple, a royal priesthood, and that they were giving acceptable sacrifices to God once again, and since Peter quotes from the Old Testament literature as his source, and since Peter also tells us that his words were the divinely inspired revelation of the Holy Spirit given to them, which had been hidden for centuries before, shouldn't we expect that the millennial period was either already taking place when Peter wrote this, or that it had already been fulfilled and that "their" sufferings and persecutions, and tribulations were the result of the millennium having already been fulfilled near the end of that age? What was it that was to take place shortly after the end of the millennium? I will attempt to show that the great tribulation was in fact already taking place when Peter wrote his letters, or that he had written his letters shortly before it had begun. If this is true, then the millennial period must be limited to the period of time during or just prior to the writing of Peter's letters some time prior to the events culminating in the destruction of the Temple and the city of Jerusalem in AD70.

The Great Tribulation and the Resurrection

As we have already seen in the previous section, Peter's letters deal a great degree with the "suffering" of God's people. Perhaps mentioned most out of any New Testament book, Peter's primary focus is on the exhortation to his audience to remain faithful despite their persecutions and trials (cf. 1 Peter 4:12). He tells them that their sufferings are going to get worse, and that more is coming to them, but he also promises them vindication, relief, and that they will only have to suffer "a little while longer" (cf. 1 Peter 1:4-6) since their salvation was ready to be revealed "in the last time." As we have already argued, Peter's letter was concerned with the promises made to Old Covenant Israel, and therefore, whatever sufferings Peter's audience was going through, they would have surely fulfilled those sufferings predicted in the Old Testament.

This period of great suffering by Israel before the coming of the Lord or Messiah is often called the Great Tribulation period. Throughout the Old Testament this idea of suffering preceding the resurrection, preceding the glory of Israel, preceding the judgment, and preceding the coming of the Messiah is unquestionable and undeniable. Peter alludes to this idea when he states that Jesus had to suffer in order to enter his glory (cf. 1 Peter 1:6-11). Daniel 12 is very clear on this issue in saying that the time of great trouble would immediately precede the resurrection of Israel.

In Isaiah 24-29, Isaiah predicts the New Covenant, the destruction of creation and the Temple, the Messianic Banquet, the Resurrection, and the Destruction of Leviathan (the Devil) and the veil that covers the people, called death. Isaiah 24:5 tells us why these things were to take place. Isaiah says that it is because God's people have "violated the everlasting Covenant." These events were promised to take place for the people who lived in "the city" and in "the land" (cf. Isaiah 24:10-13). Isaiah 29 makes it very clear which city this is, and it is called "Ariel" which means "city of peace." This is the city of "Jerusalem."

What does all this mean? It means that the promises made by Isaiah were concerning Israel and the city of Jerusalem, and that the passing away of the Temple and the everlasting Covenant of the Law was also the time of the ushering in of the New Covenant, and the Messianic Kingdom, and the resurrection, and the removal of the veil which separated God from his people and God's chosen people from the gentile nations. It also means that the power of death which was made known through the Law of the Prophets would likewise be defeated.

All throughout these chapters God declares that "in that day" when the city, temple, and people are brought low and destroyed, that He will also establish His Kingdom, raise his people from the dead, and bring them salvation. Daniel 7:21 declares that it would be in the time of the fourth beast that the little horn would rise up to persecute the Saints. Hosea 13:12-15 describes the "birth pangs" of Israel (the woman) just as Isaiah 25 did, and describes "Jacob's iniquities" as being dealt with in order to deliver them from the power of death (this is Israel's resurrection).

In Isaiah, Hosea, Daniel, and elsewhere we have clear language used by the Prophets to describe the "birth pangs" or hardships of Israel. Paul and Peter use this terminology to describe their own persecutions, and also quote from these Old Testament texts to indicate that they were fulfilling those passages in their own day. What is even more amazing, is that Paul quotes from both Hosea 13 and Isaiah 25 when he speaks of the resurrection in 1 Corinthians 15, and according to Paul in this passage, he says that after the mortal shall put on immortality "then shall come to pass what is written."

What would come to pass? Death is swallowed up in victory, which had power through the Law. In other words, the Law would not pass away, and death would not be swallowed up (thus removing the veil) until AFTER the resurrection. The common theme in all these passages does not change. The audience is the same, the context is the same, and the fulfillment is the same. The only thing that ever changed is the language that is used to describe what is taking place. First there is to be great tribulation or persecution, and then there is to be judgment or destruction, followed by the resurrection, and finally, the entrance of the Messianic Kingdom and the New Covenant Age, once and for all.

Therefore, if the millennial period is to take place prior to the great tribulation and resurrection, but if Peter and Paul both identify the time in which they lived late in their ministries as a time of great persecution during the "last time," and since they quote the Old Testament passages which deal specifically with the time of the great tribulation as that time in which they were suffering, doesn't it require that we interpret the time of the "millennium" as a period of time that had taken place already, or was coming to a close when both Peter and Paul were writing their letters?

There is no escaping this dilemma. Either a person must argue that Peter and Paul were simply using Old Testament language as a neat linguistic tool, when in fact they weren't actually speaking of the same events in the Old Testament which they quoted from, or worse they must admit that Peter and Paul may have been wrong (and thus, may not have been inspired of God), or finally, they must admit that Peter and Paul were in fact speaking of the sufferings they were enduring as those spoken of in the Old Testament! If we accept the last option, then Peter and Paul's sufferings were fulfilling those prophecies in the Old Testament which then limits the coming of the Messianic Age and Banquet, the New Covenant, the Everlasting Kingdom, and the return of the Lord at the "last time" to their own contemporary audience and generation of people "then living" 2,000 years ago.

If we accept the latter proposition, and I believe that any honest student of the Bible should, then we must also accept the period of the millennium to be limited to some period of time within the forty years from the ministry of Jesus to the time of the great tribulation (sufferings), the resurrection (glory), and the judgment and coming of the Lord in AD70. In the very least, it MUST have been fulfilled prior to this date.

It is within the pattern of the Apostles' preaching that they taught of their power through the Holy Spirit, their persecutions and sufferings, and finally the parousia (the coming or presence of the Lord) that every New Testament book is written. Jesus had commanded his disciples to preach the Gospel into all the world. They did. Jesus had told them they would receive power of the Holy Spirit. They did. Jesus told them they would suffer and even be put to death shortly before the end came. They were. And finally, Jesus told them that all these things must happen, and then comes the end. This is the framework of the entire New Testament, and it is within this structure and prophetic context that the millennium must fit in order to properly understand the nature and precise timing of the thousand year period.

──── 6 ────

THE DAY OF THE LORD

The Night and the Day

To understand the "time" context of the millennial period, or the thousand years, we must first understand the generation which Paul lived in, and the expectation that he and the other Christians and Apostles were eagerly awaiting. To help us do this we will first turn to Romans 13. In this passage Paul is going to make a reference to John 9:4-5, in addition to Psalms 90:4 to develop his primary point to the Romans.

Romans 13:8-14 – "[8]Owe no one anything, except to love each other, for the one who loves another has fulfilled the law. [9]For the commandments, "You shall not commit adultery, You shall not murder, You shall not steal, You shall not covet," and any other commandment, are summed up in this word: "You shall love your neighbor as yourself." [10]Love does no wrong to a neighbor; therefore love is the fulfilling of the law. **[11]Besides this you know the time, that the hour has come for you to wake from sleep. For salvation is nearer to us now than when we first believed. [12]The night is far gone; the day is at hand.** So then let us cast off the works of **darkness** and put on the armor of **light**. [13]Let us walk properly as in the **daytime**, not in orgies and drunkenness, not in sexual immorality and sensuality, not in quarreling and jealousy. [14]But put on the Lord Jesus Christ, and **make no provision for the flesh**, to gratify its desires."

Now, first we must understand the context of Paul's arguments throughout his letters in that he continually had to repel the idea that following the Law of Moses would continue as part of the New Covenant being brought in during this period of time. Many of the Jews believed that they could follow the Law of God (the Torah), and then continue sinning in the flesh believing that obedience to the Law would justify them and cover their sins. This was the "darkness" which Paul speaks about. Given this context, it makes perfect sense that Paul begins by explaining what the "Law" truly is.

In the New Covenant Paul explains that following the Law would no longer pertain to the old ordinances, or the Temple sacrifices, or any of those old elements (cf. Greek - Stoicheon) or rudimentary rituals. Those things simply pointed to the Spiritual reality in Christ. In the New Covenant, following the Law would consist of loving one another with a pure heart, and from this all other things that are good would flow. This is why we are told that in the New Covenant God's Law would be written on our hearts and not on tablets made with stone (cf. Romans 2:15).

Then, Paul makes some very clear statements that form a time context in which we must closely pay attention. Notice in vs. 11 that Paul says, "…you know the time, and that the hour has come for you to wake from sleep." It is clear in this passage, without developing this idea in full, that Paul is specifically referring to the end of the Old Covenant system, and that those who were once "asleep" in the earth or in the land were going to "awaken" because the time was at hand; literally that the "hour has come." Then Paul says that "salvation is nearer to us now than when we first believed."

How so many commentators miss this statement is strange, since whatever salvation Paul is talking about it is definitely something that is progressive, and it is something that in only 25-30 years after Christ died and rose again that has become "nearer" to them than it was since they had first believed. This statement truly harkens the reader to Hebrews 9:28, "So Christ, having been offered once to bear the sins of many, will appear a second time, not to deal with sin but for salvation to those who are eagerly waiting for him." Notice that in both passages this salvation was "nearer" to them, and they waited for it with eager expectation as they said they "saw the day approaching."

So again, we must see that Paul's primary focus thus far is to direct his reader's minds to the "hope" of God's people being "awakened" from sleep, and also towards their great hope of Christ's return, which they eagerly waited for and believed would commence any moment and within their lifetime. Indeed, Jesus Himself said that He would return within their generation, and so they expected as much. With this in mind Paul then goes on to say that "the night is far gone; the day is at hand. So then let us cast off the works of darkness and put on the armor of light."

Now, the question must be asked here, why would Paul use this phrase to describe the idea of the "hour which has come"? Surely this phrase isn't simply a meaningless analogy that Paul uses, or for clever linguistic appeal to his audience? When we turn our attention to John 9:4-5, I believe that our suspicion becomes much clearer as to why Paul uses this language, when we see Jesus' own words:

John 9:4-5 – "[4]We must work the works of him who sent me while it is day; night is coming, when no one can work. [5]As long as I am in the world, I am the light of the world."

Notice here that in John's Gospel Jesus declares that the "night is coming, when no one can work." It's very clear based on His statement that the "night" is the time when He wouldn't be with them anymore as He currently was. This "night" is a specific reference to the "works" of Christ not being performed (i.e. - miracles, healings, raising the dead, teaching the Gospel, etc.). So we have as a brief time frame that Jesus would not be with them from the time that Judas left the room in John 9, until the resurrection of Jesus, when he once again performed miracles for forty days among them.

When Jesus was with his disciples, it was "day." When he was no longer with them or in the world, it was "night." This is how the Gospel writers, Paul, and Peter all used the language in metaphorical terms. When Jesus left them to be crucified, it was "night." When he was raised from the dead and taught them for forth days, it was "day." When he ascended into heaven, it was once again "night." However, Jesus promised not to leave them as orphans in the world, and he said that he would send them a helper, and that they were to be a bright lamp shining in a dark place.

But then notice what Paul says approximately thirty years later in Romans 13:12, "the night is far gone, the day is at hand." Peter also emphasizes the same idea when he says in 2 Peter 1:19, "And we have something more sure, the prophetic word, to which you will do well to pay attention as to a lamp shining in a dark place, until the day dawns and the morning star rises in your hearts." So we see here that both Peter and Paul have as a current reality for them that they lived during the time of "darkness" in which they were to be "lamps" shining in a dark place.

So we may conclude then that after Jesus ascended to heaven in Luke 24 and Acts 1, He had promised them the "helper" who would be with them until the end (cf. John 9). This was a promise of the "light" in the midst of darkness. However, even after receiving the Holy Spirit at Pentecost the Apostles and disciples eagerly looked forward to a time and day very soon in their future which would only rise as the day or "morning star" when the prophetic word of Christ's return was fulfilled. So then, when Paul declares that they must "cast off the works of darkness" and put on the "armor of light," it is in the context of the time in which they lived; that is that they expected and believed that they would soon enter into the "new day" in which their Lord would bring them the fullness of salvation and into the light, apart from the works of darkness.

If you remember, the Apostles were living in coexistence with the works of the Law and its' ordinances during the time when "the light" was only being revealed to those who believed. This was the two covenant period (i.e. – Isaac and Ishmael; cf. Galatians 4). Thus, they lived in darkness or the night, but the day or light was shown to and through them, and was going to come in its fullness at the coming of the Lord. In 1 John 2:8 and Hebrews 8:13 we clearly see that the writers identify the night with the existence of the Law and it's passing away to give way to the true light, which was the New Covenant truth of the Gospel of Jesus.

"At the same time, it is a new commandment that I am writing to you, which is true in him and in you, because the darkness is passing away and the true light is already shining." (1 John 2:8)

"In speaking of a new covenant, he makes the first one obsolete. And what is becoming obsolete and growing old is ready to vanish away." (Hebrews 8:13)

The City of God

In the book of Revelation, chapters 21-22, we have a very symbolic picture of the New Jerusalem, the city of God. While some Christians who take a wooden literal approach might view these passages thinking that a glorified physical city, having four sided dimensions will actually fly out of the sky, the majority of commentators recognize this language to be a reference to the Church, the true dwelling place of God, within every believer belonging to the Body of Christ. In this view, we interpret things like jewels and golden streets representing purity and refinement, and other objects like gates and foundations representing the twelve Apostles and the twelve tribes of Israel, the foundation and establishment of the Church, the people of God. The equal sided dimensions represent the equality and unity of the Church, and thus, the city of God is a beautiful description of God's people who are in Christ.

And so as we arrive at Revelation 21:22-27, we have beautiful language describing the condition of this city (i.e. – the Church), and it says the following:

"²²And I saw no temple in the city, for its temple is the Lord God the Almighty and the Lamb. ²³And the city has no need of sun or moon to shine on it, for the glory of God gives it light, and its lamp is the Lamb. ²⁴By its light will the nations walk, and the kings of the earth will bring their glory into it, ²⁵and its gates will never be shut by day—and there will be no night there. ²⁶They will bring into it the glory and the honor of the nations. ²⁷But nothing unclean will ever enter it, nor anyone who does what is detestable or false, but only those who are written in the Lamb's book of life."

What does this passage tell us about the city, and about the condition of the city of God in the New Covenant? Well, in the Old Covenant, there was a literal temple, a literal city of Jerusalem, and literal symbols in the sky (i.e. – sun, moon, stars, etc.) which were required to keep all the festival days and ordinances under the Old Covenant Law. But notice how John uses the language here to describe life in the New Covenant of God. In this city (i.e. – the New Jerusalem, or the Church) there is no need for the physical sun or moon to guide it or to maintain the festival days and keeping of the Law. The only thing required now is that God's glory will guide and shine through the city! By the light of God John says that nations and kings will be lead, and night will not be found.

The physical creation of sun, moon, stars, and other items used in Old Covenant Temple imagery were guiding pictures or a metaphor of the reality of God and the ultimate truth of salvation in and through Christ Jesus. Those things were always just a symbol of what was true about our existence, and about what truly guides and directs our lives. As the sun provides light and life through heat and by its rays, so too does the son of God provide light and life to us as He shines through us. The same motif could be used for the other elements of creation and the Old Testament ordinances and symbols.

Remember that the "night" represented darkness, and life under the Old Covenant system brought death and bondage, and a veil that covered the eyes of the people. Now, in the New Covenant city we are told that nothing unclean will enter into it because only God's true people may be a part of it. Then in the next chapter John gives more beautiful language to describe the condition of the church after the coming of Jesus:

> "[1]Then the angel showed me the river of the water of life, bright as crystal, flowing from the throne of God and of the Lamb [2]through the middle of the street of the city; also, on either side of the river, the tree of life with its twelve kinds of fruit, yielding its fruit each month. The leaves of the tree were for the healing of the nations. [3]No longer will there be anything accursed, but the throne of God and of the Lamb will be in it, and his servants will worship him.

⁴They will see his face, and his name will be on their foreheads. ⁵And night will be no more. They will need no light of lamp or sun, for the Lord God will be their light, and they will reign forever and ever."

The river of the water of life is none other than the Word of God, and that which brings life and healing by God through His Spirit. The tree of life is Jesus, with the diverse branches growing off of it from all nations, and doing good works (i.e. – bearing fruit: Galatians 5) each month. In the Old Covenant Jewish system bringing a sacrifice of fruit or of your flock was done during certain festival holidays or times of the year. In the New Covenant Age the works that are done and the fruit that is produced comes from love and good deeds which happens all the time, without any need for a calendar or the regulation of feast days, Jewish rituals, or special recognition of one day over another.

This passage says that His servants (Christians) will worship Him, and that they will see Him face to face, and that "night" will be no more. What does that mean? It means that no longer will God's people be blinded by works of the Law, and no longer will they be restricted from coming to God directly, having a close, personal relationship with Him. Having no need of a "lamp" or "the sun" is a reference to the need of both under the Old Covenant system. But now, in the New Covenant Age, the Church Age, there is no need for the Law written on stone, or the festival days, or the ordinances, or the Old Temple, or a physical city of God to be needed to follow the one true God! Now God Himself is their light, and He reveals truth and guides His people as they need it.

The true beauty of everything that John describes in these two chapters is that he draws from the Old Covenant language to describe the conditions of the New Covenant in Christ. But the most important aspect that we have to understand about this passage is that these are the conditions AFTER the millennial period. The light of God given to the nations, kings, and His people to guide them and lead them and to dwell within them forevermore is the condition of the world after the "night" had passed away and the "dawn" or "day" had arrived. The two ideas are linked together. The light of God arrives in the world as the night passes away. The night was the period of the Old Covenant Law of bondage and sin, and the day was the entrance of the New Covenant into the world, preached by the Apostles and first-century Christians, and finally established once and for all after the Old Covenant system had been abolished in AD70.

A Watch in the Night

Given what we have already seen from John, Paul, the writer of Hebrews, and Peter's statements, what we truly need to address is an Old Testament statement in Psalms 90:4 which says, "a thousand years in your sight are but as yesterday when it is past, or as a watch in the night." The critical nature of this statement is twofold. First, the writer says that a thousand years to God are like yesterday "when it is past." The reason this is important is because the idea being expressed here is that "yesterday" must pass before God sees it as a thousand years being completed.

Or to put it another way, the thousand years is not completed until the previous day has passed. What is even more interesting about this is that a Jewish "day" never begins until sundown, or evening. The Day lasts from sunset until the following sunset, and so the Psalmist clearly utilizes the idea of the "watch in the night" to reveal that this "thousand year" period is essentially like the time from sunset to dawn of the following day. While the Psalmist is not trying to convey a literal thousand years, nor that yesterday passing is literally equivalent to one thousand years (even in God's eyes), it is important to note that the primary focus of the writer is to direct your attention to the idea that what seems to human beings to be a very long period of time is of no boundary for God.

This DOES NOT mean that time is meaningless or un-definable to God, rather, it means that God is outside of time and is able to fulfill his promises no matter how long they may take, and even if we might think that they might not come to pass. However, when God establishes a time-table for prophetic things to take place, He does not fail to make them come to pass, nor change direction without notice, nor lie or make things up as He goes, even though we think they are taking too long. In 2 Peter this was their dilemma. People were mocking Jesus' statement about His coming "in their generation" and the Christians were beginning to doubt that Jesus was in fact going to come, since it had already been around 35 years or so since Jesus uttered the words that He would come within "that generation." We will address 2 Peter 3 shortly (the day as a thousand years).

Second, the writer says that this thousand year period is also "as a watch in the night." Now this statement is crucial because it establishes a precedent for us to understand the idea that however long the period is (whether very long, or very short), in God's terms and in His grand scheme a thousand years is compared to "a watch in the night," and so the two terms or ideas may be used interchangeably. If God sets an event for us in prophetic language which shall come to pass, the amount of time it takes to be fulfilled is not a problem for God. God will keep His promises no matter what! If God says in generic terms that something will happen within a generation or within a period of time, and it nears the end of that period, while it might seem very long to human beings, it does not negate God's ability to fulfill and keep His promises!

The basic idea being conveyed with this passage is that to God time is of no regard in His eyes, however, in our eyes time is everything. Therefore, when Paul penned the letter to the Romans in or around AD60-62 (according to most credible scholars), Paul sees that the time since Christ left (called "the night") until the writing of this letter was to him as "yesterday when it is passed" or a "night far gone" (cf. Romans 13:12). Therefore, if the night was far gone to Paul, and the day was at hand and light was already shining in the place of darkness according to Paul, John, and Peter, doesn't this imply and necessitate that each of these men expected Christ to return very soon at His coming, in which He would be the permanent light of the world and the "Day Star rising"?

Of course, most futurist paradigms have us believe that the "night" is still here today, and that it is a period lasting so long that no one can ever truly know when the "dawn" might arise in our hearts (cf. 2 Peter 1:19). According to most Christians today, the light that was already beginning to shine in Paul and

Peter's day, is still just barely shinning at the end of the evening night when dawn was about to appear. Apparently we have been living in the dawn of the day for nearly 2,000 years, still waiting for the sun to finally rise over the horizon! With the idea of the "watch in the night" in your minds, a brief dialogue on 2 Peter 1:19 might be helpful. The "day dawning" or the "day star rising" is an obvious allusion to the near end of the "night" which we have already discussed, and which the whole of this section (cf. 2 Peter 1:13-20) makes abundantly clear. Therefore, the idea of the "day dawning" is a direct reference to the second coming which they eagerly looked forward to happening in their near future. It is also important to make the connection that Peter's allusion is referring to when he speaks about the "day star rising in their hearts."

The "day stars" are equivalent to the "morning stars" which, according to Job 38:7 are the "sons of God" singing together for joy. In speaking of the "morning stars" it is spoken of Jesus that He is the "bright morning star" (cf. Revelation 22:16). Therefore, we are quite certain that the "day star" rising has everything to do with the day when Christ would come again and when those Christians would become the "sons of God" and when His glory would then be theirs.

And so we are confident to make the connection that the time when Jesus would be gone is also the same time of "the night" and "the darkness" until His return. We can state clearly that the Apostles were to receive the "helper" at which time they would be used as a "light" or "lamp" in a dark place and in a dark world.

And we are finally confident to say that their eager expectations around 25-35 years later were that the "night" was far gone, or quite literally that it was essentially over, and that they could already see the day approaching, just as with the morning dawn of a new day. This was the near expectation of the coming of the Lord, and the "night and day" imagery that is used throughout the New Testament could not be any clearer on this point. For the Apostles, the sun was about to rise on the whole world, and this would be the ushering in of the Messiah for their salvation, and for the complete establishment of the Kingdom of God at the second coming of the Lord (cf. Hebrews 9:28).

A Day as a Thousand Years

Now before we get to the meat of the matter (arguing for the forty year millennium) we must consider a crucial statement made by Peter in his second letter. In this letter Peter makes the following comments (with my own comments in brackets):

"[8]But do not overlook this one fact, beloved, that with the Lord one day [when it is past, cf. Psalms 90:4] is as a thousand years, and a thousand years as one day [when it is past]. [9]The Lord is not slow to fulfill his promise as some count slowness, but is patient toward you, not wishing that any should perish, but that all should reach repentance. [10]But the day of the Lord will come like a thief [in the night], and then the heavens will pass away with a roar, and the elements will be burned up and dissolved, and the earth and the works that are done on it will be exposed." (2 Peter 3:8-10)

Two critical elements of this passage must be seen. First, when Peter draws from the analogy of the thousand years as a day, he is clearly quoting from and alluding to Psalm 90:4. Peter didn't just make this idea up. And so, when we see that this "day" is a direct allusion to a "watch in the night" we MUST see the connection between the use of "night and day" language with that of the "thousand years" and also the "watch in the night." There is also a direct allusion to the "thief in the night" related to the thousand years which I will touch on a little later. For Peter, the time that is being spoken about is the time in which they were being mocked by the scoffers because the coming of the Lord "seemed" to be taking a very long time.

The scoffers, both in Peter's epistles and in Jude, were mocking the Christians because Jesus had promised them that the destruction of the Temple and the end of the Jewish Age would occur in that generation (cf. Matthew 23-24). But Peter reassures them that for God a "thousand years" in God's eyes is like a very short period of time (i.e. - as a watch in the night, or the time from sunset to dawn or sunrise).

Since there is no doubt that the New Testament writers, including Jesus Himself, used this analogy and drew from this idea to express the time of the "night" and the "coming day," it is very likely that Peter is also doing the same thing here, and is simply attempting to "ease their minds" because what "seems" long to those Christians who are suffering and being persecuted at the hands of their enemies, is actually going to come to pass exactly as Jesus had promised.

The strength of this argument becomes even stronger when we see Peter also reference the idea of the Lord coming "like a thief" in the very same passage. What other Scriptures draw on this analogy or idea, and how do they apply it? Job 24:14, Matthew 24:43, and 1 Thessalonians 5:2 all specifically use the idea of the thief coming and they each describe this event as one which happens "during the night" when those who are not ready will be taken by surprise.

Therefore, in one chapter, and in only three verses, Peter describes the "day far gone" and the "thief in the night" and also alludes to the "thousand year" language from Psalm 90:4, which to any observant reader would recall the readers' mind to the same idea that Jesus would come at the "end of the night." What did Peter, John, and Paul say about the night in which they lived? It was ready to pass, and was growing old, and day was approaching soon!

Now, what is often said about this passage is that it may be making an argument that since a day to the Lord is also as a thousand years, that when God speaks of time in the Bible He really means "in His eyes." They might argue that when the Bible speaks of a "soon" or "near" event that it really doesn't mean what it says, even though the language indicates a soon or near event is expected. But does this idea really hold any weight? Consider for just a moment that this is even possible. How do we know which idea Peter is putting forth?

Is Peter saying that God would come "very soon" (as the night was about to pass), or was Peter saying that while it was seeming to take so long, Jesus would actually come very soon, but to God, soon can be even longer than what you think is long? For God, a single day is like a thousand years and so it is actually, potentially thousands of years or more away? Well, what does Peter himself (a man led and inspired to speak by the Holy Spirit) say about this? Again, in this very passage Peter says:

"**⁹The Lord is not slow to fulfill his promise** as some count slowness, but is patient toward you, not wishing that any should perish, but that all should reach repentance."

Again, many of the Judaizers were mocking Peter and the Apostles (cf. 2 Peter 3:1-5; Jude 18) and were saying that the promises made by Jesus were "not happening" since He had first made the predictions. Remember, Jesus said that in "this generation" these things would happen (cf. Matthew 23-24). Now, more than thirty years later these same Jews who were denying and mocking the words of Jesus were now doing the same thing to Peter and Paul.

But notice Peter's response. Peter tells his audience what he had already formerly told them in his first letter, and in fact he was reminding them that these things must happen before the coming of the Lord. What he is now saying in this second letter he had formerly already told them in his first letter (cf. 2 Peter 3:1-4)! Well, what did Peter tell them in his first letter concerning this? I'll get to this in a moment.

Now, in his second letter Peter "stirs up their remembrance" about what he had written in his first letter to let them know that while some of them were impatient, thinking that Jesus was taking far too long and was "slack concerning His promises," God does not look at time as they did, and that He was going to wait until the very last possible moment before He came as he promised. And so what appears to be a long time in "their eyes" is not at all a very long time in "God's eyes." Do you see the method of interpretation that Peter uses concerning "which" idea he has in mind about the "thousand years"? Just to be very clear I will pose the question again as I had asked before.

Question: Is Peter saying that God would come "very soon" (as the night has almost passed) even though they felt that it was taking far too long and were even being mocked for their beliefs...

...or was Peter saying to hold on just a little while longer because it will actually happen soon, but since a single day is like a thousand years to God, soon could actually be very far off, and ultimately could be many thousands of years away?

Do you see the problem when the second option is preferred? Is this really the immediate context of the passage, and is this what Peter has in mind when he is addressing his audience? Once again, I think that any astute scholar or even an unlearned student who has even the remotest amount of common sense can clearly see that Paul's audience, and the context of his statement is dealing directly with the immediacy of the coming of the Lord and that their expectations will be fulfilled soon. They were impatient and were being mocked and persecuted for believing that Jesus would come very soon as Jesus predicted, but God was not impatient and would wait till the very last possible moment of when He said He would come to them. You can sum up Peter's argument with the following paraphrase (my own words):

"You see guys, while you think it's taking a very long time because Jesus said He would come within your lifetimes, and even though it's now nearly 30 to 35 years later, this generation is coming to an end, and even though the sufferings you're going through make it even harder to endure, and since you see the things happening which Jesus promised would happen before He comes, don't think that Jesus is going to take forever, or not come at all. Just because you are impatient about it and going through these trials isn't going to change the fact that Jesus will come in this generation as He said He would. You see, Jesus doesn't live in the realm of time as we do, and so for Him to wait to the very last minute of this generation is for the simple fact that He wants as many of His people to be saved as possible. So don't worry, it's coming soon; hold fast and hang tight! I know it's been 35 years or so, but the generation isn't over yet guys, but it will be soon!"

And lastly, if it is true that since time for God is meaningless, and that since a day to the Lord can be a thousand years, and a thousand years can be as a day, then when the Bible speaks of time that is "far off" and "a long time away," is it possible that the Bible is actually talking about something very soon or near? You see, many modern commentators make the case that when the Apostle's say that the Lord's coming will be "very soon" in their own generation, that since a day to the Lord can also be a very long time off, well, don't you see that God could return in thousands or millions of years and not violate the meaning of "soon" and "near"? But does that really work? Wouldn't the opposite argument also be true? When the Bible talks about things that are "not near" and "not soon," wouldn't that also mean that those things could also actually be "very soon" and "very near" to God?

Using that sort of logic makes time meaningless in the Bible. It turns time statements into unknowable and undefined statements that no person can ever understand. The Bible wasn't written to God, nor was it written for Him to read based on His own understanding. It was inspired by God, and given to human beings in order for "them" to read and for "them" to understand using human language. Human language has real meaning, and words have actual definitions. To violate the plain and literal meaning of words like "near" and "soon" simply because they don't fit your predetermined view of Jesus' coming in your future is not using proper Biblical interpretation or hermeneutics. Any Biblical scholar and hermeneutics professor can tell you that. The logical explanations often used by prophecy pundits for 2 Peter 3 and the meaning of "a day to the Lord is as a thousand years" are in fact illogical, and they are copout excuses for what otherwise would be failed predictions by the Apostles in the view of many of these pundits and Christians.

In fact, the majority of skeptics and atheists see the validity and truthfulness of the fact that the Apostles said and believed that Jesus would return "soon" and at any moment in the first century. They understand what's at stake here. Unfortunately, they see the coming of Jesus in the same way that many Christians do today, that it must have occurred with a physical body and with a cosmological change and transformation of the universe. Atheists understand the true "timing" of the coming of the Lord and the first-century imminence of the events described in prophecy, but they completely miss the true nature of how those things were fulfilled. Because of this, they reject Scripture, since to them the events never happened as they were predicted to.

Many Christians today attempt to avoid the problem raised by many skeptics and atheists, not by correcting their false understanding of the nature of the coming of Jesus and the fulfillment of prophecy in the first century, rather, they attempt to get around the problems of the time statements made by the Apostles by changing the meaning of the words, and in turn, they spiritualize the meaning of words like "soon," "near," "at hand," "at the door," and "in a very, very little while." Now who's allegorizing and spiritualizing prophecy?

Assumptions made by Christians today like, "We know Jesus hasn't come yet," or "We know the resurrection hasn't taken place yet," or "We know the millennium hasn't begun yet," are one of the primary reasons most Christians can't get beyond the most basic aspects of truly understanding the meaning of Scripture when it talks about these issues. While needing to progress to the "meat" of the meaning of Scripture, most Christians today, even many who claim to be scholars and teachers and pastors and theologians, still require and need to go back to the milk and start all over again (cf. Hebrews 5:12).

Finally, concerning the passage in 2 Peter 3:8, Samuel Dawson had this to say in his book, "Essays on Eschatology," in response to the typical statement by Christians that "time doesn't mean anything to God":

"...[that time means nothing to God]. However, this statement is overbroad. In some senses, time doesn't mean much to God; and in others, it is tremendously important...While God is not bound by time, he communicates to [those of us] who are. When God made prophecies containing a time element, matters of days or years were incredibly significant. Indeed, the very faithfulness of God would be at stake if he made prophecies including time, and then didn't fulfill them." (pp. 21-22)

You see, God created time, and human beings live within those parameters, and we communicate understanding words that define different amounts of time. When God communicates to us in the Bible, He uses time in dealing with man and He expects man to respect time as He has created it and given us a detailed account of something that is going to happen. Additionally, God is faithful in matters of time, and when God says that He will do something in a certain period of time, His Word is validated when what He said would happen, does in fact happen exactly when and how he said it would!

When God gives a prophecy and describes the appointed time of fulfillment, there is nothing that any human being can do to delay or postpone that promise or prediction from God. If the promise is an unconditional statement like, "I will do this or that," then it will happen exactly as God says it will. For Christians today to make the bold assertion that God failed to fulfill his prophecies and that he postponed the predictions to come in that generation simply because the Jews rejected Him is a rejection of God's faithfulness to keep His own promises!

In fact, the whole reason God waited 40 years to destroy those Jews who rejected Jesus was because He was utterly patient with them, and that is exactly that 2 Peter 3:9 tells us. God was being very patient, but he would not delay his promises beyond the appointed time. While it seemed like a long time to wait, 30-40 years was nothing for God, and yet, God was going to keep His promise, and He would come to them within that generation just as Jesus had predicted. There was no delay, and there was not anything left unfulfilled.

Peter Stirs Up Their Remembrance

In my previous chapter I explained in great detail the prophetic context of the millennium with the rest of Scripture, specifically focusing on Peter's letters. My primary focus was on the context of Peter and Paul's letters, and how everything they had written was regarding the hope of Israel, and that they believed that they were receiving everything promised in the Old Testament very soon and in their own day. But one of the most often overlooked aspects of Peter's statements in 2 Peter 3 regarding how "a day to the Lord is as a thousand years," was that Peter stated that everything he was talking about here in chapter 3 was only a further development of what he had already told them in his first letter, and that both letters were simply a reminder of what had come from the predictions of the holy prophets and from Jesus himself. Remember, at the beginning of 2 Peter 3, Peter says this:

> "[1]This is now the second letter that I am writing to you, beloved. In both of them I am stirring up your sincere mind by way of reminder, [2]that you should remember the predictions of the holy prophets and the commandment of the Lord and Savior through your apostles..."

Well, when did Peter and the rest of the Apostles receive a "command of the Lord" about what Peter described as their sufferings and persecutions? In Matthew 24 and Luke 21 Jesus had told them that this would happen before the end would come. Therefore, everything that Peter continues to talk about is dealing with everything I described in the former chapter in addition to the specific things that Jesus predicted in his Olivet Discourse in Matthew 24 and Luke 21. Whatever Jesus was talking about in Matthew 24 was the same context of 2 Peter 3.

Thus, as we read 2 Peter 3, we must understand that the language Peter employs is speaking of the same context and content of the things he has already described in his first letter, and it is in relationship to all the things that the prophets of old had written about and predicted, and it was directly related to what Jesus had told them in Matthew 24 and Luke 21. If anything that you read in 2 Peter 3 differs in any way with the timing, nature, or fulfillment of the same events described in Matthew 24 and Luke 21, then your interpretation of 2 Peter 3 is wrong. The fact that Jesus used apocalyptic language and imagery in his Olivet Discourse to explain all the events leading up to and including the time of the end is also a prophetic "key" to helping the reader understand the language of 2 Peter 3. Since Peter tells us that 2 Peter 3 is a direct commentary on what Jesus had told them before, then we ought to expect that his language is also used in a similar fashion. Peter's imagery and language in this chapter is highly prophetic and apocalyptic.

Peter describes the "heavens and earth that now exist" (vs. 7) in relationship to the Old Covenant system he had spoken about in his first letter. Peter alludes to the first heavens and earth and their destruction to describe the sudden destruction that was soon coming upon his people Israel (the Heavens and Earth created at Sinai). Likewise, in vs. 10 Peter describes the "heavens passing away like a roar," the "elements burning and dissolving away," and the "earth and its works being burned up and exposed." Is Peter talking about the physical heavens, elements, and earth here? Only in the minds of modern prophecy pundits!

The truth of the matter is that Peter's language here is duplicated many other times in the New Testament in reference to Israel, the Law, and the ordinances of the Jewish system (the elements of the Law). The "works of the earth" are a direct reference to the works of the Jews, under the Law. What was going to be exposed? The fact that works and the Law could not save, but only righteousness and the work of Jesus Christ!

In case there is any doubt that what I have just said is true, here are just a few examples of what I am talking about:

"The Heavens Shall Pass Away Like a Roar"

Matthew 24:35 – "Heaven and earth will pass away, but my words will never pass away"

1 Corinthians 7:31 – "For this world in its present form is passing away"

2 Corinthians 3:12-18 – "[12]Therefore, since we have such a hope, we are very bold. [13]We are not like Moses, who would put a veil over his face to prevent the Israelites from

seeing the end of what was passing away. [14]But their minds were made dull, for to this day the same veil remains when the old covenant is read. It has not been removed, because only in Christ is it taken away. [15]Even to this day when Moses is read, a veil covers their hearts. [16]But whenever anyone turns to the Lord, the veil is taken away. [17]Now the Lord is the Spirit, and where the Spirit of the Lord is, there is freedom. [18]And we all, who with unveiled faces contemplate the Lord's glory, are being transformed into his image with ever-increasing glory"

1 John 2:8 – "At the same time, it is a new commandment that I am writing to you, which is true in him and in you, because the darkness is passing away and the true light is already shining."

1 John 2:17-18 – "[17]The world and its desires pass away, but whoever does the will of God lives forever. [18]Dear children, this is the last hour; and as you have heard that the antichrist is coming, even now many antichrists have come. This is how we know it is the last hour."

Hebrews 8:13 – "In speaking of a new covenant, he makes the first one obsolete. And what is becoming obsolete and growing old is ready to vanish away."

Clearly, the "heavens" and "world" were references to the Old Covenant world, or the old system, and the Old Law. Anyone who attempts to turn these passages into physical, cosmological definitions will completely miss the scope of Peter's intended meaning.

"The Elements Burning and Dissolving"

Galatians 4:2-4 – "[2]...but he is under guardians and managers until the date set by the father. [3]So also we, while we were children, were held in bondage under the elemental things of the world. [4]But when the fullness of the time came, God sent forth His Son, born of a woman, born under the Law..."

Colossians 2:20-23 – "²⁰If you have died with Christ to the elementary principles of the world, why, as if you were living in the world, do you submit yourself to decrees, such as, ²¹"Do not handle, do not taste, do not touch!" ²²(which all refer to things destined to perish with use)--in accordance with the commandments and teachings of men? ²³These are matters which have, to be sure, the appearance of wisdom in self-made religion and self-abasement and severe treatment of the body, but are of no value against fleshly indulgence."

Every time the Greek word "Stoicheon" is translated "elements" in the Bible, it is with reference to the rudimentary ordinances of the Law. There is never any deviation from this. Are we to believe that the only time that it supposedly refers to something different is in 2 Peter 3? Notice what Isaiah 34 has to say about the judgment coming upon the Assyrians:

Isaiah 34:2-4 – "²The LORD is angry with all nations; his wrath is on all their armies. He will totally destroy them; he will give them over to slaughter. ³Their slain will be thrown out, their dead bodies will stink; the mountains will be soaked with their blood. ⁴All the stars in the sky will be dissolved and the heavens rolled up like a scroll; all the starry host will fall like withered leaves from the vine, like shriveled figs from the fig tree."

Would anyone argue that Isaiah actually predicted the "physical" dissolution of the stars, sky, and heavens when this prediction of the destruction of the Assyrians was made? I certainly hope not! Yet, when Peter makes the identical statement, using identical language, and is saying all of these things in reference to the Old Testament prophecies and the teachings of Jesus in Matthew 24 and Luke 21, all of a sudden it's now talking about the physical cosmos? Remember what I said before about the "Analogy of Scripture"? Now would be a good time to apply that principle here!

Much more could be said about 2 Peter 3, however, a diligent study of this book in light of the few comments I have made here should be enough to get any faithful Berean Bible student to take a closer look for themselves at the true meaning and context of Peter's letters. For what it's worth, one of the best commentaries and treatments I have ever read on this subject, that is, understanding 2 Peter 3, is a book titled "The Elements Shall Burn With Fervent Heat," A Study of 2 Peter 3, by Dr. Don K. Preston. If you are interested in learning much more about this topic, do not read another book on this subject before you read this one. With that said, I have made the case and provided substantial evidence for the idea that Peter used language throughout his letters, and specifically in 2 Peter 3 that was consistent with, and in fact was tied directly to the same language that Jesus used in Matthew 24, and that the Old Testament writers used to describe judgment and apocalyptic events that were not cosmological in literal terms. I have shown that these things were to take place near the end of the millennium, and that Peter and Paul specifically refer to the time that they lived as the near end of that period, when the day or dawn was about to rise. The context of the millennium fits into this period of time, and no other. It is not, and cannot extend beyond this. Therefore, the millennium was near its end when Peter and Paul wrote those words.

——— 7 ———

THE TRANSITION PERIOD

Making the Case for a Forty Year Millennium

To this point I have already provided a large foundation for the basis of the "thousand year period" being that period of time in which the disciples and Apostles lived and ministered, expecting that its near end was imminent and that it would soon bring in the "new day." This would place the "thousand year period" at the beginning of Jesus' ministry continuing until approximately the time of the Neronian persecution of the Christians, and specifically just before the Roman armies first surrounded Jerusalem during the mid AD60's. "Revelation 20 takes us back to the beginning of the New Testament era [in which] the binding of Satan in Revelation 20:1-3 can be understood to mean that Satan cannot prevent the spread of the gospel during [that] age, that he cannot gather Christ's enemies together to attack the church, and that this binding takes place during the entire era of the New Testament church."[1] As I argued previously, the New Testament church completed its Great Commission missionary work prior to and during the time from Christ, and leading up to AD70.

Arguably, the ministry of Jesus began on or around the year AD27-29. The 3 ½ year ministry of Jesus would then place his death and resurrection at around AD30-32. Given this information, we are to conclude that the "millennial period," or the "transition period," (also called the Second Exodus by some scholars[2]) as it is often referred to was the period of time from about AD27 to about AD64 or AD67; a

---

[1] Hoekema, Anthony A., *The Meaning of the Millennium.* (Downers Grove, IL: InterVarsity Press, 1977). 56-57.

[2] See Brant Pitre's book "Jesus, the Tribulation, and the End of the Exile: Restoration Eschatology and the Origin of the Atonement."

period of approximately 37 - 40 years. Given the near unanimously accepted tradition held by Hebrew scholars that a Jewish generation was equivalent to approximately forty years, and that Jesus Himself declared that "this generation shall not pass away till all these things take place" (cf. Matthew 12:41-45; 23:36; 24:34; & the synoptic passages), it is very clear that this period of time fits very nicely within the Biblical description and framework of the period of "the night passing" and the "day rising" as the "thousand year period."

So someone may ask, "You mean to tell me that the 'thousand years' is actually only a 'forty year' period"? At the outset to many people this might seem ridiculous, especially when viewed from a Westernized, modern, American perspective; that is until one looks at the Biblical language and Scriptural precedent for this as being a very real and legitimate possibility. Remember, the idea of the thousand year period wasn't something John the revelator simply made up, nor was it just some vision that he received without any knowledge of what he was writing about or seeing. The fact that the Book of Revelation is the most Hebrew New Testament book is not disputed. Nor is it disputable that nearly two thirds of this book is either a direct quote or an allusion to an Old Testament idea, theme, or passage.

Its structure and style in the Greek is likely to have first been written in Hebrew or Aramaic and then translated into Greek, or at least the writer was so familiar with Hebrew thought that he drew from this knowledge to write the book, and it is also very intentional in the way it is grouped, structured, and written. It is my belief that the writer of the Book of Revelation was none other than John Lazarus himself, a Jewish Priest or Rabbi and brother of Martha (John 11). It is also my opinion that John Lazarus wrote the Gospel of John, in addition to 1, 2, and 3 John as well.[3]

If this is true then it is very likely that the writer of Revelation drew from the many symbols, ideas and themes of the Old Testament, and also from his contemporaries of the

---

[3] See "The Disciple Whom Jesus Loved – Who Wrote the Fourth Gospel" by David Curtis of Berean Bible Church; on audio lecture and outline form at www.bereanbiblechurch.org.

time (the disciples and Apostles) in using the phrase, "the thousand years" of Revelation 20. However, true or not, the book is clearly a Jewish work, and the language of the thousand year period unmistakably draws from Old Testament language and Jewish thought.

The fact that the number "one thousand" or "thousands" is used so often in the Bible for something OTHER THAN a literal numerical value lends credence to the idea that the phrase "thousand years" has a Jewish definition and does not refer to an exact period of exactly one thousand years. Whether it is to be interpreted as "fullness," "complete," or simply "a lot," we can only speculate, but the clear evidence seems to point to the forty year period, the generational period Jesus was speaking to, and the entirety or fullness of that period as to the time in question.

"While some might find the idea of a forty year millennium strange to the ears, it was not an uncommon thought, even among the ancient rabbis. Dr. Randall E. Otto describes the following Jewish views: 'While this interim period of the messianic age was placed at four hundred years in 4 Ezra 7:28 and Apocalypse of Baruch 29-30, 'older traditions concerning the days of the Messiah fix a very short interval for the interim period, namely, forty years (R. Eliezer ben Hyrcanus; Bar. In Sanh. 99a; R. Aqiba: Midr. The. On Ps. 90:15; Tanch. Eqeb 7b, Pes. Rabb. 4a).' Similarly, the Qumran materials indicate such a period, as for instance, the Damascus Document: 'from the day of the gathering in of the unique teacher, until destruction of all the men of war who turned back with the man of lies, there shall be about forty years; (CD xx, 14-15), and a Commentary on Ps 37:10: 'I will stare at his place and he will no longer be there. Its interpretation concerns all the evil at the end of the forty years, for they shall be devoured and upon the earth no wicked person will be found' (4QPsalms Pesher [4Q17, ii, 6-8]).' This view was not uncommon in the ancient writings."[4]

The clear coherency of Scripture on this issue seems to be apparent in light of the rest of Scripture, yet so many

[4] Preston, Don K., Who is This Babylon?, 2nd ed., (Ardmore, OK.: JaDon Management Inc., 2011). 282.

Christians in Church history have missed the argument as I have presented it. The hard and fast Western mind with all of its physical, clear cut interpretations, or even to an eastern philosophical mind with all of its seemingly spiritual or mystical interpretations, these concepts would have been completely foreign and easily misunderstood. To Hellenized Jews or Greco/Roman Christians of the 2nd through 4th centuries, many of the ideas I have presented may have been quite foreign even only one or two generations removed from the writings of the first century.

This problem isn't all too hard to see. Even in our modern culture, in the last one or two hundred years Christians have adopted all sorts of new ideas with doctrines that found their beginnings in the 1800's. Take the Jehovah's Witnesses, or Mormons, or Dispensational Premillennial Christian ideas. While some of the roots to these paradigms may have existed in earlier times, these religious systems were entirely new interpretations invented within the last 200 years, and yet, today they are nothing close to what they were 200 years ago. But how is that possible? And how is it possible that in only one or two hundred years, as advanced and sophisticated as we are, that people still believe and interpret religious ideas in ways that seem to be entirely false, even a cult?

In an age of technological advancements, with the printing press, scholarly research being performed in every field of study imaginable, and with the advent of internet and computers, surely people living today should be able to figure out exactly what it was that people were preaching and teaching only one or two hundred years ago; right? Unfortunately, what is still difficult today, that is, the ability to maintain strict coherent sound doctrinal positions across the board over hundreds of years, was even more difficult in the time of the patriarchal/early-church writers.

To a Jewish audience of the first century the idea that I have presented to you here would not have been a foreign concept at all. Or if it had been then surely the great expectation and eager waiting that took place for Christ to soon appear at His coming in the first century generation was an ill advised expectation on their part. It was one that few people today would be able to figure out if not for the fact that we are now able to understand that their concept of the "generation" and the "watch in the night" and the "day rising" and the "thousand year" period was all one and the same, and that these concepts were not new ones at all, but intrinsically tied to their first century concepts and ideas, and to the literature available to them during that time.

The Typology of the Forty Year Exodus

The charts below provide a simple picture of the typological nature of the first Exodus with the second Exodus. Notice the stark similarities between both periods and the undeniable relationship and of the nature of events which take place during these periods of time. To any observant reader, these similarities cannot be ignored. The first Exodus was a shadow, a type, or a picture of the second Exodus which was the reality, the anti-type, and the fulfillment of God's promises.

	First Passover	OLD COVENANT: COVENANT OF DEATH	
Slavery In		50 days later – the Law was given [Ex. 19:1] 3,000 die for worshipping the golden calf [Ex. 32:28]	Promised Land
EGYPT		40 YEARS TRANSITION	Crossing Jordan
	Crossing The Red Sea - Deliverance	Miraculous Evidences of God's Presence and Power SHADOW	Salvation Complete

	First Spiritual Passover	NEW COVENANT: COVENANT OF LIFE	
Slavery To SPIRITUAL		50 days later – the Spirit was given 3,000 baptized, receive life (Acts 2:41)	Christ's Kingdom
EGYPT (elements)		40 YEARS TRANSITION	End of Old Cov. Age - Salvation Complete
	Christ's Death - Deliverance	Miraculous Evidences of God's Presence and Power FULFILLMENT	

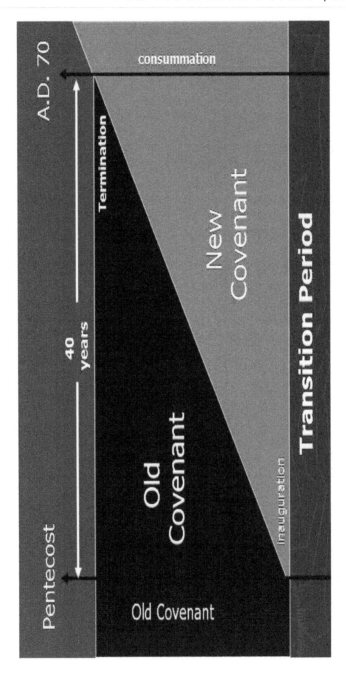

—— *8* ——

REVELATION 20

Binding, Reigning, Resurrection and Judgment

As I began presenting my arguments in the introduction to this book I made a reference to the "binding of the strong man" by Jesus in the Gospel of Matthew:

"²⁸But if it is by the Spirit of God that I cast out demons, then the kingdom of God has come upon you. ²⁹Or how can someone enter a strong man's house and plunder his goods, unless he first binds the strong man? Then indeed he may plunder his house." (Matthew 12:28-29)

We see here Jesus first giving us a glimpse into the "binding" which was currently taking place during His ministry. Jesus proclaimed that what He was doing was by the Spirit of God, therefore, the Kingdom of God was upon them, and thus, the strong man's house was being plundered through His ministry. However, the time had not yet come for this "strong man" to be completely plundered, but it would come soon (cf. Romans 16:20). And so it is that we come to Revelation 20, the great passage of the thousand year period and the binding of Satan.

It should be noted before I begin my analysis of Revelation 20, that my general approach to the book as a whole is known as *progressive parallelism*, one that is primarily defended by postmillennial scholars such as Kenneth Gentry and William Hendriksen. While I certainly have my own quirky differences (being the full preterist that I am), the framework that brings me to understand Revelation 20 in the manner that I do first derives from this general approach. I do not see Revelation as a chronological depiction from start to finish, nor a simple vision from John in which he simply records information as he sees it. I believe that John used known literary devices and apocalyptic genre to formulate the vision that was given to him, so that his readers and first century audience could understand, and so that the letters and prophecies he gave could not be deciphered or easily understood by the Roman soldiers, should any of them have captured a messenger traveling throughout the churches of Asia Minor, and the rest of the Roman Empire. During the time of the final years leading up to AD70 and the Jewish War with the Roman armies, Christian persecution by the Romans was rampant. Nero had blamed the Christians for setting fire to Rome, and Christians were taken by the thousands and killed. If any of them had been caught with a document explaining the soon defeat of the Roman Emperor and his Roman cohorts, they would have been killed or taken prisoner immediately.

It's within this context that I believe that the book of Revelation was written and delivered to the saints throughout Asia. The book of Revelation is a book written in code, in a genre that many of the Christians, especially the Jewish ones, would have readily understood and applied to their own immediate context and future.

In Revelation 20, verses 1-3 John describes the coming down from heaven of a mighty angel who lays hold upon the Devil, and binds him and casts him into the bottomless pit, "till the thousand years should be fulfilled," after which "he must be loosed a little season"; and verse 7 says: "And when the thousand years are expired, Satan shall be loosed out of his prison." When reading this passage concerning the "binding of Satan" we must regard this act as either a complete or a partial depriving of Satan of his power.

There are two primary reasons that this "binding" period was only a partial deprivation of Satan and his powers in my opinion. The first reason that this binding was not a complete deprivation of Satan's powers is that after the period of the "thousand years" Satan is THEN subjected to the judgment after he deceived the nations for the period of a "little while." During the time of a "little while" (cf. Revelation 20:3), Satan is given complete control to be able to "deceive the nations." Prior to this time the purpose of being bound was to prevent him from "deceiving the nations."

It is of note here to consider that the "nations" Satan was going to deceive were the nations that would "surround the camp of the Saints and the beloved city" (cf. Revelation 20:7-9). Interestingly, John draws from Luke 21:20-21 and uses a "double entendre" to describe the events of Revelation 20:7-9. In Luke 21, Jesus describes the "physical" armies which would surround the "physical" city of Jerusalem and bring about its eventual, natural destruction. In Revelation 20:7-9 we see John pull from this language to describe the deception of the "nations" (Jews) which would surround the saints (Christians) and the beloved city (the Church). Luke describes the physical and natural event, and John describes the spiritual and covenantal event.

What Luke described in physical terms about national Israel and the Roman armies, John describes in spiritual terms using identical language concerning spiritual Israel (i.e. – the Church) and those who were coming against them (the persecuting Jews). The direct parallel language seems to clearly depict a similar thought, event, or intention on behalf of John. Likewise, the fact that Luke 21 is "Luke's Olivet Discourse", and that Revelation is "John's Olivet Discourse" (argued earlier in this book) seems to be a perfectly clear connection between Luke's description of the "binding of the strong man," compared with John's description in Revelation 20.

The fact that Rome actually limited Jewish persecution against the Christians prior to AD64 tells us that the "deceiver" was indeed limited in his power. Satan and his subjects did not have power to deceive the nations, nor to stop the Gospel from spreading throughout Syria, Judea, and to the ends of the earth. As reported by Paul in his own letters, and also Luke's record about Paul's ministry in the book of Acts, Paul's Roman citizenship protected him from Jewish persecution (cf. Acts 23-28). In the last verse in the book of Acts (cf. Acts 28:31) Luke records for us that Paul was able to preach the Gospel to the whole world with boldness and without hindrance up until the end of his recorded ministry. Additionally, I have already provided substantial evidence in this book that the Gospel was preached throughout the whole world during the Apostles ministry, known as the "Great Commission." During this time, thousands and thousands of Jews and new gentile believers came to believe in Christ and had seen the light of the Gospel message.

Given that most Biblical scholars agree that the book of Acts was written in or around the years AD60-62, we have grounds therefore to suggest that the Biblical account is in agreement that from the time of Christ's ministry (around AD27-33) to the period of the Neronian persecutions (AD63-64), there was little resistance keeping the Christians from expanding and performing the Great Commission (a period lasting about 34-37 years without hindrance). Could it be that the reason Paul was uninhibited up to this point was because Satan (the adversary) had been bound and had no power over Jesus' ministry and the ministry of the Apostles and disciples?

Remember, the outpouring of the Spirit at Pentecost gave the Apostles the power and authority to "bind or loose" whatever they chose (cf. Matthew 16:19, 18:18). They were empowered with the same authority and ability that Jesus enjoyed during his earthly ministry, and even more. Jesus told them they would be given the keys to bind or lose whatever they chose, and that nothing would overcome the church, which they were entrusted to establish and uphold. In fact, Jesus told them that they would be given "the keys" to bind and loose. What was it that Satan would be bound with? You got it! KEYS to the bottomless pit! At Pentecost in Acts chapter 2, three thousand Jews from every nation, tribe, and tongue under heaven were saved and believed in the Gospel message. Thousands more were to follow after this.

The veil, deception, and blindness of the Jews was being lifted, and this could only be so if the great deceiver was being held back, bound, and kept from his work of deception among the Jewish nations. Also, remember that "something" was holding back the "man of sin" according to Paul (cf. 2 Thessalonians 2) in his own day, and that the disciples knew who he was, or at the very least that he was alive and that they were aware of who or what was holding him back, but that he would not be revealed until "the rebellion comes" (cf. 2 Thessalonians 2:1-12).

Some people may argue that this cannot be true because during their ministry Satan was "roaring around like a lion seeking to devour whomever he could" (cf. 1 Peter 5:8). And Paul said that they fought against "principalities and powers not of this world" (cf. Ephesians 6:12-13). The problem with this is two-fold. First, some of the letters in the New Testament were written after the end of the millennial period according to my argumentation, or they were written at the very beginning of the loosing period during the great tribulation and the great falling away, in which Christians would suffer at the hands of their adversaries, the Jews, as well as the Roman authorities. This was the "little while." In the Afterword of this book, Dr. Don K. Preston substantiates this argument more fully. But secondly, in Ephesians 6:12-13, Paul tells them to be ready to fight against these powers "in the day of the evil one." What day was that? It was the day when the evil one would be let loose upon them!

Anyone familiar with Jewish history knows that the great rebellion or the great falling away began to take place in and around AD66, and that it culminated in the final destruction of the national people of Israel and the Temple at the hands of the Roman armies beginning in AD70 and concluding in AD73. Is it possible then that the "great deception" of the "nations" was the beginning of the "great rebellion" by the Jews? The Bible nearly always speaks of "the nations" as the Jewish nations, or as the Diaspora Israelites who lived among the gentile nations (Jews who had been scattered and rejected by God as foreigners). In his book "War of the Jews," Josephus recorded that they had been deceived into thinking that their savior was going to come to save and regather them and that he would thwart the Romans and establish his national Kingdom forever. We'll have much to say about Josephus and this great deception and the rebellion in just a bit.

The binding of Satan was therefore something less than a complete taking-away of his power during the forty year period because Paul, during his own ministry, said that he still fought against principalities and powers, and he said that Satan would "soon be crushed under your feet" (cf. Romans 16:20) during that time. If being bound completely prohibited Satan from any action, there would have been nothing for Paul and the Apostles to have fought against during this time, however, the power of the great Prince (Jesus Himself) gave them strength through the Holy Spirit to overcome so that no evil would defeat or overpower them. Thus, just as a handcuffed prisoner can still cause havoc and kick the window from inside the police car, or spit on officers, or cuss and scream, his ultimate authority and power is negated by the restraints holding him back, and by the overarching legal authority of the officers who are arresting him.

The strong man depicted in Scripture is clearly Satan, and would have included the Jewish adversarial authorities who chased, persecuted and tortured the Apostles and first century Christians (cf. Revelation 2:9, 3:9); no commentator I am familiar with disagrees with this. The one who is strong enough to bind Satan is none other than Jesus himself. But Satan is not so bound as to have no effect at all as I have previously stated. It is the limitation of his power and authority; it is a usurping of his former role as a dominant figure and accuser through the Old Covenant Law; it was the lessening of his influence and activities which could not be overcome since the "stronger" man had all the power.

The binding period therefore was not a complete wiping out of Satan's powers; it was however a complete prohibition of his powers through the ministry of Jesus Christ, and through the power that was given to the Apostles over Satan and his works. This was necessary in order for the Gospel to be spread to the entire known Jewish world. Jesus commanded them to take the message of the Gospel everywhere, and if Satan had been allowed to deceive the nations, and also to wreak havoc on the Christians (prohibiting them from spreading the Gospel message), this feat would not have been accomplished.

A passage in Hebrews will help us at this point:

"For as much then as the children are partakers of flesh and blood, He also Himself likewise took part of the same; that through (His own) death He might destroy him that had the power of death, that is the Devil; and deliver them who through fear of death were all their lifetime subject to bondage." (cf. Hebrews 2:14-15)

This passage clearly refers to the same truth as that declared by Jesus in Matthew 12:29; for the one whose power was destroyed by Jesus is expressly said to be "the Devil," and those who are delivered from his power, "the children," are "the goods" of which Jesus, by His death, has stripped him of his former powers. It is evident too, that "destroy him" does not mean the complete deprivation of his power or his existence, nor his judgment in a single moment, for he still exercises the power of death in the Law on a large scale after Jesus dies and is resurrected (i.e. - the Temple and Jewish nation, and the legal ordinances still stood after the crucifixion); but it means the crippling and limiting of that power, which Satan could then only partially exercise against those who chose not to believe in Jesus Christ, until the final destruction at the end of the Old Covenant Age in AD70.

The above statement is in full agreement with the words of Jesus to the seventy when they returned to Him with joy saying:

"Lord, even the devils are subject unto us through your Name. And He said unto them, I beheld Satan as lightning fall from heaven. Behold, I give you power to tread on serpents and scorpions, and over all the power of the enemy." (cf. Luke 10:19)

Here was the binding of Satan, in that his power was greatly restricted through the Apostles' works during the next 34-37 years. In John's vision of the Revelation, the binding of Satan was done by the instrumentality of an angel from heaven; and by the passage in Hebrews we learn that the effective cause of the breaking of his power was the death and resurrection of Jesus Christ. It is pertinent therefore to recall that on the morning of His resurrection, "the angel of the Lord descended from heaven, and came and rolled back the stone from the door" (cf. Matthew 28:2). There is a suggestive correspondence between the action of opening the door of the tomb of the Lord Jesus, rolling away the great stone by means of which His body had been sealed therein, and the action of shutting Satan up in the abyss and setting a seal upon him. It suggests that both actions were performed by the same mighty angel and at the same time.

The same suggestive correspondence also applies with the giving of the keys to the disciples to "bind and lose" whatever they chose. It is no coincidence that Satan was bound by keys, and that the disciples were allowed to bind and loose with the keys given to them by God. That Satan's power is greatly limited during the ministry of the disciples, but not wholly destroyed until the end, is certainly the fact. Consider what Jesus said as He approached His death on the cross, "Now is the judgment of this world; now will the ruler of this world be cast out" (cf. John 12:31, 16:11). But He did not cast him out in every sense; for He said afterward, "The ruler of this world is coming, and he has no claim on me" (cf. John 14:30). Here are the conceptions of the limiting of Satan, or the casting out of Satan, which should guide us in interpreting Revelation 20.

If we have reasoned correctly up to this point, then it is easy to say what "the thousand years" signifies. It is quite surely the time from the binding of Satan (the beginning of Jesus' ministry) and through the period of time in which Paul and the Apostles preached and had authority over Satan keeping him bound, and up until the time that the "deceiver" was allowed to go out for "a little while" (i.e. AD66-70) to deceive the nations (i.e. the Jews), and to bring about the destruction upon the Jewish nation and Jerusalem, and the Herodian Temple by the Roman armies.

Consider the following interpretation for the unfolding of events in Revelation 20:

> Revelation 20:4-10 – "⁴Then I saw thrones, and seated on them were those to whom the authority to judge was committed. Also I saw the souls of those who had been beheaded for the testimony of Jesus and for the word of God, and those who had not worshiped the beast or its image and had not received its mark on their foreheads or their hands. They came to life and reigned with Christ for a thousand years."

In the first four verses the people in question are the Christians who received salvation during and after the ministry of Christ who came to life and reigned with Him during the millennial period (the forty years). Many of them were killed for their faith near the end of this forty year period, most of who died during the seven year Jewish revolt against Rome, and during the great tribulation from AD63-70.

"...⁵(~~The rest of the dead did not come to life until the thousand years were ended~~). This is the first resurrection. ⁶Blessed and holy is the one who shares in the first resurrection! Over such the second death has no power, but they will be priests of God and of Christ, and they will reign with him for a thousand years."

Verse 5 is somewhat of a quagmire. As you can see, I've taken the liberty of deleting (with a strikethrough) the beginning of Revelation 20:5 because this statement is likely a commentary added later by an early church scribe. The primary reasons the words are in question here are because they aren't found in any of the oldest manuscripts of the book of Revelation in the Bible. Those manuscripts include the Codex Sinaiticus, the Codex Alexandrine, in addition to the earliest Syriac and Aramaic manuscripts. Not only was this part of the verse not originally included in those early manuscripts, but it simply does not fit the clear and normal flow of the context of the verse. In fact, many translators recognize the problem immediately and often place this part of the verse in parenthesis to indicate the apparent problem. Yet, even with so much controversy surrounding this questionable passage many commentators have quoted it for years as a basis for many end times religious doctrines and schemes.

The NIV and NLT are two of those translations which place the beginning of verse 5 in parenthesis to make this abundantly clear. The reason this is important is to avoid the misunderstanding that the "first resurrection" took place at the "end" of the thousand years. Read as a parenthetical statement, or one that should not be in the text at all, the first resurrection refers to those who "came to life in Christ," throughout the thousand year period.

Now, if we make a succession for the addition of the parenthetical statement, then it is my opinion that the writer (or scribe) is suggesting that the "first resurrection to life" which the New Testament Saints were experiencing during the millennial period would not be experienced for the "rest of the dead" until after the period of the "thousand years" was over. We are then told that the ones who share in the "first resurrection" are blessed and holy and that they will reign with Christ during the thousand years over their enemies. We see in Revelation 22 that John describes all the saints of the Church as reigning forevermore with the Lord, and that this takes place after the millennial period, but John is also clear to point out in Revelation 20 that during the millennial period the saints who are alive during this time (which included those who were persecuted and martyred) would also reign with Christ during that period of time. This would be true despite many of their sufferings and the existence of the Old Covenant and Temple, which was passing away, alongside the New Covenant which was being established.

There is one group of Christians, some of whom would be martyred, who would be resurrected and reign with Christ during the millennial period, and then there is the rest of the dead who would not experience this resurrection life until the end of the millennium. For both groups this is the first resurrection (being raised to life in Christ). For the former group of Christians, coming to life occurred while they were alive to hear the Gospel. For the rest of the dead (the Old Covenant Saints), coming to life in Christ at the end of the millennium was the result of their faith in God throughout the Old Testament (cf. Romans 4:1ff; Galatians 3:11, 24; Hebrews 3:2-5, 11:9-20). This group was also knows as the faithful remnant (cf. Isaiah 10:21, 28:5, 37:32; Jeremiah 31:7; Micah 2:12, 5:7-8; Romans 9:27, 11:1, 5).

In Revelation 20 there is strong evidence to support the idea that the first-century Christians were experiencing the "first resurrection" during the ministry of Jesus and after Jesus' ascension (cf. John 3:15-16, 36, 4:14, 5:24, 6:40-54, 10:28; 11:17-27, 17:2-3; Acts 13:46-48; Romans 2:7, 5:21, 6:4, 11-13, 22-23; 8:11; 2 Corinthians 5:17; Galatians 2:19; 6:8, 15; Ephesians 2:1-6; 4:22-24; 5:14; Colossians 2:12-13; 3:1-3, 10; 1 Timothy 6:12; Titus 1:2, 3:7; 1 John 1:2, 2:25, 3:15; 1 Peter 2:24; Jude 1:21). Therefore, if the first century Apostles, disciples, and Christians were coming to life then, and were reigning and ruling with Christ already, what reason do we have to believe that they were not taking part of the first resurrection spoken about in Revelation 20?

Revelation 20 specifically says that during the thousand year period those who experienced this "first resurrection" would be those who reigned and ruled with Christ OVER HIS ENEMIES (cf. Matthew 22:44; Mark 12:36; 1 Corinthians 15:25) until the loosing of Satan and the judgment of the city of Jerusalem, the beast, the false prophet, and Satan himself.

Jesus even predicted His wrath, or Day of Judgment, and said that it would come upon "that evil generation" (cf. Matthew 23). In Matthew 3:7 Jesus condemned the Pharisees and Sadducees and asked them who warned them of the wrath they would soon face? Matthew 12:41-42 also describes this wrath and says that something greater than Solomon and Jonah was present with them, and yet they rejected Him, and so "that generation" would be judged for it.

In Matthew 23 Jesus gives the Pharisees seven woes (remember the seven seals of Revelation, and the seven scrolls?), the harshest of rebukes, and even declares that "they" would fill up the measure of their sin, and that "they" were guilty of the blood of all the martyred saints from Abel to Zechariah. If this wrath was to occur in their lifetime how then could the thousand year period be anything other than the generational period of nearly forty years from AD27-30 to AD64-67 when the judgment of Revelation 20 takes place AFTER the millennium? Notice EXACTLY what Jesus said to "them":

"[33]You snakes! You brood of vipers! How will you escape the judgment of gehenna? [34]Therefore I am sending you prophets and wise men and teachers. Some of them you will kill and crucify; others you will flog in your synagogues and pursue from town to town. [35]And so upon you will come all the righteous blood that has been shed on earth, from the blood of righteous Abel to the blood of Zechariah son of Berekiah, whom you murdered between the temple and the altar. [36]Truly I tell you, all this will come on this generation." (Matthew 23:33-36)

Therefore, the context of the judgment of Revelation 20 is none other than the fulfillment of the decree of judgment by Jesus in Matthew 3, 12, and chapters 23-25. To apply Matthews' judgment texts or Revelation 20 for that matter, to an end of time judgment rather than a first-century judgment is to completely take the issue entirely out of context and is a direct failure to consistently interpret Scripture with Scripture using the rule of the "Analogy of Scripture" which we discussed earlier in this book.

Remember also that earlier in this book I argued for the ancient life-spans of the Hebrew people in the book of Genesis, and that in ancient Sumerian texts it was recorded that Kings had lived long lives for thousands of years? Well, remember that in Revelation 20 John said that these resurrected saints would "reign and rule" with Christ during the thousand years? Why is that significant? Because only Kings can reign and rule! Thus, New Testament, first century Christians were going to be reigning and ruling as Kings, and the ancient idea of millennial age (completely symbolic) represented this group as being those who would first experience eternal life, who would be given crowns, and who would be raised from the dead, and who would express authority over their enemies through the power of God. The Apostles were given authority by Jesus, and they were in fact reigning and ruling with Christ throughout the Great Commission and the ministry of the Apostles and first century disciples.

"...[7]And when the thousand years are ended, Satan will be released from his prison [8]and will come out to deceive the nations that are at the four corners of the earth, Gog and Magog, to gather them for battle; their number is like the sand of the sea. [9]And they marched up over the broad plain of the earth and surrounded the camp of the holy people and the beloved city, but fire came down from heaven and consumed them, [10]and the devil who had deceived them was thrown into the lake of fire and sulfur where the beast and the false prophet were, and they will be tormented day and night forever and ever."

This passage is really very clear in light of history, and Jesus' own statements pertaining to the "surrounding of the holy city by armies" (cf. Luke 19:43, 21:20; Daniel 9:27). The "nations" of verse 8 speak of the Jewish nations who are deceived by Satan (the adversary) into gathering for battle and persecuting the Christians. However, as they gathered for battle thinking they would overcome and Christians (the camp of the holy people and the beloved city of God), the exact opposite occurs, and the Jewish nation is utterly destroyed by the Roman Emperor Vespasian, and his son Titus, the Roman Army Commander, and all the Roman armies. And so John's description of the battle between the Jews and the Christians ultimately results in the actual scene of Luke 17 where the Jews are instead surrounded and destroyed.

The circumstances are quite ironic to say the least. The nationalistic "holy people" of God are utterly destroyed or shattered (cf. Daniel 12), while the spiritual "holy people" of God are preserved and saved. Daniel 12 predicted that Israel would be completely shattered during these events, and that the judgment and resurrection would take place for all these people, and that Satan, and the beast, and the false prophet would be tormented forever, day and night, without ceasing.

If there is any doubt as to whether or not the historical account of the destruction of the city of Jerusalem, and the nation of Israel, and the temple in AD70, does not fit the description above as I have interpreted it, I suggest a quick reading of the historian Flavius Josephus in his account of the "War of the Jews." Take special note of the fact that Josephus records that the Jewish nations were deceived by a great "false prophet" into "gathering for battle" against the Romans. Then notice the outcome and the stark similarities in the language Josephus uses as it compares with Luke 17 and Revelation 20.

Josephus, War of the Jews, Book VI, Chapter 5:1-3

1. WHILE the holy house [the Jewish Temple] was on fire, everything was plundered that came to hand, and ten thousand of those that were caught were slain; nor was there a commiseration of any age, or any reverence of gravity, but children, and old men, and profane persons, and priests were

all slain in the same manner; so that this war went round all sorts of men, and brought them to destruction, and as well those that made supplication for their lives, as those that defended themselves by fighting.

The flame was also carried a long way, and made an echo, together with the groans of those that were slain; and because this hill was high, and the works at the temple were very great, one would have thought the whole city had been on fire. Nor can one imagine anything either greater or more terrible than this noise; for there was at once a shout of the Roman legions, who were marching all together, and a sad clamor of the seditious [the Jewish revolters], who were now surrounded with fire and sword.

The people also that were left above were beaten back upon the enemy, and under a great consternation, and made sad moans at the calamity they were under; the multitude also that was in the city joined in this outcry with those that were upon the hill. And besides, many of those that were worn away by the famine, and their mouths almost closed, when they saw the fire of the holy house, they exerted their utmost strength, and brake out into groans and outcries again [cf. Zechariah 12:9-11; Jeremiah 6:26; Amos 8:10; Revelation 1:7]: Pera did also return the echo, as well as the mountains round about [the city,] and augmented the force of the entire noise.

Yet was the misery itself more terrible than this disorder; for one would have thought that the hill itself, on which the temple stood, was seething hot, as full of fire on every part of it, that the blood was larger in quantity than the fire, and those that were slain more in number than those that slew them; for the ground did no where appear visible, for the dead bodies that lay on it; but the soldiers went over heaps of those bodies, as they ran upon such as fled from them.

And now it was that the multitudes of the robbers were thrust out [of the inner court of the temple by the Romans,] and had much ado to get into the outward court and from thence into the city, while the remainder of the populace fled into the cloister of that outer court. As for the priests, some of them plucked up from the holy house the spikes that were upon it, with their bases, which were made of lead, and shot them at the Romans instead of darts.

But then as they gained nothing by so doing, and as the fire burst out upon them, they retired to the wall that was eight cubits broad, and there they tarried; yet did two of these of eminence among them, who might have saved themselves by going over to the Romans, or have borne up with courage, and taken their fortune with the others, throw themselves into the fire, and were burnt together with the holy house; their names were Meirus the son of Belgas, and Joseph the son of Daleus.

2. And now the Romans, judging that it was in vain to spare what was round about the holy house, burnt all those places, as also the remains of the cloisters and the gates, two excepted; the one on the east side, and the other on the south; both which, however, they burnt afterward. They also burnt down the treasury chambers, in which was an immense quantity of money, and an immense number of garments, and other precious goods there reposited; and, to speak all in a few words, there it was that the entire riches of the Jews were heaped up together, while the rich people had there built themselves chambers [to contain such furniture].

The soldiers also came to the rest of the cloisters that were in the outer [court of the] temple, whither the women and children, and a great mixed multitude of the people, fled, in number about six thousand. But before Caesar had determined anything about these people, or given the commanders any orders relating to them, the soldiers were in such a rage, that they set that cloister on fire; by which means it came to pass that some of these were destroyed by throwing themselves down headlong, and some were burnt in the cloisters themselves. Nor did any one of them escape with his life.

A false prophet was the occasion of these people's destruction, who had made a public proclamation in the city that very day, that God commanded them to get upon the temple, and that there they should receive miraculous signs of their deliverance. Now **there was then a great number of false prophets** suborned by the tyrants to impose on the people, who denounced this to them, that they should wait for deliverance from God; and this was in order to keep them from deserting, and that they might be buoyed up above fear and care by such hopes. Now a man that is in adversity does easily comply with such promises; for when **such a seducer** makes him believe that he shall be delivered from those miseries which oppress him, then it is that the patient is full of hopes of such his deliverance.

3. **Thus were the miserable people persuaded by these deceivers**, and such as belied God himself; while they did not attend nor give credit to **the signs** that were so evident, and **did so plainly foretell their future desolation**, but, like men infatuated, **without either eyes to see or minds to consider, did not regard the denunciations that God made to them**. Thus there was a star resembling a sword, which stood over the city, and a comet, that continued a whole year. Thus also before the Jews' rebellion, and before those commotions which preceded the war, when the people were come in great crowds to the feast of unleavened bread, on the eighth day of the month Xanthicus, [Nisan,] and at the ninth hour of the night, so great a light shone round the altar and the holy house, that it appeared to be bright day time; which lasted for half an hour. This light seemed to be a good sign to the unskillful, but was so interpreted by the sacred scribes, as to portend those events that followed immediately upon it.

At the same festival also, a heifer, as she was led by the high priest to be sacrificed, brought forth a lamb in the midst of the temple. Moreover, the eastern gate of the inner [court of the] temple, which was of brass, and vastly heavy, and had been with difficulty shut by twenty men, and rested upon a basis armed with iron, and had bolts fastened very deep into the firm floor, which was there made of one entire stone, was seen to be opened of its own accord about the sixth hour of the night.

Now those that kept watch in the temple came hereupon running to the captain of the temple, and told him of it; who then came up thither, and not without great difficulty was able to shut the gate again. This also appeared to the vulgar to be a very happy prodigy, as if God did thereby open them the gate of happiness. But the men of learning understood it, that the security of their holy house was dissolved of its own accord, and that the gate was opened for the advantage of their enemies.

So these publicly declared that **the signal foreshowed the desolation that was coming upon them**. Besides these, a few days after that feast, on the one and twentieth day of the month Artemisius, [Jyar,] a certain prodigious and incredible phenomenon appeared: I suppose the account of it would seem to be a fable, were it not related by those that saw it, and were not the events that followed it of so considerable a nature as to deserve such signals; for, before sun-setting, chariots and troops of soldiers in their armor were seen running about among the clouds, and surrounding of cities.

Moreover, at that feast which we call Pentecost, as the priests were going by night into the inner [court of the temple,] as their custom was, to perform their sacred ministrations, they said that, in the first place, they felt a quaking, and heard a great noise, and after that they heard a sound as of a great multitude, saying, "Let us remove hence."

But, what is still more terrible, there was one Jesus, the son of Ananus, a plebeian and a husbandman, who, **four years before the war began**, and at a time when **the city was in very great peace and prosperity**, came to that feast whereon it is our custom for everyone to make tabernacles to God in the temple, began on a sudden to cry aloud, "A voice from the east, a voice from the west, a voice from the four winds, a voice against Jerusalem and the holy house, a voice against the bridegrooms and the brides, and a voice against this whole people!"

This was his cry, as he went about by day and by night, in all the lanes of the city. However, certain of the most eminent among the populace had great indignation at this dire cry of his, and took up the man, and gave him a great number of severe stripes; yet did not he either say anything for himself, or anything peculiar to those that chastised him, but still went on with the same words which he cried before.

Hereupon our rulers, supposing, as the case proved to be, that this was a sort of divine fury in the man, brought him to the Roman procurator, where he was whipped till his bones were laid bare; yet he did not make any supplication for himself, nor shed any tears, but turning his voice to the most lamentable tone possible, at every stroke of the whip his answer was, "Woe, woe to Jerusalem!" And when Albinus (for he was then our procurator) asked him, who he was and whence he came and why he uttered such words? He made no manner of reply to what he said, but still did not leave off his melancholy ditty, till Albinus took him to be a madman, and dismissed him.

Now, during all the time that passed before the war began, this man did not go near any of the citizens, nor was seen by them while he said so; but he every day uttered these lamentable words, as if it were his premeditated vow, "Woe, woe to Jerusalem!" Nor did he give ill words to any of those that beat him every day, nor good words to those that gave him food; but this was his reply to all men, and indeed no other than a melancholy presage of what was to come.

This cry of his was the loudest at the festivals; and he continued this ditty for seven years and five months, without growing hoarse, or being tired therewith, until the very time that he saw his presage in earnest fulfilled in our siege, when it ceased; for as he was going round upon the wall, he cried out with his utmost force, "Woe, woe to the city again, and to the people, and to the holy house!" And just as he added at the last, "Woe, woe to myself also!" there came a stone out of one of the engines, and smote him, and killed him immediately; and as he was uttering the very same presages he gave up the ghost.

Revelation 20 and Parallel Passages

From the preponderance of evidence we have seen thus far concerning the context and language of Revelation 20, there is one final linguistic piece of the puzzle that is of utmost importance. For anyone who has already come to conclusion that Revelation 12 is speaking about events in the first century (such as the majority of our postmillennial friends), consider the direct parallels that exist between Revelation 20 and Revelation 12.

The chart below needs no explanation, and what is most important to keep in mind when reviewing it, is that the context of the "millennium" is what Revelation 20 is all about, therefore, if Revelation 20 is speaking of the same events as those mentioned in Revelation 12, and if Revelation 12 has already been fulfilled prior to AD70, then that would place all of the events of Revelation 20 prior to AD70 as well, and thus, the millennium would be a past event, already fulfilled.

Revelation 12:7-11	Revelation 20:1-6
Heavenly scene (v. 7)	Heavenly scene (v. 1)
Angelic battle against Satan and his host (vv. 7-8)	Presupposed angelic battle with Satan (v. 2)
Satan cast to earth (v. 9)	Satan cast into the abyss (vs. 3
The angels' evil opponent called "the great dragon,...that ancient serpent called the devil or Satan, who leads the whole world astray" (v. 9)	The angels' evil opponent called "the dragon, that ancient serpent, who is the devil, or Satan," restrained from "deceiving the nations anymore" (vv. 2-3), to be released later "to deceive the nations in the four corners of the earth" (vv. 3, 7-8)
Satan "is filled with fury, because he knows that his time is short" (v. 12)	Satan to be "set free for a short time" after his imprisonment (v. 3)
Satan's fall, resulting in the kingdom of Christ and his saints (v. 10)	Satan's fall, resulting in the kingdom of Christ and his saints (vs. 4)
The Saints' kingship, based not only on the fall of Satan and Christ's victory but also on the saints' faithfulness even to death in holding to "the word of their testimony" (v. 11)	The saint's kingship, based on only on the fall of Satan but also on their faithfulness even to death because of their "testimony for Jesus and because of the word of God" (v. 4)

Consider also the two charts developed by Dr. Don K. Preston in his book, "Who is This Babylon" (pgs. 265-266). In these charts, Dr. Preston provides us with concise parallels of Revelation 6, 12, 20, and also shows how Matthew 23 also fits into the picture. Since nearly all of our reformed, postmillennial and amillennial friends agree that Matthew 23 was fulfilled in the first century before and during AD70, wouldn't you think that they would be consistent in applying the Revelation texts in the same way?

Revelation 6	Revelation 12	Revelation 20
Past suffering (v. 9f)	Past suffering (v. 5-6)	Past suffering (v. 4)
Satan defeated, (v. 10)-(robes given); cf. Luke 10:18	Satan defeated, (cast out, vs. 7f); time of the kingdom (12:10)	Satan defeated (bound, vs. 2-3) this is the millennium
More suffering to come (v. 10-11)	More suffering to come (v. 12)	More Suffering to come (v. 7-9) after the millennium
Suffer only "a little while" (kronon mikron, vs.11)	Satan has but "a little while," (oligon mikron, v. 12)	Satan loosed a "little while," (kronon mikron, (v.3, 7-9)

Matthew 23	Revelation 6	Revelation 20
Past Suffering, (v. 29-31)	Past Suffering, (v. 9)	Past Suffering, (v. 4)
Satan Bound, Matthew (12:28); saints "raised from dead"; on thrones in early church period (Ephesians 2:5-7)	Satan bound; white robes given, symbol of victory (v. 10)	Satan bound for thousand years, (v. 2)
More suffering to come (v. 34)	More suffering to come (v. 11)	More suffering to come (v. 3, 7-9)
Final victory in Jesus' generation (v. 35-39)	Final victory in "a little while" (v. 10-17)	Final victory in a little while, after the little season of Satan's loosing (vs. 3, 9-10) "Behold, I come quickly!"

———— *9* ————

THE DAYS OF VENGEANCE

These Days or Those Days?

In addition to all of the previous Biblical and historical evidence I've provided for the thousand year period taking place prior to AD70, consider these additional evidences. Luke 21:20-24 says that the days when Jerusalem would be surrounded by armies were the "days of vengeance" to "fulfill all things that were written." If the book of Revelation is a prediction of the things spoken of by the prophets in the Old Testament, then it must be included as part of "all things that were written." And so the question must be asked, are "the days of vengeance to fulfill all that had been written" speaking about the days of the first century, or are they speaking about the future days for us today and at the end of time"?

Unless we are to believe that this book was a new writing and that the Old Testament does not speak of its contents (which few scholars believe or even lend credence to), then it must follow that that contents which are found in the book of Revelation are in fact speaking about those events which the Old Testament prophets spoke about and foretold. Therefore, when the book of Revelation includes the thousand year period spoken of by John, it follows that the days in which vengeance came upon Israel when Rome surrounded the city and destroyed it were during or shortly after the "thousand year period." Revelation 20 speaks of the judgment that was to come, and this follows immediately after the millennial period. Unless someone tries to argue that there are two distinctly different judgments that Jesus had in mind, there is no way that anyone can deny that the judgment of Israel in AD70 was fulfilled, and therefore, the millennium had to have taken place prior to that event.

In addition to this, John begins the Revelation in verses 1:1-3 and also closes the Revelation in verses 22:6-7 and verse

20, by saying that it is the Revelation of things "which must soon take place" because "the time is near" and that "He [Jesus] comes quickly." If John wrote this book prior to AD70 (and recent, credible scholarship suggests that he did) then the events found within the Book of Revelation clearly describe the "thousand year period" as being a period of time prior to the destruction of Jerusalem and the Temple in AD70.

Also, in Revelation 1:19 John is told to write "things that were, things that are, and things which must soon take place." In any of the three periods which John describes here, the thousand year period is either a period of time limited to John's past, or it is limited to John's own present day in which he is writing this Apocalyptic letter, or it is limited to John's very near future in which all things were to be fulfilled. Most scholars admit that the book of Revelation was written no earlier than AD64, and no later than AD96. If this book was written prior to AD70 then John's words concerning the thousand year period could not have been a period of time "about to take place" since this would limit the "thousand years" to no more than approximately 3-7 years prior to AD70.

Surely a long period of time in any interpretation could not have been limited to a period of seven or fewer years, and even if it were, we have no Biblical precedence to determine whether or not this is so. If however, the book of Revelation was speaking of a period of time concerning John's own day (i.e. – write about "things that are"), it could quite easily fit the description of the time discussed earlier in this presentation, that it is the time between AD27-30 to AD64-67 (approximately); a near complete forty (40) year period or generation in the Jewish framework.

If this is the case then John is indeed writing about a thousand year generational period in Revelation 20 which was to be over very shortly after he had written the book (around AD62-65). John said that he was writing during the time of the 6th Emperor (cf. Revelation 17:10), which many scholars attribute to the reign of Nero Caesar.[1] Thus, in John's scheme,

---

[1] Kenneth Gentry, in his book "The Beast of Revelation," makes a very compelling case substantiating this view and argues that the

he is writing the book near the end of the millennial period, around AD62-65, and is already experiencing tribulation with his brethren during the seven year period of persecution (cf. Revelation 1:9). Ultimately, John depicts the events as culminating in the loosing of Satan, and the ultimate judgment of Jerusalem and the coming of the Lord (which the book itself would indicate was about to take place when John wrote it).

The Resurrection

While it is not the intent of this book to explain in great detail the nature or manner of the resurrection, there are many passages that deal with the "resurrection" where it is directly associated with the "millennium" and the "judgment." The reason this is so important to take note of is because the millennium is supposed to occur prior to the final or second resurrection and judgment period. Remember, Acts 24:15 and John 5:29 describe both a resurrection of the just (First Resurrection), and a resurrection of the unjust (Second Resurrection). Therefore, if it can be shown that the Apostles and first-century disciples expected this final resurrection and judgment to happen very soon, we can then determine two things:

1. That the thousand year period must have been something other than a literal rendering of the number one thousand in actual, physical 365 day years.

2. That they understood the thousand year period to be something other than a very long period of time (much longer than forty years anyway), since we already know that a very near occurrence of the resurrection and judgment for the disciples requires a limited span of forty or fewer years for the millennial period to have been fulfilled during their ministries.

---

identity of the Beast, 666, when calculated using the ancient system of Gematria, belongs to the Roman Emperor Nero Caesar.

We would surely not accuse the disciples of being liars, confused, or uninspired when they wrote about these events, would we? Certainly they were aware of the "thousand year" language, and yet they still chose to accept that its fulfillment was very near to them (as nearly all the New Testament letters and epistles indicate). This fact alone is strong evidence that the language of a thousand year period is certainly not a physical period of an exact number of one thousand years or more, but rather, that this phrase was used in its "occasional" and "literal" sense, meaning that it was "literally" a symbolic phrase used in a symbolic book, written in coded form with vast amounts of representative imagery throughout. In short, the "millennial period" represented the fullness of the generation which was to experience all the things Jesus had formerly predicted. It would not come early, nor would it come late, but it would occur at exactly the appointed time.

Matthew records in chapter 12:41-42 that the faithful ones of the Old Testament would "rise up" in that generation to judge the wicked Jews because they rejected Jesus. Again, if the thousand year period does not speak of the forty year period ending in AD70, how could this have been possible to say? Even Felix was warned about the "coming judgment" in Acts 24:25. Paul told him of those things that were going to happen and Felix was alarmed at the news of what he had been told. James likewise warned that while they were suffering greatly, those Christians were not going to have to wait long for their vindication because the Lord was "standing at the door" and that the "coming of the Lord was at hand" (James 5). Paul also, in writing 2 Thessalonians 1, speaks of their suffering, afflictions, and persecution and he tells them that "those who persecute you" would be repaid with vengeance for what they had done to them.

Jesus told His disciples that "These are the days of vengeance, to fulfill all that is written" (cf. Luke 21:22). The writer of Hebrews also declared this same judgment upon those who killed and rejected Jesus by saying that Jesus would judge His people for what they had done (cf. Hebrews 10:29-31). The Gospel of John tells us that the same resurrection of life would be accompanied by a resurrection of judgment. The resurrection after the thousand year period would occur in the "last day" (cf. John 6:39-54; 12:48). Furthermore, in Matthew 3:10 and Luke 3:9 John the Baptist declared that the "axe was already laid at the root of the tree," speaking of the judgment that was about to come upon the nation of Israel. It was so near that the blade was about to chop the root! A very strong evidence that the resurrection was about to occur during this period of time (after the book of Acts was written in or about AD62-64) is the statement made by Luke in Acts 23:6 concerning Paul,

"It is with respect to the hope and the resurrection of the dead that I am on trial." Concerning this resurrection Luke then records in Acts 24:15, "...having a hope in God, which these men themselves accept, that there is about to be a resurrection of both the just and the unjust."

What an amazing statement! Luke records that the very thing Paul defended and explained to Felix was exactly what he believed was "about" to happen! He believed that the resurrection and the coming judgment was about to take place. The word Paul uses in the Greek text is "mello," and I explained earlier in this book that it means an eager expectation of imminence or of something about to take place at the appointed time. Since Paul said in these same passages to Felix and Agrippa that his doctrine of the Resurrection was "nothing but the hope of Israel," and since Paul further believed that this resurrection was "about to take place," are we going to suggest that Paul's expectation of a SOON resurrection was false?

Furthermore, the timing of the Resurrection is linked with the timing of the end of the millennium. If it can be shown that the millennium ended prior to AD70, then it proves that the Resurrection was also fulfilled prior to AD70. Likewise, if it can be shown that the Resurrection took place prior to AD70, it proves that the millennium also took place and ended prior to AD70. Either view proves the timing of the other. But what else do we know about the Resurrection as it pertains to the millennium?

The Resurrection was the salvation and hope of Israel (cf. Isaiah 25:8; Acts 26:6-8; Romans 11:25ff). According to

Revelation 20:10ff, the Second Resurrection is supposed to take place AFTER the millennial period. Therefore, the Resurrection of Revelation 20 was the salvation and hope of Israel. Additionally, Daniel 12:2-7 places the fulfillment of the Resurrection and salvation/hope of Israel at the destruction and shattering of the Holy people (national Israel). Since the destruction and shattering of national Israel took place in and around AD70 we can surely state with obvious conviction that the Resurrection and the end of the millennial period took place prior to AD70!

Remember, in the book of Revelation John did not say that only some, or most of the book was near or imminent when he wrote it. John said that the coming of the Lord and ALL of the contents of his book were things that were (in the past), things that are (currently taking place), and things that were near (things about to take place). Therefore, if this book includes the coming of the Lord, the resurrection, the judgment, and the millennial period, then everything in this book had to be nearly completed since he wrote the book prior to AD70. If the millennial period lasts thousands of years or more, how could John truly say that everything in the book was imminent and about to take place? Either he would be a liar, or he was very confused, or the millennium is something OTHER THAN a literal thousand years or longer.

If the coming of Jesus in judgment and the resurrection has not yet happened, then how these events could be regarded as being "imminent" for John when he wrote the book is mind boggling. You can't say in one breath that everything else in the book of Revelation was imminent, and in the next breath say that the millennial period, followed by the resurrection and judgment and the coming of the Lord were not imminent or about to be fulfilled for John and the Apostles! Which is it? Were the events in the book of Revelation imminent or were they not imminent? You can't say that "some were" and that "others were not." Most popular commentaries attempt to get around this problem by "re-defining" the meaning of the word "imminent," because without doing so, they have a theological problem that they cannot solve, and that does not fit their illogical paradigm.

Therefore, based on the simple and logical arguments that I have made in this chapter, the resurrection was an event that the Apostles and disciples of the first century expected to occur very soon in their generation. They also expected that the judgment and millennial period would also be fulfilled very near in their future. Since all of this is true, the Apostles and disciples COULD NOT HAVE considered the millennium to be very long, or at least beyond a period of about 40 years. They could not have, and would not have perceived of it this way. Either they were greatly deceived, or they were greatly misinformed, or they knew that these events were truly going to be fulfilled in the near future, within their lifetimes, and their expectations were not incorrect. If that is true then the millennium cannot be, and is not a future occurrence, and it is not a period of thousands of years that we currently live in. It was fulfilled exactly on time, as the Apostles and disciples expected and predicted, during the time of the first century, and prior to AD70.

———— *10* ————

OBJECTIONS

Objection Overruled!

Of the many millennial interpretations that exist in the popular Christian community today, the most often of those that are the most critical of the transmillennial view typically come from within the postmillennial circles. While this is somewhat surprising given that the transmillennial view is most closely related to the postmillennial view, some of the harshest objections come from critical scholars within the postmillennial fields of study. The only primary difference between transmillennial and postmillennial schemes is in the length and duration of the millennial period, and our final future expectation. While we do take great issue with those of premillennial, amillennial, and historicist schemes, our greatest differences exist because of our overall difference in approach to hermeneutical methods of Biblical interpretation.

Since we begin with vastly different methods of interpretive rules, we will naturally come to great differences in understanding. For example, "[t]he kingdom expected by the premillennialist is quite different from the kingdom anticipated by the postmillennialist, not only with respect to the time and manner in which it will be established but also in regard to its nature and the way Christ will exercise control over it."[1] It is not our objective in this book to explain all of those differences, or to address them. Our focus is on a positive affirmation of our approach, seeking to provide a defense for what we believe, not a defense against all the views of the other schemes. There are plenty of books written by those within the views described above written against one

---

[1] Clouse G., Robert, *The Meaning of the Millennium.* (Downers Grove, IL: InterVarsity Press, 1977). 7.

another, and there are reasonable and plausible arguments against each of them. I do not wish to re-hash those arguments here. However, I would like to answer just a couple of objections raised against our fellow brothers and sisters in Christ who are closely related to our own view, and use a similar hermeneutical approach to Biblical interpretation.

Both the postmillennial and the transmillennial schemes see Jesus returning at the conclusion of the millennium, and both schemes see Christians having dominion and reigning with Jesus during that period of time. However, as we have argued before, the transmillennial view places the duration of the millennial period at about forty (40) years, or at some point between the ministry of Jesus and AD70. The postmillennial view places the duration of the millennial period long after the coming of Jesus in AD70, as it continues until a future "end of time" at yet another, final coming of the Lord. But what are the major objections offered up by postmillennial scholars regarding the transmillennial view?

In his book "When Shall These Things Be?" (WSTTB), Keith Mathison writes:

> "…[T]he [transmillennial] interpretations of the millennium fail to take seriously the long-term time text involved…When the word thousand is used in Scripture, it refers either to a literal thousand or to an indefinite, but very large, number" (209).

But what evidence does Mathison give to confirm his statement? According to Mathison the idea of a millennium requires a "very long period of time" or a "very large number." But is this in fact true? To support his claim, Mathison cites Psalm 50:10, which states:

> "For every beast of the forest is Mine, and the cattle upon a thousand hills. (Psalm 50:10)

The argument goes something like this: "since God owns the cattle on all the hills, and since 'a thousand hills' represents all of the hills, obviously we're talking about millions of hills here. And using this logic, they argue that in the same way

Revelation 20 uses "a thousand years," we should then assume that the symbolism of that phrase must be speaking about a very long period of time, potentially lasting as long as thousands or millions of years, or even longer.

However, the faulty logic in that argument is this. The context of Psalm 50:10 and the language that is being employed by the writer of this passage does not lead to the principle that "thousand" always signified "a very large number" as in "millions" or more. The context of Psalm 50:10 uses the principle of "completeness" or "fullness." In fact, only two verses later, the passage interprets itself:

"The world is Mine, and the *fullness* thereof." (Psalm 50:12b).

In the Bible the symbolic reference to "thousand" can be used a number of different ways. It can refer to "one" (day/yesterday/a watch in the night), or it can be used in reference to millions of hills, or even to eternity (cf. Psalm 105:8). There is nothing about the reference to a "thousand" by itself that tells anyone what it is referring to. Only the context of the passage where this phrase is written can determine its intended meaning; but in nearly every case the primary idea that is being communicated is the expression of "fullness" and "completeness," not necessarily "a very large number."

In G.K. Beale's book "*The New International Greek Testament Commentary: The Book of Revelation*," Beale (a reformed scholar of the same tradition as Mathison) states that some of the Jews considered the length of the intermediate messianic reign to be forty years. He also adds that one Jewish tradition made an anti-type connection between Adam's lifespan (930 years, only 70 short of a thousand) and a reign of Messiah for a (possibly symbolic) thousand year period (p. 1018-1019).

In the book written against Mathison's WSTTB, titled "House Divided: Bridging the Gap in Reformed Eschatology," the following observation is made:

"Adam falling short of the 1,000-year lifespan by 70 years (Genesis 5:5) may represent his being created a mortal being and perishing in sin outside of God's presence. If this is the case, then it is more than reasonable that the number 1,000 took on the symbolism and representation of Christ's and the church's victory over Death in contrast to Adamic man's vain existence apart from God's salvation (Ecclesiastes 6:6).

Some Evangelicals and Reformed theologians along with some preterists such as Milton Terry [and Carol A. Hill] do not understand the long lifespans in the early chapters of Genesis to be literal. They believe that the lifespans were symbolic and contained numerological elements. But even if Adam's lifespan was a literal 930 years, this does not exclude an anti-typical, symbolic 1,000 years in Revelation 20.

When Messiah came as 'the last Adam,' His reign in and through the church for a symbolic thousand years brought the church, not to the dust of the earth separated from God's presence, but to the Tree of Life and into the very presence of God (Revelation 20-22:12). Through faith in and union with Christ as the last Adam (the Tree of Life and New Creation), Christians have achieved what Adam could not. The church was clothed with 'immortality'; it attained unto the 'fullness of life' in AD70; and it will never die for the aeons of the aeons (2 Corinthians 1:20; 1 Corinthians 15:45-53; Revelation 21-22; John 11:26-27)."

As the authors of "House Divided" make so plainly clear, the only future coming of Jesus discussed in the book of Revelation is the one that would take place within the generation of the first century Christians, nearly 2,000 years ago. Mathison, and even the popular reformed writer and theologian Dr. Kenneth Gentry, agree that the imminent coming of Jesus took place in AD70. But then they make the startling conclusion that the imminent coming of Jesus in Revelation 20 and following was not referring to the same events described nearly everywhere else throughout Scripture and in reference to His coming in Matthew 24 and in AD70.

What evidence do they provide to argue for an additional third coming at the end of time beyond the second coming of AD70? Very little at all that is based on Biblical exegesis; rather, the often employed argumentation is that since they know the millennium is a current reality, and since it must last a very long time, His final coming must still be in our future. Its one assumption built onto another, and ultimately, their house of cards falls flat on the table. The typical evidence provided by those within the postmillennial schemes is the traditional statements from orthodoxy concerning the understanding of the millennium from the views they staunchly support. Never mind the orthodox views that greatly disagree with their own view; they prefer to use the ones that support their paradigm. Their claim of orthodoxy and creedal authority to support their view is founded on shaky soil that is so hotly contested in the annals of history and church tradition that it is no wonder that there is so much confusion on the matter!

But an even greater admission by Mathison in his book WSTTB can be found on pg. 194. Here Mathison states that, "As far as Paul knew, Christ could have returned in his lifetime." Apparently Mathison doesn't even realize the crux to his own belief system while making this statement. If Paul had any thought at all that Jesus "could" return in his own lifetime, there is absolutely no way at all that Paul, or any other New Testament Apostle or disciple would have or could have viewed the millennial scheme in a manner that agrees with any of the popular views today, including Mathison's own view of postmillennialism. What is Mathison's only other option? Does he believe that Paul was confused, or that he had no idea of this millennial doctrine John espoused? If any of the first century Christians had ANY idea of a millennial period that would last hundreds, or thousands of years long and into the future, they could not have expected the return of Christ within their own lifetimes. But they did.

"Amazingly, [Mathison] has evidently forgotten to leave room for his millennium. He knows the millennium must be complete before the second coming, but concedes Paul thought the second coming could have taken place within his lifetime. So he must believe that Paul considered it possible for the entire millennium to be fulfilled in the first century. That would make Paul a full-preterist, not a Mathison-style postmillennialist. Mathison complains that preterists compress the 1,000 years down to 40 (WSTTB, 209), but now he has Paul doing it too. We are in good company!"[2]

And so Mathison, and others from the reformed persuasions are left to defend a position that posits the Apostles as confused, and apparently wrong concerning the time of the Second Coming. Why would Paul tell his first-century audience to expect the appearing of the Lord soon in their future if he knew that thousands of years had to pass, including a millennial period, before the time would come? So the questions that must be asked are, were they wrong, and were they confused about the timing of the Day of the Lord and Christ's Parousia?

If Mathison and others from his persuasion wish to believe this sort of logic, then that is where we will have to part ways with one another. I believe in the full inspiration and reliability of Scripture, and if the Apostles and disciples believed that Jesus was to return within their own lifetimes, and if they believe that the millennial scheme is included within that time-frame, then I stand by their own statements, not church tradition or dogma. Mathison's hopeless and inconsistent postmillennial system allows for both a first-century return of Jesus (one the Apostles expected), while at the same time requiring thousands of years and a world-wide conversion to take place first. If this is the system that Mathison and others expect us to adopt, he has some serious exegetical work, and some explaining to do.

---

[2] Fenemore, Michael A. & Simmons, Kurt M., *The Twilight of Postmillennialism. Fatal errors in the teachings of Keith A. Mathison, Kenneth L. Gentry, Jr. et al.* (Preterism.info Publishing.: CreateSpace, 2010), 48-49.

------ *11* ------

CONCLUSION

Final Thoughts

The church in Smyrna was promised a crown of life that would not be hurt by the second death (cf. Revelation 2:10-11). Paul expected this crown also (cf. 1 Corinthians 9:25) and even associated his receiving it at the coming of Christ (cf. 1 Thessalonians 2:19; 2 Timothy 4:8). Peter also associated this awarded crown with the coming of Christ (cf. 1 Peter 5:4). Why is it that they all seemed to expect all of this at the coming of Jesus very soon in their own lifetimes? Because Jesus told them that when He came in His glory that He would reward every man according to his works and then He told them that some of them would be alive when this occurred (cf. Matthew 16:27-28)! When do we see this event being fulfilled? Revelation 20:6-15 and 21:8 places the rewards at the end of the book where the definition of the "second death" and judgment is also given.

Thus, the reward of the crown of life for those who were still alive, and for those who were dead in Christ, along with those who would participate in the millennium, the resurrection, and the judgment, are associated as occurring at the same period of time, or so closely together that there is little distinguishing them apart from one another, and those events included the coming of Jesus in AD70. All of those things are tied together in Matthew 16:27-28. Again, if the disciples' and Apostles' expectations were for these events to occur in their own lifetimes, very soon, were they wrong? Was their idea of the thousand year period of time wrong or so completely foreign that they did not understand it even until the very end of their ministries? Is their inspiration and divine authorship to be rejected as faulty, uninspired, and not divine? I think not!

I would rather reconsider my own presuppositions concerning the second coming, the thousand year period, the binding and loosing of Satan, the judgment, and the resurrection, before I fall into the category of rejecting Scripture simply to fit and conform to my own paradigm and view of these events. Sadly, most Christians today fall into the category of "panmillennial" and simply suggest that no one can truly figure it all out. It's too confusing; too elaborate, and too ancient to even begin to try to understand. And sadly, they are mistaken, and there is no reason to be panmillennial about God's eschatological and redemptive scheme for humanity at all. There is reason to celebrate, to leap for joy, and to be excited about being able to understand something that has confused many Christians in the church since its' inception.

A dear friend of mine here in town, Charlie, an avid student of God's Word with an astute Reformed background, had this to say concerning the fulfilled or Preterist interpretation of Scripture:

"The consistent [full] preterist agrees with the creedal writers to the number of [future and prophetic] "comings" of Christ (there is only one) along with its accompanying events. The creedal writers simply misunderstood the nature of that coming and were thereby forced to postpone it. One error led to the other. On the other hand, the partial preterist teaches two New Testament comings of Christ; one that is within the Scriptural time-frame and nature of fulfillment [the first century generation], and another that is foreign to Scripture [at the end of time].

The partial preterist position is merely an attempt to satisfy the time-statements [like soon, near, at hand, etc.] and still maintain the predilection [or former view] they had prior to 'seeing' those time-statements. It's nothing more than a compromise. But with its denial of the fulfillment of significant eschatological events (i.e. - the Second Coming, resurrection, and judgment), it is still the integrity of Christ and His apostles that is compromised.

If the partial preterist is convinced that partial preterism is the truth, then the creeds and confessions missed it. Partial preterism is just as out of accord with (if not more so) the creeds and confessions as [they would claim] consistent preterism is. The difference is that the consistent [or full] preterist admits it, while the partial preterist plays the 'within creedal orthodoxy' shell-game."

Just as Dr. Berkhof said, "The Reformation adopted what the early Church taught respecting the return of Christ, the resurrection, the final judgment, and eternal life... It can hardly be said that the Churches of the Reformation did much for the development of eschatology. There has never been a period in the history of the Christian Church in which eschatology was the center of Christian thought." I believe that "period" is upon us! And I would further agree with Gentry's assessment concerning the movement or development of progress in our understanding concerning eschatological doctrines. "[W]e should expect to find a gradual development of the millennial schemes, rather than a fully functioning system in early Christian history. For example, Walvoord confesses when defending dispensationalism: 'It must be conceded that the advanced and detailed theology of pretribulationism is not found in the Fathers, but neither is any other detailed and 'established' exposition of premillennialism. The development of the most important doctrines took centuries.'"[1] Indeed, I would argue that the doctrine of eschatology has taken nearly two-millennia to fully develop!

On the Other Side of the Millennium: Revelation 20-22

Now, if you're reading this still, it means that you've taken the journey with me through all of my arguments and "reasoning through the Scriptures." But, you might ask the question, "...if all of this is fulfilled, how then should we live, and why does any of this even matter, and is the Bible even still relevant to us today?" 2 Peter 3:11 asks the question of what manner of persons ought we be to live in holy conduct and godliness? If sin and death is defeated, can we just live as we please?

---

[1] Gentry, Kenneth L. Jr., Three Views on the Millennium and Beyond, (Grand Rapids, MI.: Zondervan, 1999). 15.

What did the Apostles believe life would be like after the millennium and after the second coming had occurred? Is holiness and godliness only to last up to the time of Jesus' coming, but not afterward? Grant it, most people believe that there is no need to live for Christ after His coming since we're in heaven already without the existence of sin or evil. It's hard to sin when you're already made physically and spiritually perfect without fleshly desires impeding your progress! However, given my arguments, the Kingdom of Jesus was being fully revealed during the ministry of Jesus and the Apostles, and the New Covenant Church was being established during that same period of time, leading up to an including AD70, and thus, life after the millennium and in the Kingdom of God during the New Covenant Age was and is not an escape from the physical reality of life on planet earth. Indeed, the Kingdom of God and of Christ includes the entire creation, both in heaven and on earth! You cannot separate the physical creation from the spiritual reality of heaven. God's Kingdom includes all of it!

The truth of the matter is that the Kingdom of God reigns and rules throughout the entire creation It permeates each of us, and it causes us to be placed into action where real change can take place in the world. It is a Spiritual reality that becomes a physical reality and is made manifest and can be seen through the outworking of the people of God in our everyday lives. It reigns in heaven, and it reigns on earth. As Revelation 11:15 says, "The kingdom of the world has become the kingdom of our Lord and of his Messiah, and he will reign forever and ever." The Kingdom of God is at work in every aspect of our lives today. When something good happens, or when something bad happens, everything works together for good and for the glory of God and for the purposes of God's ultimate plan. Everything that happens is within the divine scope of God's authority and nothing takes place outside of his Kingdom dominion and control.

1 Peter 1:15-16 gives us the "reason" for godly living beyond the millennium and the coming of the Lord in AD70: "Be Holy for I am Holy." Morality is based on the character of God, not the fairness of God or life from the human perspective. In Romans 13 Paul tells them to walk "as in the

day" which was approaching! They were to "put on Christ" in order to live as they should in the "age to come." Did you catch that? Do you see that Paul has in mind what life in Christ will be like IN THE AGE TO COME? Paul expects life to go on in the New Covenant Age! Paul isn't expecting the worldwide cosmological transformation of the physical universe at the Lord's coming any more than he is expecting rabbits to turn into penguins!

Paul says they were to walk "properly" as a child of God. There is a proper way to live as a Christian, and there is an improper way to live. You could put it this way, "walk now AS THOUGH you were already there." Or Paul might have said, "...fake it until you make it." But one thing is certain, Paul expected that some of them would live beyond the coming of the Lord, and he expected that planet earth would remain as well. And he expected that the people he originally wrote to would live as they should "IN THE AGE TO COME" (which those of us today current live in, and have now been living in for almost the last 2,000 years).

Thus, Paul did not believe in or expect an "end of time" scenario as so many prophecy pundits would have you believe today. Paul's doctrine of transformation was covenantal, and his message of the Kingdom was no different than Jesus' message. While Jesus stated that the Kingdom of God is not of this world, John adamantly stated that the Kingdom of this world has become the Kingdom of God and of His Christ! That includes everything, both the spiritual-heavenly reality, and the physical creation itself. Nothing is outside of the Kingdom of God; it all belongs to Him!

We are told that God's Word abides forever. If it abides forever, doesn't its' principles abide for us today also, even though all prophecy may have been fulfilled 2,000 years ago? We are to always be "REMINDED" of the "present truth" (cf. 2 Peter 1:12-15). We are told to grow in the grace and knowledge of the Lord (cf. Peter 3:16). We are told that the nations shall walk after me (cf. Micah 4:2; Psalm 37:31). In the New Heavens and Earth nations are being "healed" and saved, and walk by "His" light (cf. Revelation 21).

Nothing which defiles shall enter His Holy City; evil will only exist outside of the city of God (cf. Revelation 21:27;

22:14-15). Is everyone inside the City of God in the New Heavens and Earth? Revelation 21-22 says that there are those who live like dogs outside the city gates in the New Heavens and Earth! Hardly a cosmological transformation where everyone physically living is perfected! And is all evil burning in the Lake of Fire? Not at all! There are people "LIVING" outside the City's gates! How then are we to live; like dogs, or like Kings and Priests within the Holy City of God (The New Jerusalem)?

In the New Covenant Age, we are supposed to "return" to the Land of Israel to be restored. It's not a physical land, or a physical city that you can visit or travel to. The physical land and city is us! The Kingdom of God and the Holy City is the Promised Land, and we are all a part of it! The New Testament writer said that we have come to a heavenly city and a New Jerusalem (cf. Hebrews 11:16, 12:22). Jesus declared that he would build a different temple "not made with hands," and that "we are His temple" and that He would dwell in us, and we in Him (cf. Mark 15:58; 1 Corinthians 3:16; 2 Corinthians 6:16).

Once the regathering of God's people took place (the Great Commission), and the Church was established, how are we to live? According to the promises of the Old Testament, we are to have one King over us, with one Shepherd (cf. Ezekiel 37:24; 1 Peter 2:25), and we are to receive our salvation in the Messiah and in the land of God (cf. Isaiah 49:5-12; 2 Corinthians 6:1-2, 16; 1 Peter 1:9).

According to all these passages (and there are many more), God is going to multiply his people, dwell with them, lead them, guide them, heal them, and He is supposed to "be our light" continually. If this is true, how is it that we would not walk in holiness according to the character of God, but make the argument that once all is fulfilled we might walk as dogs and evil doers, and according to our own desires?

What About Israel Today?

The worldwide support and the establishment of the state and nation of Israel is a fraud perpetrated on the world and fueled by the fanaticism of Dispensational Zionists. The year

1948 originated with a lie, and it continues its' existence with a lie, and it offers the world a Zionistic national hope based on atheism and unbelief rather than a hope in God! The fact of the matter is that most Jews in Israel are atheistic, unbelieving, and are not Jewish at all, neither by blood decent nor by religion. To support them on the basis of a zealous religious doctrine of futurist, dispensational, premillennial theology ought to cause an outcry from true followers of Jesus. The Bible NEVER promises that Israel would be given blessings or redemption while she was in a state of utter rebellion and unbelief in God. That is her current Spiritual condition today, though Israel today is not even the same people of God that existed 2,000 years ago and before that time. Israel today IS NOT the Israel of the Bible.

The popular Christian mainstream teachers like Hal Lindsey, Tim LaHaye, Jerry Jenkins, Thomas Ice, and a myriad of others, teaches that we need to support national Israel no matter the cost and no matter the method to achieve her success, primarily so that the end times may begin for Christians. According to this view, it makes no difference to God or us whether or not the people of national Israel today are atheist, non-believing, criminal, vial, or adulterous against God. It is a view that essentially places a national group of people above God's true people, true Israel, or the Church, and above other nationalities or groups who have been oppressed by Israel's attempt to become a nation once again.

Often people say, "Does eschatology really matter"? Why is all this stuff so serious to you? And what is my response? If your eschatology changes how you involve yourself in politics and government, and world affairs, is that not important? If your "end times" view changes whether or not you choose to go to college, to invest in your future, or your children's future, shouldn't that be a major problem or issue to consider? Is a future, physical land of Israel really our blessed hope? Are these the types of issues that "aren't a big deal"? John 4:21-24 says that we shall worship, neither in this mountain, nor in Jerusalem, but we shall worship God "in Spirit and truth."

The promise of the restoration of true Israel was to be fulfilled by faith in Abraham's SEED (NOT PLURAL), (cf. Galatians 3:16, 26-29). That seed was fulfilled in Christ Jesus, not the nation of Israel in the Middle East today. If your end time's view changes your view of the world, how you involve yourself in social and political issues, and how you view the future of our country and of your own life in general, doesn't "eschatology" matter a great deal?

Galatians 4:21-31 shows us the picture of Hagar in bondage with her children, and it tells us that the Jerusalem above is true. Hebrews 12:18-28 shows us the true land, the true Israel, the true Jerusalem and the city of God. It was the city that was still very near to come according to Hebrews 13:14, and it was a city that would last forever, opposite of the one which they currently inhabited (Old Covenant Jerusalem). Hebrews 11:16 describes this city, and the writer tells us that it is a better country, a heavenly city! Hebrews 12:28 says that they were "receiving a Kingdom that cannot be shaken," and indeed, it is a Kingdom that permeates all of creation, both in heaven and on earth, and it is expressed in the world through the healing of the nations and through the fruit of the Spirit (cf. John 15; Galatians 5; Revelation 22).

And so we come to the conclusion of this book, and we implore you to reconsider any theology which places the millennial period outside the period of the first century. If you have ever believed that the hopes and goals of the Church ought to be in a future period where the Church is truly not fully reigning now with Christ on His throne, and if you have ever believed that we are still fighting against the powers of Satan and the Old Covenant Law of sin and death, praying for Jesus to come again and snatch us up out of the world, and if you are still acting as though we are not yet conquerors, having complete Kingdom dominion, and lacking authentic power to bring change and healing to the world, then please reconsider!

Indeed, Revelation 22 says that we are to be a healing to all nations! God's original mandate in the garden in the book of Genesis was to have dominion over the earth and to greatly multiply and increase, eating daily from the tree of life. If this is still future for us today, how can we possibly bring fulfillment to this saying? How can the Church truly bring healing to all nations through the Gospel message and through the river of life (Jesus) if we haven't even obtained the promises in this chapter yet? In fact, according to most popular commentaries and pastors today, no matter what we do the world is only going to get worse and worse, and less and less Godly. Is that the kind of future you believe we are really destined for? When Revelation speaks of the "leaves of the Tree" bringing healing to all nations, it speaks in Jewish imagery. A leaf is a manuscript or ancient insert written in a scroll or document. The leaves of the tree are representative of the "Word of God" bringing healing to all nations.

It is my hope and goal that if you've read this book, you will at least challenge your presuppositions or previous beliefs about the millennium, the future, and even the coming of Jesus in general, and that you will consider that Jesus is already reigning and ruling from His throne, completely, entirely, lacking nothing, and that the only future hope that you need to worry about is the hope of making a difference in the world through the power of the Lord Jesus Christ, and bringing healing to all nations through the message of love and of the Gospel. "The fact that different views concerning the Second Coming of Christ and the millennium have been and are held should not discourage anyone from making an earnest search for the truth...It is to be regretted that these differences of opinion even among those who accept the Bible as the inspired and authorative Word of God cannot always be dealt with by unprejudiced exegesis and friendly discussion rather than made the basis for quarrels or tests of orthodoxy...It should be added that the church has debated and reached conclusions and has embodied these conclusions in her creeds as the other great doctrines of the faith. But the subject of eschatology still remains in dispute."[2] I concur with Lorraine Boettener's statements, and I believe that this is one area where the Church could still use a little help!

The truth of the matter is that "[in] the midst of the current climate of uncertainty, however, Christians who have earnestly sought to remain true to the great doctrines of biblical and historic Christianity find themselves unable to articulate with one voice a message of hope for our world. Among the areas dividing the Christian ranks, few have been as explosive as

---

[2] Boettner, Loraine, *The Meaning of the Millennium.* (Downers Grove, IL: InterVarsity Press, 1977). 138-141.

those surrounding the doctrine of 'last things,' or eschatology...The anticipation of the climax to human history—a corporate eschatology—and the resultant question concerning the millennium as a specific state in that climax cannot be relegated to the fringes of the biblical proclamation. On the contrary, it belongs to the heart of what the Bible intends to teach."[3]

Amen.

[3] Grenz, Stanley J., *The Millennial Maze: Sorting out Evangelical Options*. (Downers Grove, IL: InterVarsity Press, 1992). 23-27.

AFTERWORD

By Dr. Don K. Preston

The Forty-Year Millennium

Our purpose is to demonstrate two things: 1) the Millennium of Revelation 20 began with the ministry/passion/resurrection of Christ, and; 2) the Millennium terminated forty years later at the resurrection and termination of the Old Covenant age in AD 70.

- **The Elements of the Millennium are the Elements of the Forty Years from Jesus' Ministry to AD70**

The axiom that if A=C and B=C, then A=B, can be applied to the Millennium. Here is what we mean: if the Millennium (A) is described by events (C) which also describe first-century events (B), then the Millennium took place during the first century (A=B). Revelation describes the Millennium as containing certain elements, such as:

- The *initial* vindication/resurrection of the martyrs with Christ.
- The binding of Satan.
- The rule of the saints with Christ: "I saw thrones on which were seated those who had been given authority to judge."
- The saints as a priesthood.
- The loosing of Satan.
- The destruction of Satan and the resurrection of "the rest of the dead" at the end of the Millennium.

According to Hebrews 11:39-40, the living and the dead would receive their blessings *at the same time*. Thus, if the martyrs of Revelation received thrones, priesthood, and authority, then the living saints should receive those very things *at the same time*, and *this is precisely what we find.* Note the harmony with the living during the forty-year period:

- The living saints were *resurrected*, awaiting the consummation of the resurrection at the last hour (John 5:24-28; 6:44). Notice Jesus stated "the hour is coming and *now is*" and again "the hour is coming." John later wrote: "It is the last hour" (1 John 2:18). The resurrection scenario of Revelation is as that found in John 5. The fact that 1 John says the consummative "last hour" was upon them proves that *the end of the Millennium was near.*

- The martyrs *sat on thrones* and were given *authority to judge* (Rev 20:4). The martyrs were told that they would only have to wait a little while before their full victory was achieved. However, their living brethren first had to suffer to fill the measure of suffering (Rev 6:9-11).

- The living and the dead had been enthroned with Christ "in the heavenlies" (Eph 2:1-6).

- The living had been given the authority to judge (Matt 19:28; 1 Cor 6; 2 Cor 2:15-16). In Matthew 19:28, Jesus told the apostles that they would sit on twelve thrones, judging the twelve tribes of Israel. This judgment would take place *through the message they preached* (Matt 16:19; cf. 2 Cor 2:15f).

- The living saints had to experience the suffering already experienced by the martyrs.

- The living would only have to suffer for a little while (Rev 6:9-11; 1 Peter 1:4f).

Some falsely claim that Jesus and the saints did not truly reign during the forty-year period. Paul, commenting on Christ's status during that forty-year period, wrote, "He must reign until His enemies are put under His feet" (1 Cor 15:24).

Paul uses the *present infinitive*, which means Christ was currently reigning, and *would continue to reign until his enemies were put under Him. The time of His rule is the time of the putting down of His enemies.* If He was not ruling before AD 70 then He was not putting down His enemies before AD 70; yet 1 Corinthians 15:24, Colossians 2:14f, Hebrews 10:13, etc., all speak of how Christ had *begun* to put all enemies under Him. He was *ruling in the midst of those enemies, awaiting the consummation of His conquering work.*

William Bell astutely notes that if Christ did not begin to rule until AD 70, then the putting down of His enemies, and ruling in the midst of His enemies, did not begin until AD 70. Yet Paul wrote "He must reign *until His enemies are put under Him.*" His reign and the putting down of His enemies are synchronous events. The Psalmist wrote, "Rule thou, *in the midst of your enemies*" (Psalm 110:2). The "ruling until the enemies were put under Him" and the "ruling in the midst of His enemies" are parallel statements. Paul makes it indisputably clear that Christ had begun the work of putting His enemies under Him: "He has put all things under Him, but we do not yet see all things put under Him" (1 Cor 15:27; cf. Col 2:14f).

The time of the *end* (1 Cor 15:24) is when Messiah *finalized His triumph over His enemies*—*not* the time when he would *begin* to put down His enemies. Revelation depicts that final victory, "when the thousand years are finished" (20:7). So, in Revelation, the beginning of the Millennium is the beginning of Messiah's conquering work. The Millennium reign is the *consolidation of Messiah's rule.* The *end of the Millennium* is when that work was perfected.

John says the martyrs were *priests* who *reigned* with Christ *for the Millennium.* In this they share an organic unity with Christ. Zechariah foretold that in the Messianic Temple, Messiah would be *both priest and king on His throne* (6:13). Hebrews 8:1-3 tells us that Jesus was serving as High Priest over the True Tabernacle, as He sat at "the right hand of the throne of majesty"—exactly where the Psalmist said he would *rule* in the midst of His enemies (Psalm 110:1-2).

In Revelation 20, just as their Lord sat on the throne as king and priest, so also the saints sat on thrones and served as priests. This was not only true of the dead. The living saints were priests as well (Heb 13:15, 1 Peter 2:4; Rev 1:5).

Satan was bound for the Millennium. Here too we find common ground with the ministry of Jesus and the forty years between His ascension and coming (ca. AD 30-70). When Jesus cast a demon out of a man, the disciples marveled. Jesus said that this was not possible unless the strong man was being bound (Matt 12:29). After Jesus sent His disciples out on the "limited commission," they returned incredulous at their success. Jesus told them, "I saw Satan fall like lightning from heaven" (Luke 10:18; cf. Rev 12).

Note the similarities between 2 Thessalonians 1-2 and Revelation:

- Suffering and martyrdom: in the first century (2 Thess 1; 2:7f); in the Millennium (Rev 20:1-4; cf. Rev 6:9-11; 12:12).
- The binding of the enemy of God: in the first century, "You know what is restraining him . . . . The one who *now restrains him* will do so until he is taken out of the way" (2 Thess 2:6-7); in the Millennium Satan is bound (Rev 20:1-4).
- The release (revealing) of the man of sin in the first century (2 Thess 2:8); the releasing of Satan after the Millennium (Rev 20).
- The destruction of the enemy at the end: in the first century (2 Thess 2:8); at the end of the Millennium (Rev 20:10).

Christ's Parousia, which would be the vindication of the suffering Thessalonians and the destruction of the persecuting enemy, was to occur *in the lifetime of the Thessalonians* (2 Thessalonians 1:4-10). The Lord's coming in judgment of the man of sin would be the final vindication of the martyrs in Revelation 20. Therefore:

- The destruction of the man of sin is the conquering of Satan at the end of the Millennium.
- The destruction of the man of sin of 2 Thessalonians 2

is the Parousia of 2 Thessalonians 1.

The coming of the Lord in 2 Thessalonians 1 was to be in the lifetime of the Thessalonians, when the Lord would give them relief from the persecution they were then experiencing. Therefore:

- The destruction of the man of sin, *at the end of the Millennium*, would occur in the lifetime of the Thessalonians.

Notice also that while Paul wrote that the last enemy, death, would be put down at Christ's Parousia (1 Cor 15:19-25), John wrote that death would be destroyed *at the end of the Millennium* (Rev 20:10f). Therefore, Christ's Parousia would be at the end of the Millennium. Thus, Jesus' statement "Behold, I come quickly!" meant that the end of the Millennium was near when John wrote.

So we see that every constituent element John used to describe the Millennium is also applied to the period of time from the ministry of Christ until AD 70. These thematic and temporal parallels demonstrate that the Millennium extended from Jesus' ministry until AD 70.

When the Thousand Years Are Over

Another way to determine whether or not the forty-year period was the Millennium is to compare what was to happen *at the end of the Millennium* with the language of imminence found in the New Testament. If the events in Revelation posited at the end of the Millennium were considered imminent in other books of the New Testament, this constitutes *prima facie* evidence that the end of the Millennium was near. At the end of the Millennium we see: Satan released; his making war with the saints; his final destruction. In the New Testament we see: Satan released ("The Devil walks around seeking whom he may devour" 1 Peter 5:8)[5]; his making war with the saints (the saints had to suffer "a little while" 1 Peter 1:4f; cf Rev 12:10); the destruction of Satan ("the God of peace shall crush Satan under your feet shortly" Rom 16:20). Simply stated:

- The destruction of Satan would be at the end of the Millennium.
- The destruction of Satan was near when Paul wrote Romans.
- Therefore, the end of the Millennium was near when Paul wrote Romans.

The end of the Millennium is also the time of The Resurrection (i.e. "the rest of the dead," who came to life *after the thousand years*; Rev 20:7-12), yet Peter wrote that Christ was "ready (Gk. *hetoimos*) to judge the living and the dead" in the first century (1 Peter 4:5). We also see the opening of the books to judge who would or would not enter the kingdom, while Jesus told His disciples that "there are some standing here that shall not taste of death till they see the Son of Man coming in His kingdom" (Matt 16:27-28). Lastly, we see that Heaven and earth fled away, and the arrival of the New Creation in which God dwells with man—all things which "must shortly come to pass" (Rev 22:6, 10-12).

The Millennium and Israel's Festal Calendar

In Israel's festal calendar, the New Creation would come at the climax of the last three feast days—Trumpets (Rosh HaShanah, i.e. judgment), Atonement, and Harvest/Tabernacles. *Tabernacles is when God's presence would be restored to man through resurrection.*[8]

In Revelation 14:1-4 we see the first fruits of the harvest (cf. John 5:24f), which corresponds to the enthronement of the martyrs in Revelation 20:1-4. The martyrs were awaiting the harvest (Feast of Tabernacles), which would occur at the destruction of Babylon, the city guilty of killing the saints (14:6f). *This is the end of the Millennium* (Rev 20:10f). In Revelation 20-21, *at the end of The Millennial resurrection*, we hear the victory declaration: "The tabernacle of God is with man!" (Rev 21:3). *This is the fulfillment of Israel's festal calendar, the Feast of Tabernacles!*

It is commonly argued that the "ceremonial aspects" of Torah ended at the cross, and that Israel ceased to be God's covenant people at the cross, while Old Testament prophecy remained valid to AD 70 (some Preterists), or still remains valid (Futurism). However, nothing was more "ceremonial" or *prophetic*, than Israel's *covenantal* feast days! The fact that Revelation 20-21 depicts the fulfillment of Israel's last three feast days *at the end of the Millennium* proves that the "ceremonial" aspects of Torah remained valid when John wrote. Watch carefully:

- Israel's Feast Days (*and thus, Torah itself*) would remain valid *until what the Feast Days foreshadowed* was fulfilled (Matt 5:17-18; Col 2:14-16; Heb 9:6-10).
- Those feast days foreshadowed the resurrection—the hope of Israel—*at the end of the Millennium.*
- Therefore, Israel's Feast Days (*and thus, Torah itself*) would remain valid *until* the end of the Millennium.[9]

Clearly, the consummation of Israel's age and the end of Torah is inseparably tied to the end of the Millennium. We offer one final syllogism:

- The Resurrection was *the salvation hope of Israel* (Isa 25:8; Acts 26:6-8; Rom 11:25f).
- The Resurrection of Revelation 20:10f— *at the end of the Millennium*—was therefore the salvation hope of Israel.
- Daniel 12:2-7 posits the fulfillment of the resurrection/salvation hope of Israel in AD 70.
- Therefore, the end of the Millennium was in AD 70.

Biblically, there was no resurrection *apart from Israel's hope*. Thus, the resurrection of the "rest of the dead" at the end of the Millennium must be interpreted within that framework. In summary, we note that every element of the Millennium was present for the saints living during the 40 years between Jesus' ministry and AD 70, and that the end of the Millennium resurrection was the hope of Israel. If that resurrection has not happened, Torah remains valid and *Israel remains God's covenant people*. As we have seen, Daniel 12 falsifies this idea.

Although much more could be said, all of the evidence presented points irrefutably to the fact that the Millennium began in the ministry of Christ and extended for the forty years lasting till AD 70.

The Epistles of Peter, Revelation and the Millennium

In studies of the millennium, it is somewhat amazing to me that so little attention is given to the direct parallels between the other New Testament epistles and the book of Revelation. Yet, the parallels are undeniable and substantive. While a great deal of time could be devoted to examining the parallels with the other books, e.g. the book of Ephesians, I will offer a parallel description here (see table below) demonstrating the links between Peter's two epistles and the Apocalypse. I am confident that this is not an exhaustive list of the parallels, but it is suffice for our purposes here as to briefly cover the primary parallels that do exist.

It is more than obvious that Peter and John wrote of the same pressing issues and made the same promises. When this is recognized it becomes more than clear that the end of the millennium was near during the latter half of the first century.

PETER'S LETTERS   **JOHN'S REVELATION**

PETER'S LETTERS	JOHN'S REVELATION
To the "diaspora"	Concerning the twelve tribes (7, 14)
To the saints in Asia	To the churches of Asia
Fulfillment of Israel's promises– at the parousia	Fulfillment of all that the prophets foretold (10.7; 22.6)
Written from "Babylon"	Written About Babylon

Peter calls on the Transfiguration as vision of Christ's parousia– at the end of the millennium	Vision of Christ is like the Transfiguration (19)
Resurrection (salvation) the hope of Israel (1.9-12)	Resurrection at the end of the millennium- the Hope of Israel (10.7; 11:15-19; 20.10-12)
Present Suffering (1.4f; 4:12; 5:9)	Brother in the tribulation (1:9)
Suffer for a little while (1:4f)	Suffer for a little while (6.11; 12:10; 20– the millennium!)[2]
Filling the measure of suffering (1:4f; 5:9)	Filling the measure of suffering (6.11; 20:1-12)
Eternal inheritance- at the parousia	Eternal Inheritance (7:14f– 20:12f)
Exodus motif (time of your sojourn 1:17; strangers and pilgrims 2:11)	Rev. 15– Song of Moses– Second Exodus
Spiritual priesthood (2.5)	Kingdom of priests (1:9); Priests on the thrones (20:1f)
Spiritual temple (2.5)	Spiritual temple – Christ is the Temple!
Rejected stone– chief of corner (2.4f)	Rejected Stone– Chief Corner – 21– He is the temple!

---

[2] See my *Who Is This Babylon?* or Chapter 20 of this book for a demonstration of the direct parallels between Revelation 6, 12, & 20. When these parallels are recognized, it demands that the millennium had all but expired when John wrote, and that it would be consummated in the Day of the Lord in vindication of the martyrs, which Jesus unambiguously posited in THAT generation at AD70 (cf. Matthew 23).

Judgment on those who rejected the Stone (2:4-8)	Judgment on those who pierced him (1.7; Babylon, the city where the Lord was slain, 11:8)
Isaiah 49– I will lead them to living waters	7.14– I will lead them to living waters– 21.2f– *at the end of the millennium*
Isaiah 49– (1:5:1-3-- Chief Shepherd brings Salvation of the remnant of all tribes– and then to the nations	144,00 out of the 12 tribes- the remnant– and then the salvation of the nations (7:, 14, 21:25ff)
Messianic Woes (The Tribulation they were enduring)	Great Tribulation (7.14; 16:16f)[3]
Satan walks about (5:8)	War with Satan (Satan cast to earth...–> Satan loosed at the end of the millennium
Fiery trial is among you (present tense, not future, 4:12) –> What John foretold was now present	Fiery trial was coming (3:10– about to come)
Thief Coming (2 Peter 3)	Coming as a thief (3:1-2; 16:15)
New Heavens and Earth following the Day of the Lord[4]	New Heavens and Earth following the millennium

---

[3] See my *Blast From the Past: The Truth About Armageddon*, for an exposition on the Tribulation and how it was fulfilled in the first century. That book is available from www.store.bibleprophecy.com, Amazon, and other internet book retailers.

[4] See my *The Elements Shall Melt With Fervent Heat*, for an in-depth study of 2 Peter 3 demonstrating fulfillment in AD 70, with the dissolution of Israel's Old Covenant "heaven and earth."

Christ was "ready" (*hetoimos*) to judge the living and the dead– (4.5– Rev. 20.10-12)- "The End of all things (the millennium) has drawn near (4.7)	These things must shortly come to pass

One thing to notice in these comparisons is that Peter gives no indication of a protracted period of time before the consummation of the end. In other words, he was anticipating the imminent consummation of his eschatological hope in the near future. Now, since he and John patently wrote of the same identical topics, themes and motifs, then since Peter gives us no hint, clue, or suggestion of a protracted delay before that climax (especially one of over 2,000 years), this is a powerful indication concerning the end of the millennium, "the end of all things, has drawn near" (1 Peter 4:7). In light of these parallels, consider then:

- Peter and John wrote to the same audiences
- They addressed the identical topics, themes, motifs
- They called on the identical prophetic background
- The both wrote concerning the hope of Israel
- They both made the identical promises
- They both posited fulfillment OF ALL THINGS within an imminent time frame in their near future

In light of these indisputable facts, it is relevant to ask: What method of hermeneutical principles are we using whereby we can delineate between Peter's epistles and John's Revelation in regard to the time of fulfillment (of those identical subjects and promises of which they both spoke)?

Since Peter and John patently wrote to the same people, about the same things, and since they both wrote of the imminent consummation of the end of all things (i.e. the New Creation that follows the millennium), this demands that the end of the millennium was near to both Peter and John when they wrote their epistles.

GLOSSARY

The words listed below are provided to assist the reader and to help with understanding the meaning of various definitions found throughout this book, in addition to other important words and ideas that are helpful with regard to end times and the study of eschatology (last things). It is certainly not a complete list, nor is it comprehensive of the entire field of study.

Allegory: a representation of an abstract or spiritual meaning through concrete or material forms; figurative treatment of one subject under the guise of another. Used in Galatians 4:24, where the apostle refers to the history of Isaac the free-born, and Ishmael the slave-born, and makes use of it allegorically. Every parable is an allegory. Nathan (2 Samuel 12:1-4) addresses David in an allegorical narrative. In the eightieth Psalm there is a beautiful allegory: "Thou broughtest a vine out of Egypt," etc. In Ecclesiastes 12:2-6, there is a striking allegorical description of old age.

Amillennialism: does not believe in a literal or earthly physical millennial Kingdom. Followers of this view hold that the millennium was inaugurated with Christ's resurrection. In an "already/not yet" sense, Christ already reigns over all and is already victorious over Satan. Christ currently reigns in the hearts of Christians and there is no need for a physical reign of Christ on the earth until the end of time. In this view, the future reign with Christ described in Revelation 20 is considered to be ruling with Christ in heaven and not on earth. Because there are promises to Israel that are to take place in the millennial Kingdom, this view holds that the promises to Israel have been transferred to the church. God is done with Israel as they have rejected their Messiah. There will be a progressive decline in the morality of the world until the Rapture: The saints, living and dead shall meet the Lord in the clouds and immediately proceed to judge the nations of the world with Christ and then follow Him into their eternal state.

Anti-type (see Typology Principle): something that is foreshadowed by a type or symbol, as a New Testament event prefigured in the Old Testament. For example, when Abraham was given a ram in place of sacrificing his son Isaac on the mountain, this was a "type" of the ultimate sacrifice of Jesus, the "Lamb of God," on Mount Moriah. Also, the forty year Exodus period was a "type" of the New Testament Exodus period. During this time there was manna (Spiritual Food – Gospel), miracles (outpouring of the Holy Spirit), wandering in the wilderness (great commission), and entering the Promised Land (entering into the New Covenant Age of Christ).

Apocalypse: a prophetic revelation, especially concerning a cataclysm in which the forces of good permanently triumph over the forces of evil. From the Greek word apocalupsis, meaning to "uncover" or "disclose" some new revelation. It is the term found in the opening titular phrase of the introduction to the book of Revelation (The Apocalypse of Jesus Christ).

Apocalyptic: a literary genre used to describe prophetic literature composed in highly metaphorical and symbolic language system used within post-exilic Judaism and early Christianity.

Apocalyptic prophecy: a category of prophetic pronouncement concerned with the eschatological hope in God's blessing and vindication of the redeemed, and His righteous judgment of the wicked. It often employs hyperbolic cosmic imagery (e.g., darkening sun, blood-red moon, stars falling from the sky, foreboding clouds) and fantasy imagery (e.g., red dragons with seven heads, locusts with human faces, leopards with bear's feet and lion's teeth) to invest earthly, historical, sociopolitical events with their full theological and eternal significance.

Archetype (type, typology): the original pattern or model from which all things of the same kind are copied or on which they are based; a model or first form; a prototype.

Canon: a body of books accepted as authoritative by some religious body. Most modern Protestants, and Protestant churches historically accept exactly sixty-six books, thirty-nine books from Hebrew, which they call the Old Testament, and twenty-seven books written in Greek, which they call the New Testament. The term means "measuring stick" or "measuring rod" and was given to define the standard or method which the early church used to establish which documents were or were not to be included in the Bible that we read today.

Christian Zionism: is a belief among some Christians that the return of the Jews to the Holy Land, and the establishment of the State of Israel in 1948, is in accordance with Biblical prophecy. It overlaps with, but is distinct from, the nineteenth century movement for the Restoration of the Jews to the Holy Land, which had both religiously and politically motivated supporters. The term Christian Zionism was popularized in the mid-twentieth century. Prior to that time the common term was Restorationism. Some Christian Zionists believe that the "ingathering" of Jews in Israel is a prerequisite for the Second Coming of Jesus. This belief is primarily, though not exclusively, associated with Christian Dispensationalism. The idea that Christians should actively support a Jewish return to the Land of Israel, along with the parallel idea that the Jews ought to be encouraged to become Christian, as a means fulfilling a Biblical prophecy has been common in Protestant circles since the Reformation.

Day of the Lord: is an eschatological day of ultimate judgment and salvation bringing deliverance or doom. It is also called the Day of Yahweh (in Old Testament eschatology) and a day of final judgment (Amos 5:18–21; Ezek. 30). It is also called the Day of Christ, or Day of Jesus Christ, and the day of the Second Advent (II Peter 3:10; I Cor. 1:14; Phil. 1:10, 2:16).

Dogmatics (dogma): is the established belief or doctrine held by a religion, or a particular group or organization. It is authoritative and not to be disputed, doubted, or diverged from, by the practitioners or believers. Although it generally refers to religious beliefs that are accepted without reason or evidence, they can refer to acceptable opinions of philosophers or philosophical schools, public decrees, or issued decisions of political authorities. The term derives from Greek δόγμα "that which seems to one, opinion or belief" and that from δοκέω (dokeo), "to think, to suppose, to imagine." Dogma came to signify laws or ordinances adjudged and imposed upon others by the First Century. The plural is either dogmas or dogmata, from Greek δόγματα. Today, it is sometimes used as a synonym for systematic theology.

Dispensationalism: a biblical hermeneutic paradigm common in conservative fundamentalist and Evangelical Christian theology. Originating from the Plymouth Brethren in the nineteenth century and popularized in the *Scofield Reference Bible* in the twentieth century, dispensationalism has three primary characteristics: 1) the call for a consistent literal or "normal" hermeneutic, 2) the separation of Israel from the church, 3) the separation of human history into several distinct epics, "economies," or dispensations in which God relates to mankind in a distinct way. With regard to soteriological history (history of salvation), dispensationalism teaches that salvation has always been by faith alone, by grace alone, yet the content of the Gospel has been progressively revealed through biblical history. Dispensationalism has a variety of forms.

Eisegesis (see Exegesis): the interpretation of a text (as of the Bible) by reading into it one's own ideas. It is the approach to Bible interpretation where the interpreter tries to "force" the Bible to mean something that fits their existing belief or understanding of a particular issue or doctrine. People who interpret the Bible this way are usually not willing to let the Bible speak for itself and let the chips fall where they may. They start off with the up-front goal of trying to prove a point they already believe in, and everything they read and interpret is filtered through that paradigm. Stated another way, they engage in what the Bible refers to as "private interpretation."

Eschatology: is a major branch of study within Christian theology. Eschatology, from two Greek words meaning *last* (ἔσχατος, last) and *study* (λογία, lit. discourse), is the study of the end of things, whether the end of an individual life, the end of the age, or the end of the world. Broadly speaking, Christian eschatology is the study of the destiny of man as it is revealed in the Bible, which is the primary source for all Christian eschatological studies. The major issues and events in Christian eschatology are death and the afterlife, Heaven and Hell, the Second Coming of Jesus, the Resurrection of the Dead, the Rapture, the Tribulation, Millennialism, the end of the world, the Last Judgment, and the New Heaven and New Earth.

Exegesis (see Eisegesis): is a theological term used to describe an approach to interpreting a passage in the Bible by critical analysis. Proper exegesis includes using the context around the passage, comparing it with other parts of the Bible, and applying an understanding of the language and customs of the time of the writing, in an attempt to understand clearly what the original writer intended to convey. In other words, it is trying to "pull out" of the passage the meaning inherent within it. The opposite of exegesis is eisegesis, which is a person's particular interpretation of scriptures that are not evident in the text itself.

First Coming (1ˢᵗ Advent): the First Coming of Jesus Christ entailed the fulfillment of the Old Testament prophecies of the Messiah to come to earth as a baby in a manger in Bethlehem, just as prophesied. Jesus fulfilled many of the prophecies of the Messiah during his birth, life, ministry, death, and resurrection. However, there are some prophecies regarding the Messiah that Jesus had not yet fulfilled by the time of his ascension, which is generally referred to as **The Second Coming** of Christ, when all prophecy would be fulfilled. In His first coming, Jesus was the suffering Servant and sacrificial eternal High Priest. In His second coming, Jesus was to be the conquering King and judge. In His first coming, Jesus arrived in the most humble of circumstances. In His second coming, Jesus was to arrive with power and glory in judgment against his enemies, and to establish a New Covenant Kingdom age and reign that has no end.

Full Preterism (a.k.a. – Consistent Preterism, Covenant Eschatology, Realized Eschatology): is the view that all Biblical prophecy was fulfilled at or before AD70, including the judgment, the resurrection, and the coming of the Lord, and that the ongoing relevance and practical application of all Scripture continues since that time, and that the primary function of the Church is to bring healing to all nations, continually bearing good fruit as Revelation 21-22 states.

Gematria: is a system of assigning numerical value to a word or phrase, in the belief that words or phrases with identical numerical values bear some relation to each other, or bear some relation to the number itself as it may apply to a person's age, the calendar year, or the like. It is believed that this system was used in the book of Revelation to enable Christians to "calculate" the number 666, to reveal to them who John was talking about.

Historical-Grammatical Principle: is a Christian hermeneutical method that strives to discover the Biblical author's original intended meaning in the text. The aim of the historical-grammatical method is to discover the meaning of the passage as the original author would have intended and what the original hearers would have understood.

Great Tribulation: the Great Tribulation was a series of events concerning the time when the Roman legions destroyed Jerusalem and its temple in AD70 during the end stages of the First Jewish–Roman War, and it only affected the Jewish people rather than all mankind. This period of time was a divine judgment visited upon the Jews for their sins, including the rejection of Jesus as the promised Messiah. It occurred during the first century, during the 3 ½ years prior to 70AD when the armed forces of the Roman Empire destroyed

Jerusalem and its temple. Also known as the time of great distress, or Jacob's Trouble, this period is primarily discussed in the Gospels, and in particular the prophetic passages in Matthew 24, Mark 13 and Luke 21.

Heresy: is an accusation levied against members of another group which has beliefs which conflict with those of the accusers. It is usually used to discuss violations of religious or traditional laws or codes, and was primarily first introduced in Christian circles by Irenaeus in which his primary argument was the support of the concept of apostolic succession which he believed carried the weight of Scripture itself to teach and interpret all truth throughout each generation.

Biblical Hermeneutics: is the study of the principles of interpretation concerning the books of the Bible. It is part of the broader field of hermeneutics which involves the study of principles for the text and includes all forms of communication: verbal and nonverbal. In the interpretation of a text, hermeneutics considers the original medium as well as what language says, supposes, doesn't say, and implies. The process consists of several steps for best attaining the Scriptural author's intended meaning(s), such as Lexical-Syntactical Analysis, Historical-Cultural Analysis, Contextual Analysis, Theological Analysis, and Special Literary Analysis.

Idiom: is an expression, word, or phrase that has a figurative meaning that is comprehended in regard to a common use of that expression that is separate from the literal meaning or definition of the words of which it is made.

Motif: is a recurring subject, theme, idea, etc., especially in a literary, artistic, or musical work. It is a distinctive and recurring form, shape, figure, etc., in a design, as in a painting or on wallpaper, or in a literary device, and it is a dominant idea or feature that repeats throughout the text of Scripture.

Olivet Discourse: is a biblical passage found in the Synoptic Gospels of Mark 13, Matthew 24, Luke 21. It is known as the "Little Apocalypse" because it includes Jesus' descriptions of the end of the Jewish Old Covenant age, the use of apocalyptic language, and Jesus' warning to his followers that they will suffer tribulation and persecution before the ultimate triumph of the Kingdom of God. The *Olivet discourse* is the last of the five discourses of Matthew and occurs just prior to the narrative of Jesus' passion beginning with the anointing of Jesus. In the narrative is a discourse or sermon given by Jesus on the Mount of Olives, hence the name. It is also presumed by many scholars that the Book of Revelation was John's "Olivet Discourse" written in apocalyptic literary style, and in expanded form, since his Gospel is the only one of the four that does not contain this portion of the accounts of Jesus' ministry.

Partial Preterism (a.k.a. – Historic Preterism, Orthodox Preterism): holds that most eschatological prophecies, such as the destruction of Jerusalem, the Antichrists, the Great Tribulation, and the advent of the Day of the Lord as a "judgment-coming" of Christ were fulfilled either in AD70 or during the persecution of Christians under the Emperor Nero. Most partial preterists believe that there are still some prophecies left to be fulfilled near the end of time, and they typically assert that we are currently living in the millennial Kingdom Age at the present time.

Postmillennialism: is an interpretation of chapter 20 of the Book of Revelation which sees Christ's second coming as occurring after (Latin post-) the Millennium, a Golden Age in which Christian ethics prosper in this view. Although some postmillennialists hold to a literal millennium of 1,000 years, most postmillennialists see the thousand years more as a figurative term for a long period of time (similar in that respect to amillennialism). Among those holding to a non-literal millennium it is usually understood to have already begun sometime in the past, which implies a less obvious and less dramatic kind of millennium than that typically envisioned by premillennialists, as well as a more unexpected return of Christ. Postmillennialism also teaches that the forces of Satan will gradually be defeated by the expansion of the Kingdom of God throughout history up until the second coming of Christ at the end of time. This belief that good will gradually triumph over evil has led proponents of postmillennialism to label themselves "optimillennialists" in contrast to "pessimillennial" premillennialists and amillennialists. Many postmillennialists also adopt some form of preterism, which holds that many of the end-time's prophecies in the Bible have already been fulfilled. Several key postmillennialists, however, did not adopt preterism with respect to the Book of Revelation, among them B. B. Warfield, Francis Nigel Lee, and Rousas John Rushdoony.

Premillennialism: is the belief that Jesus Christ will literally and physically be on the earth for his millennial reign at his second coming. The doctrine is called premillennialism because it holds that Jesus' physical return to earth will occur prior to the inauguration of the millennium. Premillennialism is based upon what is claimed to be a literal or "straight forward" interpretation of Revelation 20:1-6 in the New Testament which describes Jesus's coming to the earth and subsequent reign at the end of an apocalyptic period of 7 years of tribulation. It views this future age as a time of fulfillment for the prophetic hope of God's people as given in the Old Testament. Most adherents of this view believe that the Saints on the earth will be raptured up at some point before, during or near the end of the tribulational period, at which time the millennial reign of Christ is to begin.

Preterism: is a Christian eschatological view that interprets prophecies of the Bible, especially Daniel and Revelation, as events which have already happened in the first century A.D. Preterism holds that Ancient Israel finds its continuation or fulfillment in the Christian church at the destruction of Jerusalem in AD70. The term preterism comes from the Latin *praeter*, which is listed in Webster's 1913 dictionary as a prefix denoting that something is "past" or "beyond," signifying that either all or a majority of Bible prophecy was fulfilled by AD 70. Adherents of preterism are commonly known as *preterists*.

Promised Land: refers to all the literal Old Testament prophecies concerning the physical Israel promised to the nation of Israel, which the people received before the end of King Solomon's reign. Some futurists deny the passages in Joshua, I Kings, II Chronicles, and Jeremiah which clearly state that the descendants of Israel did possess all the territory promised to them, and believe that the land promises are still unfulfilled. The promise is first made to Abraham (Genesis 15:18-21) and then renewed to his son Isaac, and to Isaac's son Jacob (Genesis 28:13), Abraham's grandson. The Promised Land was described in terms of the territory from the River of Egypt to the Euphrates river (Exodus 23:31) and was given to their descendants after the Exodus. (Deuteronomy 1:8). The Promised Land is also a type or picture of the ultimate eternal promised land that relates to the new heavens and new earth, and the "Jerusalem which is above" whose builder is God, or the "New Jerusalem" which the saints of God are to receive.

Prophecy: is a process in which one or more messages that have been communicated to a prophet are then communicated to others. Such messages typically involve divine inspiration, interpretation, or revelation of conditioned events to come (cf. divine knowledge) as well as testimonies or repeated revelations of the future, referred to as forth-telling or foretelling.

Rapture (Pre-Trib, Mid-Trib, Post-Trib, Pre-Wrath): refers to the "being caught up" discussed in 1 Thessalonians 4:17. The Rapture is used in at least two senses in modern traditions of Christian eschatology: in pre-tribulationist views, in which a group of people will be "left behind," and as a synonym for the final, general resurrection. Pre-tribulation rapture theology was developed in the 1830s by John Nelson Darby and the Plymouth Brethren, and popularized in the United States in the early 20th century by the wide circulation of the Scofield Reference Bible, which ultimately led to what is currently known as "dispensational pre-tribulationism." Within pre-tribulational views, there are a variety of beliefs regarding the time general events surrounding the rapture. These views are known as pre-, mid-, post-, and partial rapture theories, along with the pre-wrath rapture theory. The primary essence of the view is that there is to be two major events leading up to the return of Jesus, including the rapture, followed by or coinciding with the tribulation period, and then followed by the millennial period of 1000 years, and consummating with the final judgment and resurrection.

Resurrection: is the idea that Christians will be raised up at the last day to their ultimate glory. In a futurist framework, resurrection is primarily something that takes place at the end of time or at the return of Jesus when the physical bodies of the dead rise up and meet their spiritual counterparts in the sky, or in heaven, in a new, glorified state. It also accompanies the resurrection of the unjust that are raised to suffer eternal death. In a preterist framework resurrection was explained using natural resurrection language, but was metaphorical in its application in speaking of the hope of Israel, or the corporate resurrection of the people of God from their dead state, or their lost condition. It includes conversion of the unbeliever to a believer (being "raised to life" in Christ) as well as the corporate resurrection of the "body of Christ" which was to include gentiles and Jews into one new body or one new man in Christ.

Scriptural Synergy (Analogy of Scripture): is a basic principle of Biblical interpretation (hermeneutics) which says that Scripture must interpret Scripture; the scope and significance of one passage is to be brought out by relating it to others. Typically, this rule is most often useful to help in understanding more difficult passages by first applying easy to understand passages that speak to the same topic, but in much more clear or understood language. This principle is helpful to prevent the student of the Bible from creating entire systems or false doctrines from obscure or hard to understand passages.

Second Coming (2nd Advent): *See "First Coming."*

Sola Scriptura: is the doctrine that the Bible contains all knowledge necessary for salvation and holiness. Consequently, sola scriptura demands only those doctrines are to be admitted or confessed that are found directly within or indirectly by using valid logical deduction or valid deductive reasoning from scripture, and no other source. However, sola scriptura is not a denial of other authorities governing Christian life and devotion. Rather, it simply demands that all other authorities are subordinate to, and are to be corrected by, the written word of God, whenever necessary. Sola scriptura was a foundational doctrinal principle of the Protestant Reformation held by the Reformers and is a formal principle of Protestantism today. Beyond the Reformation, as in some Evangelical and Baptist denominations, sola scriptura is stated even more strongly: it is self-authenticating, clear (perspicuous) to the rational reader, its own interpreter ("Scripture interprets Scripture"), and sufficient of itself to be the final authority of Christian doctrine without the necessity of creed, tradition, or confession.

Transmillennialism (a.k.a. – the Transition Period, the 2nd Exodus, the Bi-Covenant Period): is the millennial scheme that interprets the thousand year period of Revelation 20 as a symbolic reference to a complete and full generation of approximately forty years from the beginning of Jesus' ministry, until the 3 ½ year war of the Jews from 66AD-70AD.

Tribulation: is the general term for distress or trials that Jesus predicted would come upon his people before the great and terrible day of the Lord and the Great Tribulation period. Christian tribulation and suffering is not to be confused with the Great Tribulation, in that the Great Tribulation is a specific 3 ½ year period of wrath and judgment delivered upon the Jews by God at the hands of the Roman Armies during the Jewish-Roman war from AD66-AD70. Christian tribulation is something all Christians are expected to be willing to endure on behalf of our faith, since Jesus said that we might be hated on account of His name, as he was hated by many.

Typology Principle: is a method of biblical interpretation whereby an element found in the Old Testament is seen to prefigure one found in the New Testament. The initial one is called the *type* and the fulfillment is designated the *antitype*. Either type or antitype may be a person, thing, or event, but often the type is messianic and frequently related to the idea of salvation. The use of Biblical typology enjoyed greater popularity in previous centuries, although even now it is by no means ignored as a hermeneutic. Typological interpretation is specifically the interpretation of the Old Testament based on the fundamental theological unity of the two Testaments whereby something in the Old shadows, prefigures, adumbrates something in the New. Hence, what is interpreted in the Old is not foreign or peculiar or hidden, but arises naturally out of the text due to the relationship of the two Testaments.

Christian Zionism: is a belief among some Christians that the return of the Jews to the Holy Land, and the establishment of the State of Israel in 1948, is in accordance with Biblical prophecy. Some Christian Zionists believe that the "ingathering" of Jews in Israel is a prerequisite for the Second Coming of Jesus. This belief is primarily, though not exclusively, associated with Christian Dispensationalism. The idea that Christians should actively support a Jewish return to the Land of Israel, along with the parallel idea that the Jews ought to be encouraged to become Christian, as a means fulfilling a Biblical prophecy has been common in Protestant circles since the Reformation.

SELECTED BIBLIOGRAPHY

The books, articles and videos listed below have been instrumental in shaping the views and opinions of the author of this book with regard to eschatology and related subject matter.

Books

Adams, Jay Edward. *The Time Is At Hand*. Woodruff, SC: Timeless Texts, 2000.

_____, and Milton C. Fisher. *The Time of the End: Daniel's Prophecy Reclaimed*. Woodruff, SC: Timeless Texts, 2004.

_____. *Signs and Wonders: In the Last Days*. Woodruff, SC: Timeless Texts, 2000.

Aune, David Edward. *Prophecy in Early Christianity and the Ancient Mediterranean World*. Grand Rapids, MI: Eerdmans, 1983.

Bahnsen, Greg L. *Victory in Jesus: The Bright Hope of Postmillennialism*. Nacogdoches, TX: Covenant Media Press, 1999.

Berkof, Louis. *Systematic Theology*. Grand Rapids, Michigan: William B. Eerdmans, 1941.

Best, Robert M. *Noah's Ark and the Ziusudra Epic: Sumerian Origins of the Flood Myth*. Unabridged ed. Fort Myers, FL: Eisenbrauns, 1999.

Bettenson, Henry, and Chris Maunder, eds. *Documents of the Christian Church*. 3 ed. Oxford: Oxford University Press, USA, 1999.

Blaising, Craig A., Kenneth L. Gentry, Robert B. Strimple, and Darrell L. Bock. *Three Views on the Millennium and beyond*. Grand Rapids, MI: Zondervan, 1999.

Boettner, Loraine. *The Millennium*. Philadelphia: Presbyterian and Reformed Pub., 1958.

Bondar, Alan. *Reading the Bible Through New Covenant Eyes*. N.p.: PublishAmerica, 2010.

Bray, John L. *Matthew 24 Fulfilled*. 5th ed. Grand Rapids, MI: American Vision, 2009.

Canfield, Joseph M. *The Incredible Scofield and His Book*. 2nd ed. N.p.: Ross House Books, 2005.

Chilton, David. *The Great Tribulation*. Tyler, TX: Institute for Christian Economics, 1996.

_____. *Paradise Restored: A Biblical Theology of Dominion*. Waterbury Center, VT: Dominion Press, 2007.

_____. *The Days of Vengeance: An Exposition of the Book of Revelation*. Waterbury Center, VT: Dominion Press, 2006.

Clouse, Robert G., George Eldon Ladd, Herman Arthur Hoyt, Loraine Boettner, and Anthony A. Hoekema. *The Meaning of the Millennium: Four Views*. Downers Grove, IL: InterVarsity, 1977.

Collins, C. John. *Genesis 1-4: A Linguistic, Literary, and Theological Commentary*. Phillipsburg, NJ: P & R Pub., 2006.

Dawson, Samuel G. *Essays on Eschatology: An Introductory Overview of the Study of Last Things*. Charleston, SC: CreateSpace, 2009.

DeMar, Gary. *End Times Fiction: A Biblical Consideration Of The Left Behind Theology*. Nashville, TN: Thomas Nelson, 2001.

_____. *Is Jesus Coming Soon?* Atlanta, GA: American Vision, 1999.

_____. *Last Days Madness: Obsession of the Modern Church*. 4th ed. Atlanta, GA: American Vision, 1999.

_____. *Left Behind: Separating Fact From Fiction*. Atlanta, GA: American Vision, 2010.

_____. *10 Popular Prophecy Myths Exposed*. Atlanta, GA: American Vision, 2010.

_____, and Francis X. Gummerlock. *The Early Church and the End of the World*. Atlanta, GA: American Vision, 2006.

_____. *Why the End of the World is Not in Your Future*. Atlanta, GA: American Vision, 2010.

Dembski, William A., Wayne J. Downs, and Justin B. A.
Frederick. *The Patristic Understanding of Creation:
An Anthology of Writings from the Church Fathers on
Creation and Design.* Riesel, TX: Erasmus, 2008.

Ehrman, Bart D. *Lost Scriptures: Books that Did Not Make
It into the New Testament.* Oxford: Oxford University
Press, USA, 2005.

Ellis, James. *The Last Days Are Left Behind: Refuting
End-Time Fallacies.* Tucson, AZ: Wheatmark, 2008.

Erickson, Millard J., and Millard J. Erickson. *A Basic
Guide to Eschatology: Making Sense of the
Millennium.* Grand Rapids, MI: Baker Book House,
1998.

Fee, Gordon D. *Revelation: A New Covenant
Commentary.* Eugene, Or.: Cascade, 2011.

Fenemore, Michael A., and Kurt M. Simmons. *The
Twilight of Postmillennialism: Fatal errors in the
teachings of Keith A. Mathison, Kenneth L. Gentry, Jr.
et al.* Preterism.info Publishing.: CreateSpace, 2010.

Fischer, Richard James. *Historical Genesis: from Adam to
Abraham.* Lanham, MD: University Press of America,
2008.

Frost, Samuel M. *Exegetical Essays on the Resurrection.*
Ardmore, OK: JaDon Management, 2010.

_____. *Misplaced Hope: The Origins of First
and Second Century Eschatology.* Colorado Springs,
CO: Presence (USA), 2002.

_____, Edward Hassertt, and Michael Sullivan.
*House Divided: Bridging the Gap in Reformed
Eschatology - a Preterist Response to When Shall
These Things Be?* Ramona, CA: Vision Publishing,
2009.

Gentry, Kenneth L. *Before Jerusalem Fell: Dating the
Book of Revelation.* 3rd ed. N.p.: Victorious Hope
Publishing, 2010.

_____. *He Shall Have Dominion: A
Postmillennial Eschatology.* 3rd ed. Draper, VA:
Apologetics Group Media, 2009.

_____. *Navigating the Book of Revelation.* 1st ed.
Fountain Inn, SC: GoodBirth Ministries, 2009.

_____. *Perilous Times: A Study in Eschatological Evil*. Nacogdoches, TX: Covenant Media Press, 1999.

_____. *The Beast of Revelation*. Grand Rapids, MI: American Vision, 2002.

_____. *The Book of Revelation Made Easy*. Atlanta, GA: American Vision, 2009.

Gonzalez, Justo L. *Story of Christianity: Volume 1, The: The Early Church to the Dawn of the Reformation*. 2 Rev Upd ed. New York, NY: HarperOne, 2010.

_____. *The Story of Christianity: Volume 2: The Reformation to the Present Day*. Rev Upd ed. New York, NY: HarperOne, 2010.

Gregg, Steve, ed. *Revelation: Four Views: A Parallel Commentary*. Nashville, TN: Thomas Nelson, 1997.

Grenz, Stanley J. *The Millennial Maze: Sorting out Evangelical Options*. Downers Grove, IL: InterVarsity, 1992.

Gundry, Stanley N., and Darrell L. Bock. *Three Views on the Millennium and Beyond*. Grand Rapids, MI: Zondervan, 1999.

Hanegraaff, Hank. *Christianity In Crisis: The 21st Century*. Waco, TX: Thomas Nelson, 2009.

_____. *Counterfeit Revival*. Waco, TX: Thomas Nelson, 2001.

_____. *The Apocalypse Code: Find Out What the Bible Really Says About the End Times And Why It Matters Today*. Nashville, TN: Thomas Nelson, 2007.

Hendriksen, William. *More Than Conquerors*. Grand Rapids, Michigan: Baker Book House, 1939.

Hill, Glenn L. *Christianity's Great Dilemma: Is Jesus Coming Again or Is He Not?: One Pastor's Story of His Search for the Answer*. Lexington, KY: Moonbeam Publications, 2010.

Hoekema, Anthony A. *The Meaning of the Millennium: Four Views*. Downers Grove, Ill: IVP Books, 1977.

Hone, William. *Lost Books of the Bible*. Old Saybrook, CT: Konecky & Konecky, 2010.

Hyers, M. Conrad. *The Meaning of Creation: Genesis and Modern Science*. Atlanta: John Knox, 1984.

Jordan, James B. *Primeval Saints: Studies in the Patriarchs of Genesis.* Moscow, ID: Canon Press, 2001.

_____. *The Handwriting on the Wall: A Commentary on the Book of Daniel.* Atlanta, GA: American Vision, 2007.

_____. *The Vindication of Jesus Christ: A Brief Reader's Guide to Revelation.* Third ed. Monroe, LA: Athanasius Press, 2009.

Josephus, Flavius. *The New Complete Works of Josephus.* Rev Exp Su ed. Grand Rapids, MI: Kregel Academic & Professional, 1999.

King, Max R. *The Cross and the Parousia of Christ: The Two Dimensions of One Age-Changing Eschaton.* Warren, OH: Parkman Road Church of Christ, 1987.

_____. *The Spirit of Prophecy.* Warren, OH: Parkman Road Church of Christ, 1971.

_____. *The Spirit of Prophecy.* N.p.: Bimillennial Press, 2002.

Ladd, George E. *A Commentary on the Revelation of St. John.* Grand Rapids, Michigan: William B. Eerdmans, 1972.

_____. *The Blessed Hope.* Grand Rapids, Michigan: William B. Eerdmans, 1956.

_____. Revelation 20 and the Millennium. Review and Expositor 57 (1960). 167-75.

MacCulloch, J. A. "Eschatology." In *Encyclopaedia of Religion and Ethics*, edited by James Hastings, 12 vols., 5:375-91. New York, N.Y.: Scribner's, 1913-1922.

Martin, Brian L. *Behind the Veil of Moses.* Longwood, FL: Xulon Press, 2009.

Martin, Timothy P., and PhD Jeffrey L. Vaughn. *Beyond Creation Science.* 3rd ed. N.p.: Apocalyptic Vision Press, 2007.

Martin, Walter, and Zacharias Ravi. *Kingdom of the Cults, The.* Rev Upd ed. Minneapolis, MN: Bethany House, 2003.

Mathison, Keith A. *Postmillennialism: An Eschatology of Hope.* Phillipsburg, N.J.: P & R Publishing, 1999.

_____. *When Shall These Things Be: A Reformed Response to Hyper-Preterism*. Phillipsburg, N.J.: P & R Publishing, 2004.

McKenzie, Duncan W. *The Antichrist and the Second Coming: A Preterist Examination*. Longwood, FL: Xulon Press, 2009.

Morris, Leon. *The Revelation of St. John*. Grand Rapids, Michigan: William B. Eerdmans, 1969.

Noe, John. *Beyond the End Times*. 2 ed. Bradford, PA.: International Preterist Association, 2000.

_____. *The Apocalypse Conspiracy*. Brentwood, TN: Wolgemuth & Hyatt, 1991.

_____. *Shattering the Left Behind Delusion*. Bradford, PA: International Preterist Association, 2000.

Noll, Mark A. *America's God: From Jonathan Edwards to Abraham Lincoln*. Oxford: Oxford University Press, USA, 2005.

North, Gary. *Rapture Fever: Why Dispensationalism Is Paralyzed*. Tyler, TX: Institute for Christian Economics, 1993.

Preston, Don K. *The Elements Shall Melt With Fervent Heat: A Study of 2 Peter 3*. Ardmore, OK: JaDon Productions, 2006.

_____. *Have Heaven and Earth Passed Away?* Ardmore, OK: JaDon Productions, 2003.

_____. *How Is This Possible?* 3rd ed. Ardmore, OK: JaDon Management, 2009.

_____. *Israel 1948, Countdown to Nowhere*. Ardmore, OK: JaDon Productions, 2002.

_____. *Like Father, Like Son, on Clouds of Glory*. Admore, OK: JaDon Productions, 2007.

_____. *The Last Days Identified*. Ardmore, OK: JaDon Productions, 2004.

_____. *70 Weeks Are Determined for the Resurrection*. Ardmore, OK: JaDon Productions, 2007.

_____. *We Shall Meet Him In The Air, The Wedding of the King of kings (Volume 1)*. Ardmore, OK: JaDon Productions, 2010.

_____. *Who Is This Babylon?* Ardmore, OK: JaDon Productions, 2006.

Russell, J. Stuart. *Parousia: The New Testament Doctrine of Our Lord's Second Coming.* Grand Rapids, MI: Baker Books, 1999.

Shelley, Bruce L. *Church History in Plain Language, 3rd Edition.* 3rd ed. N.p.: Thomas Nelson, 2008.

Simmons, Kurt M. *The Consummation of the Ages (AD70 and the Second Coming in the Book of Revelation).* Carlsbad, N.M.: Bimillennial Peterist Association, 2003.

_____. *The Road Back to Preterism.* Carlsbad, N.M.: Bimillennial Peterist Association, 2006.

Sizer, Stephen. *Christian Zionism: Road-map to Armageddon?* UK ed. Downers Grove, Ill: IVP Books, 2005.

_____. *Zion's Christian Soldiers?: The Bible, Israel and the Church.* UK ed. Nottingham: IVP Books, 2008.

Spector, Stephen. *Evangelicals and Israel: The Story of American Christian Zionism.* Oxford: Oxford University Press, USA, 2008.

Sproul, R. C. *Last Days according to Jesus, The.* Grand Rapids, MI: Baker Books, 2000.

Terry, Milton S. *Biblical Apocalyptics: A Study of the Most Notable Revelations of God and of Christ in the Canonical Scriptures.* N.p.: Wipf & Stock Publishers, 2001.

_____. *Biblical Dogmatics: An Exposition of the Principal Doctrines of the Holy Scriptures.* N.p.: Wipf & Stock Publishers, 2002.

_____. *Biblical Hermeneutics: A Treatise on the Interpretation of the Old and New Testaments.* N.p.: Wipf & Stock Publishers, 2003.

Van, Impe Jack. *Millennium: Beginning or End?* Nashville, TN: Word Pub., 1999.

Wagner, C. Peter. *Dominion!: How Kingdom Action Can Change the World.* Grand Rapids, MI: Chosen, 2008.

Walton, John H. *Ancient Israelite Literature in Its Cultural Context: A Survey of Parallels between Biblical and*

Ancient Near Eastern Texts. Grand Rapids, MI:
Regency Reference Library, 1989.

_____. *Ancient Near Eastern Thought and the Old Testament: Introducing the Conceptual World of the Hebrew Bible.* Grand Rapids, MI: Baker Academic, 2006.

_____. *The Lost World of Genesis One: Ancient Cosmology and the Origins Debate.* Downers Grove, IL: IVP Academic, 2009.

Warfield, Benjamin B. *Biblical Doctrines.* New York, N.Y.: Oxford University Press, 1929.

_____. "The Millennium and the Apocalypse." In *Biblical Doctrines*, pp. 643-64. New York, N.Y.: Oxford University, 1929.

Articles and Videos

Against Dispensationalism: Israel, the Church & Bible Prophecy. DVD. Directed by Kenneth Gentry Th.D. and Kenneth Talbot Ph.D. Apologetics Group, 2008.

Basic Training for Understanding Bible Prophecy. DVD. By Gary DeMar. American Vision.

The Late Great Planet Church: The Rise of Dispensationalism. DVD. Directed by Tyler Johnson. The Apologetics Group, 2009.

Letting the Bible Speak for Itself-The Literal Meaning of 'This Generation': A Response to Ed Hindon's 'The New Last Days Scoffers,'- Part 6. By Gary DeMar. American Vision, 2006.

AUTHOR BIO

Joseph M. Vincent II served in the United States Marine Corps until 2002 when he was honorably discharged as a Sergeant, and later went on to receive a Bachelor of Science degree in Public Administration from Park University in 2005, with an Associates' Degree in Criminal Justice, and minors in Medical Radiology, Journalism, Public Relations, and Broadcasting. Joseph also studied for one year at Liberty Baptist Theological Seminary towards a Master's Degree in Biblical Studies.

Joseph has authored several articles which can be found on his website at www.thewellkc.com, including topics such as Acts 1:11 and the manner of Christ's coming, women in the church, water baptism, and others. He has appeared on several radio programs hosted on Preterist Radio (www.ad70.net), along with appearing in Fulfilled Magazine as a contributing author. Joseph also organized and hosted the 2011 Kansas City Prophecy Conference which saw speakers such as Dr. Don K. Preston of PRI, Pastor David Curtis of Berean Bible Church, Pastor Alan Bondar of New Covenant Eyes Church, Ed Stevens of the IPA, and William Bell of All Things Fulfilled Ministries.

Joseph came to believe in Jesus from the young age of five years old, and has been a diligent student of the Bible and religion since that time. His primary focus has been in the areas of apologetics, church history, cult evangelism, and eschatology. He has served and matured in various capacities through the years beginning in charismatic churches, followed by ten years in a Southern Baptist Church, four years at Vineyard KC North, and he has been a member and leader at Mercy Church in Prairie Village, KS since 2010, where he currently serves alongside his wife Lauren as the Children's Director for Kid's Life Ministry.

Joseph and his wife Lauren have been married since 2002, and live with their four boys, Iassic, Joseph Jr., Elijah, and Seth in the Kansas City area. Joseph is a free-lance graphics designer, webmaster for www.bibleprophecy.com, he coaches little league baseball and football, and he enjoys playing guitar, singing, blogging, facebooking, painting miniature figurines, fishing, board games, x-box, playing pick-up basketball, and anything else recreational! Joseph's full-time employment is currently as a quality control inspector for the NNSA.

Made in the USA
Middletown, DE
20 September 2020